Chicken Soup for the Soul®

All in the Family

Chicken Soup for the Soul: All in the Family
101 Incredible Stories about Our Funny, Quirky, Lovable & "Dysfunctional" Families
Jack Canfield, Mark Victor Hansen, Amy Newmark, Susan M. Heim

Published by Chicken Soup for the Soul Publishing, LLC   www.chickensoup.com

The publisher gratefully acknowledges the many publishers and individuals who granted Chicken Soup for the Soul permission to reprint the cited material.

Front cover illustration courtesy of Jerry Miller. Back cover illustration courtesy of John Rockwell. Interior spot illustration courtesy of Jerry Miller. Interior photo courtesy of iStockphoto.com/ NinaMalyna

Cover and Interior Design & Layout by Pneuma Books, LLC
For more info on Pneuma Books, visit www.pneumabooks.com

Distributed to the booktrade by Simon & Schuster. SAN: 200-2442

Publisher's Cataloging-in-Publication Data
(Prepared by The Donohue Group)

Chicken soup for the soul : all in the family : 101 incredible stories about our funny, quirky, lovable & "dysfunctional" families / [compiled by] Jack Canfield ... [et al].

p. ; cm.

ISBN: 978-1-935096-39-9

1. Family--Literary collections. 2. Family--Anecdotes. I. Canfield, Jack, 1944-

PN6071.F2 C455 2009
810.8/02/03525   2009934271

PRINTED IN THE UNITED STATES OF AMERICA
on acid∞free paper

18 17 16 15 14 13 12 11 10 09   02 03 04 05 06 07 08 09 10

Chicken Soup for the Soul

All in the Family

101 Incredible Stories
about Our Funny, Quirky, Lovable
& "Dysfunctional" Families

Jack Canfield
Mark Victor Hansen
Amy Newmark
Susan M. Heim

Chicken Soup for the Soul Publishing, LLC
Cos Cob, CT

Contents

❶
~Eccentrics Are Us~

❷
~In-Laws and Outlaws~

❸
~Family Vacations and Reunions~

❹
~Forgiveness~

❺
~Thanks for the Memories~

❻

~Putting the Fun in Dysfunctional~

❼

~Family Secrets~

❽
~Happy, Horrible Holidays~

❾
~Reunited~

❿
~Brothers and Sisters~

⑪

~Parents and Kids~

Introduction

You don't choose your family. They are God's gift to you, as you are to them.
~Desmond Tutu

*F*amily. One simple word can mean so many things! What do you think about when you hear the word "family"? Love. Sibling rivalry. Blessings. Memories. Secrets. Fun. Security. Pain. Wisdom. Drama.

Families are fascinating to us, whether they're ours or someone else's. Perhaps that's why so many TV shows and movies, both comedies and dramas, focus on families. Most of us can relate to the adventures of the Griswold family as they take one disastrous family vacation after another or celebrate the holidays with (lovable but crazy) relatives. And, like Dorothy in *The Wizard of Oz*, we usually come to the realization at some point in our lives that there's no place like home.

Our families complete us. They offer acceptance. They provide a history. They shape who we are, the good and the bad. They are, as Desmond Tutu says, "God's gift to you." Sometimes we may have to tear off a lot of wrapping paper to find the goodness inside! But think about how boring life would be without family.

Another amazing thing about families is that they're all so different and yet the same. They're complicated and yet simple. They're a burden, but also a blessing. They're often the source of our greatest joys, but also our deepest pain. They can build us up and tear us down. Families add richness and complexity to our lives.

Clearly, our families are "all." Perhaps that's why we received several thousand stories for this book. Yes, thousands! In reading these stories (and, indeed, we read every single one), we wiped away a lot of tears, fell off our chairs from laughter, and were deeply moved by the courage and strength displayed by so many. It wasn't easy narrowing the selection down to 101 stories.

Many of the stories we received for this book (and weren't able to use) will show up in other *Chicken Soup for the Soul* books because, if you've been reading *Chicken Soup for the Soul* books for a while, you've probably figured out that we like families a lot. We've got books about mothers and sons, dads and daughters, twins and multiples, preteens and teens, grandparents and grandchildren, and much more. And we're going to keep publishing family stories because they really are central to our existence as human beings.

So, gather your loved ones around you and crack open this book. See if you recognize any of your siblings in the "Brothers and Sisters" chapter. Laugh along with the characters you'll read about in "Putting the Fun in Dysfunctional" and "Eccentrics Are Us." Revisit family celebrations in "Happy, Horrible Holidays" and "Family Vacations and Reunions." Or take a walk on the serious side in "Forgiveness" or "Family Secrets." There's something for everyone in *Chicken Soup for the Soul: All in the Family*.

~Susan and Amy

All in the Family

Chapter 1

Eccentrics Are Us

*Like all the best families,
we have our share of eccentricities,
of impetuous and wayward youngsters
and of family disagreements.*

~Queen Elizabeth II

On Preserving the Family Plastic

All marriages are happy.
It's the living together afterward that causes all the trouble.
~Raymond Hull

I'm visiting home for the first time in six months, and my mother is sitting outside on the concrete stoop.

"What happened to the outdoor furniture?" I ask, hoping to join her on this pleasant July day and drink some raspberry lemonade on the concrete slab that constitutes my father's version of a "deck."

My mother shakes her head.

"I don't want to talk about it," she says gloomily.

I can't imagine what could possibly be so bad, for even if her two plastic white chairs and matching table were stolen, they were ten-year-old grocery store specials worth only a few dollars.

"We got a new set from Rob," she says hesitantly, after a while.

When I asked where the set was, she just points to the garage.

"And the old set's in the basement," she calls after me, as I go to investigate.

But I don't see any new outdoor furniture in the garage, only big trash bags. However, I do find the old set in the basement and take it upstairs, piece by piece. After all, it is summer in Chicago. What could be so wrong about a little outdoor furniture?

My mother protests when she sees me carrying it out, but I am determined to have somewhere to sit outside, so I persevere.

That night, after my father returns from work and we sit down to dinner, I look out at the porch and see three black garbage bags, each carefully covering the plastic furniture.

And then I understand my mother's distress.

For as long as I can remember, my father has wrapped things in plastic. As a child, I thought it was normal. He kept his phone wrapped in not one, but two plastic zip-lock bags. He kept the bocce ball set not only in the special Eddie Bauer canvas case it came in, but also kept each ball carefully wrapped in its original plastic bag. He kept souvenir T-shirts in their plastic wrappings while wearing threadbare polos from the 1970s. It's a miracle I was allowed to venture into the world without being wrapped in bubble wrap.

"Dad, there's a reason outdoor furniture is called 'outdoor,'" I try to reason with him.

But this concept escapes him, so I continue.

"It looks like you live next to a trash dump. I can't even see your flowers anymore," I say.

"Now do you see?" says my mother wearily. "I'd rather have nothing on the porch than have to look at big black trash bags all day."

My father looks at us like we are crazy and counters with the fact that the chairs would get dirty and wet otherwise.

I point out that they are ten years old, plastic and worth a total of $10. Plus, they ruin the ambiance of the entire backyard.

Instead of agreeing with reason, he loses his temper and stomps out of the room while my mother heads over to the neighbor's to sit on a porch that looks like something other than a trash dump.

The next day, I start to tell my mother that I agree that my father has finally lost it, once and for all, when something in my parents' bedroom catches my eye. It is a drawing of a caterpillar made out of hearts that I had done as a five-year-old. There it was, faded, but in otherwise perfect condition—proudly preserved in a plastic sandwich bag on my dad's dresser. I pick it up and hold it in my hand. Suddenly, my attitude toward my father's plastic obsession becomes slightly more tolerant. I grab a book, head outside, peel off a garbage bag, and enjoy the summer sun, sitting in an old plastic chair that looks brand-new.

~Chantal Panozzo

My Obsessive-Compulsive Darling

March to the beat of your own drum.
~English Proverb

first started noticing it soon after we were married. It was important to Fred that the sponge always be placed in its "home spot" on the sink after use—the exact same place every time. I thought he was just a neatnik or his training in the Navy made him super-organized. I discovered that putting the sponge in the wrong spot on the sink was a great way to get him flustered. It was fun, and he was really cute when he was flustered!

Through the years, other "habits" began to surface that I questioned. Every night before going to bed, he would check to make sure that the doors were locked. He did this by locking and unlocking each door several times. I learned that there was no point in my locking the doors at all before I went to bed because he'd be unlocking them anyway to check them later.

He sorted his socks by color in his sock drawer, and sorted his underwear by size and type in his underwear drawer. He couldn't just loosely place his belongings into his drawers like I did. Mine would start out organized, but not stay that way for long. He needed the two largest drawers in our chest of drawers so that he could separate his things, even though I was the woman and had more stuff! I gave in to him because it was the path of least resistance.

We were always late going places because his routines for getting ready took him so long, and he invariably lost track of time. I didn't realize that he just couldn't stop himself from following his routines religiously. If I tried to rush him, he always became flustered and upset with me. I eventually learned to keep my mouth shut and took up crocheting to help me relax while I was waiting.

His need for control became the most obvious one year when we took a trip with my sister and brother-in-law. We traveled in a van from Phoenix to a time-share cabin in the mountains. We stuck Fred in the back of the van since I tend to get carsick when I ride in the back. My sister also stuck her boxer back there. By the time we reached the cabin, Fred was absolutely freaked out from having to stare at the dog's butt for three hours.

A few days later, we traveled on to Las Vegas. My sister had made the hotel reservations for us and got us a great deal. At the reception desk, Fred realized that our room was going to be on the 16th floor. I had forgotten that he doesn't like to stay above the 7th floor because that is the highest the ladders on the fire trucks can reach. This was more serious than him not "liking" to stay above the 7th floor. He was actually afraid. We went up to our room and began to unpack but he kept looking out the window and fretting. Finally, he told me that he just couldn't do this anymore and wanted to fly home immediately.

I didn't know how to react. Why couldn't he just "man up" and get over it? Why was he making such a big deal about this? Luckily, we were able to move to a room on the 6th floor and enjoy our days in Vegas, exploring the amazing buildings of the casinos and eating until we burst.

After that trip, I thought about what had happened. He and I had taken many vacations together, and there were never any signs of anxiety attacks. Then it hit me—he had always made all the arrangements. We always stayed in nice motels with no more than a couple of floors. He had always been in control on those trips!

Talk about control—it even affects his eating habits. One of his favorite things to do is take a drive out in the country, sip on a Dr. Pepper and eat M&Ms. I joined him one day and, as we were driving along, the smell of his M&Ms wafted over to my side of the car and I asked for a couple. He hesitated at first and told me that it was going to mess up his system. System?! He explained that his Dr. Pepper and M&Ms had to come out even. His last M&M and last sip of Dr. Pepper had to end together. If I took some of his M&Ms, it would mess things up. It just seemed so silly that I had to laugh! Fortunately, he has been able to laugh at himself as well. Now I just tell him if I want some M&Ms before we get in the car. Of course, he needs to know the exact number. If you say "a handful" it messes with his mind.

Before leaving the house, Fred always packs his pockets with the exact same items in the exact same pockets. When we go on a walk around the block, we can't leave until he packs his pockets. His lack of spontaneity is frustrating to me, but packing his pockets is something that he has to do. One day, our youngest son fell outside and busted his chin open. Fred couldn't just grab his keys and wallet and run out the door to take our son to the emergency room. We had to wait for him to pack his pockets.

Now, Fred has his redeeming qualities. He is pure gold as a father and husband. No other dad could have spent more time with his children than Fred did. He was always ready to play with them and spend time with them, even when he was tired to the bone. The grandchildren love him to death and always run to him when they visit. He's been a loving, faithful husband who has always made family his first priority. I love him dearly, in spite of his quirks.

Yes, we have come to realize that he has obsessive-compulsive disorder. When we were first married, in the 1970s, nobody had heard of it. He has admitted to me that he cannot stop himself from going through his little routines and really wishes that he could. But now we know about it, and it's just a part of Fred. He wouldn't be as much fun without it! And what would the family tease him about? It's all good-natured, of course, and it has been easy for the family to learn to live with his habits because he is so lovable otherwise. We wouldn't do a thing to change him! And I've completed many beautiful afghans while waiting.

~Kay Johnson

The Cleaning Lady

You sometimes see a woman who would have made a Joan of Arc in another century and climate, threshing herself to pieces over all the mean worry of housekeeping.
~Rudyard Kipling

I can't tell you exactly when it was my aunt was bitten by the bug. As far as I can remember, that's just the way she had always been. No one in her neat little circle of family and friends ever really made a major production over her behavior. Most of us just accepted her condition as sort of quirky in a roll-your-eyes kind of way. Upon meeting her for the first time, however, there were those who just assumed she was from a military family or spent some time herself in the armed forces. My aunt had the Windex-holstered, Swifter-toting cleaning bug. And its work was never done.

My earliest memory of Aunt Helen is a continuous swirl of moving parts. She was half-woman, half-machine. One moment, she would be mopping the floor, and the next moment she'd be shoveling snow off the driveway before it even had time to decide whether to melt or stick. She resembled the very appliances she was so enamored of—single-minded, smooth-running, and effectively serving the home's occupants. This polishing act was not limited to her own home. In fact, she carried the bug to our house on a daily basis. Since my parents divorced when my sister and I were quite young, my aunt felt an obligation to "help out" around the house. It was either the selfless act of a caring sister, or a window of opportunity that was streaky and in need of cleaning. My mother went with the latter.

"Don't let her fool you," my mother would say. "She wouldn't miss being here for the world."

There were days that my aunt hardly spoke a word to us when she was, as my mother would say, "on the clock." Mostly, her self-imposed duties hardly interfered with our daily routine of doing homework, playing Yahtzee, or reading comic books. That is, unless my sister and I were watching Scooby-Doo in the living room when Aunt Helen came chugging through with the vacuum cleaner in high gear. We would race to pull the plug on her so as not to miss a single "Zoinks!" or "Jinkies" from Shaggy and the gang.

"Didn't you hear that?" my aunt might ask, referring to the crackling noise going up the tube before she was suddenly silenced by me or my sister. "That's dirt!"

"No," my sister might calmly reply, settling into her spot on the couch. "That's popcorn."

As kids, we never really felt a dust-speck of guilt for this voluntary servitude. We sensed she was happiest when doing her thing. So why not enjoy the benefits of a loved one's compulsions? We never thought that maybe there just might be other forces at work behind her Mrs. Clean exterior. We were kids, after all—kids who made messes. The relationship worked great for us. Apart from vacuuming at critical times of the day like cartoon hour, the disturbances caused by Aunt Helen's compulsions were fairly minor. While eating dinner with her mopping around us, we might occasionally feel a bump against our chair or be asked to raise our feet. However, if I spilled something on my shirt, I would be ordered to immediately hand the soiled garment over while she prepped her cleaning products and filled the kitchen sink with hot water, since time was apparently of the essence.

My mother wasn't one to complain about my aunt's antiseptic behavior either. Free maid service with two kids was a blessing, and when she came home from working at a high school cafeteria all day, the last thing she wanted to do was wait on a couple more kids, even if they were her own.

"You really don't need to organize that pantry again," my mother might say. "Johnny's uniform is grass-stained, and he has a game tomorrow."

"Oh, sure, what do you take me for? I have to get home for Bob," my aunt might shoot back, referring to my uncle, who we really only saw in her wallet and on holidays and birthdays.

But the exchange between sisters was short-lived, lasting no longer than a puff of steam from an upturned iron. If there was a job to do, Aunt Helen would do it and do it right. Uncle Bob could wait a few more minutes. What no one, not even my mother, really understood at the time was that Bob probably wouldn't be there waiting anyway.

Some twenty years later, some things have certainly changed, and some have remained pretty much the same. My aunt no longer has Uncle Bob to go home to. He met a high school sweetheart at a class reunion during my sophomore year in high school and promptly moved 1,500 miles away, catching everyone, except maybe my aunt, by complete surprise. Did the cleaning bug cause him to look outside the no-dirt zone or did his wandering eye give birth to the little bugger that gripped my aunt all these years? Maybe she saw her home coming apart and did everything she could to put things in order—literally. I guess we all deal with disorder in our own way.

One would think that with a new, visible husband, a happy marriage, and a little rust now on her bones that my aunt and her bug would have mellowed. Not exactly. My wife is in her glory when Aunt Helen visits. She purposefully neglects to clean our Lazy Susan because she knows that is what my aunt has been thinking about from the moment she was invited over, considering the effort she put into it during her last visit. That and whether or not we finally purchased a can of furniture polish since "Windex is for windows!"

Her next visit will be particularly pleasing, though. It will be my son's three-year birthday party, and with him leaving debris and bits of wreckage in his wake, now could not be a better time for a visit from Aunt Helen and her little friend. I'll stand a safe distance away behind my camcorder as I film my son tearing open gifts like Jaws on spring break in Cancun. Occasionally, the blur of a hand will dart into the frame and deftly catch bits of wrapping paper before they even hit the floor. Off-frame, they will be neatly folded and placed in a white plastic trash bag. The cleaning bug is alive and well.

~John MacDonald

Imaginary Friends

*Imagination and fiction make up more than
three-quarters of our real life.*
~Simone Weil

At four feet, nine inches and barely ninety pounds, Grandmother was a powerhouse of energy. Wearing white bobby socks and canvas tennis shoes, she rambled through her two-story brick home, sanitizing each room and washing her hands every hour over the kitchen sink.

As Grandmother scrubbed her palms raw with lye soup and a dishrag, she whispered, "What did y'all say? Hee, hee. You comin'? We need you here."

Curious about her company, I raced into the kitchen to investigate. Upon hearing my footsteps, she abruptly ceased her muffled chatter as if I had interrupted an appointment with a good friend. Turning toward me while continuing to scour her hands, she'd say, "Dwan, what can I get for you? Why don't you go out and play?"

On my way out the door, I would hear her resume the conversation. "What did y'all say? Hee, hee. I'm washing, washing. No, I didn't hear from her. Where is she?" Grandmother seemed to be having so much fun. I always wondered what her invisible friends were saying, but I didn't dare ask. I was told at an early age that it wasn't polite to speak of her companions.

I liked visiting Grandmother but noticed, when not in the company of her make-believe friends, she seemed melancholy and distant.

She seldom left the house and often told me of plots against her. She'd say, "The lady next door is making moonshine and wants me to leave town so I won't tell the police" or "Brother Brown has been sending people to watch me because I saw him steal money buried in the cemetery." I struggled to separate reality from counterfeit in her world.

After long visits with Grandmother, I breathed a sigh of relief to be free of fantasy. This reprieve ended the day my sister introduced me to Tyler. Like many young children, six-year-old Bonnie had conceived an imaginary friend. Unlike our grandmother's private companions, who only dwelled within the confines of her walls, Tyler went with us everywhere.

When we sat down to eat at McDonald's, Bonnie announced, "He's eating my hamburger." When we drove through town, "Tyler, look at the big buildings." When it was time to go to bed, "Brush your teeth, boy."

One day while visiting Grandmother, I said, "Bonnie is crazy, Grandmother. She has an imaginary friend. She talks to him all the time, and it is driving me nuts. I'm embarrassed to have my friends over because they may see her talking to him."

Grandmother clenched her raw fists and looked up at me. (I was already taller than her at age eleven.) "Now, just you listen. You better not say that to her. Don't you know that imaginary friends are a sign of creativity? Very intelligent people have imaginary companions, and Bonnie is a very smart girl. She reminds me of me. So you hush."

I pondered what my grandmother said. Creativity? Intelligence? I had never associated them with incessant chatter to invisible people.

Thirty years later, as I replay this conversation in my mind, I realize that fantasy serves distinct purposes for different people.

For my grandmother, her invisible friends were her escape. They were pleasure, solace, and an expression of the joys and pain of her existence. They held her within the walls of mental illness, yet permitted her to maintain contact with her true identity as a wife, mother and grandmother. Her companions soothed her compulsions and gave her courage to face contrived conspiracies.

For Bonnie, Tyler was truly an expression of her creativity and intelligence. He was a temporary stage in the adventures of childhood. He entertained, while enabling her to expand her communication and social skills. He comforted my sister at a time when the world seemed too large for little girls.

Tyler eventually faded from Bonnie's imagination. My grandmother's companions remained until her death. In many ways, I wish life could have been different for Grandmother, but I'm thankful for the simple pleasures she received from her imaginary friends. In some odd way, I believe God allowed them to comfort her soul and lighten the burden of her mental disorders.

~Dwan Reed

"Any more roughhousing in here and I'm sending your imaginary brother to his imaginary room!"

Just Because

If God had wanted me otherwise,
He would have created me otherwise.
~Johann von Goethe

I grew up in a world where "crazy" was served up daily as a plateful of dysfunction. Years later, at the age of thirty-four, I had a name for my illness. I was bipolar.

During my chaotic life, I managed to give birth to a ten-pound, ten-ounce bundle of love, Shayla Rae Dawn. To me, she was sheer perfection. Many times throughout the years of raising my daughter, the walls I had built up from a lifetime of abuse dissolved when I held her in my arms. Like a waterfall that had been turned off, my bipolar was evaporated by the love of my child.

As a little girl, Shayla depended on me for both love and security. Although these were things I had never received, I was able to create them in the deep bond I shared with my daughter.

Looking back, my daughter never thought something was wrong with Mommy, because my erratic behavior was simply normal to her. We would play together like two schoolmates, skipping along the sidewalk, singing and laughing. If she climbed a tree, I was right behind her, imagining the spectacular tree house we could build in its towering limbs. Shayla would awake in the middle of the night to the wondrous aromas of freshly baked cinnamon buns, whipped shortbread and banana muffins. It never occurred to her that regular people do not start baking at 3:00 A.M.

Then, there were times when my bipolar was infused with such creativity that it seemed like pure brilliance. I would write, compose and submerge myself in the gift that my mental illness allowed me to share with the world. Long before I was diagnosed, my bipolar was like a mischievous child, coming out to play whenever it desired.

During her childhood, Shayla took delight in my unusual parenting methods. One of her favourite memories was of the "Just Because" parties I would host on a whim. While my daughter was at the neighbour's, I would contact her friends and invite them over for the next day, "just because." They would arrive to find our home adorned with colorful decorations. I would have craft projects set up for the girls, and a homemade angel food cake with marshmallow icing, complete with sprinkles and sparklers. The girls would hide behind the couch, and when Shayla entered, her friends would jump out and yell, "Surprise!"

Since being diagnosed with bipolar and properly medicated, my life has changed in dramatic ways. I have clarity where racing thoughts once existed. I have stability where chaos resided. I have been a spokesperson for mental health issues, sharing my troubled past with those wanting to see me as a person coping with a mental illness. Additionally, I have spoken at my daughter's former high school twice and watched with great pride how accommodating Shayla has been with my bipolar.

Stepping out from behind the shadows of my bipolar, I have positioned myself to be scrutinized. To openly announce to the world that I have a mental illness is not an easy task, yet I gain control over my life when I share my journey with strangers. The realization that my "mental imperfection" is the foundation of my dysfunction now gives me hope! My daughter, Shayla Rae Dawn, has taught me that there are no limitations in life, only recognition that there is freedom in embracing our differences!

~Tonya L. Alton

Never Late

Punctuality is the politeness of kings.
~Louis XVIII

The family curse began when my twin brother and I were about five years old. Our mother took on us on shopping trips to town. We had to drive several miles to catch a bus that would take us to Gay Street, the main street in downtown Knoxville, Tennessee. From the time we exited the bus until we caught one for a return ride, Mother marched us up and down every street in the city. She stood only five feet two inches, but her short legs covered more territory than people much taller. She never bought much because money was in short supply, but Mother had an itinerary she had to cover before the homeward bus ran. Don't be late for the bus; don't be late getting home. "Don't be late" became our family's mantra, and it's caused plenty of grief over the years.

Mother began her twenty-year career as an elementary school teacher when my twin brother and I started first grade. Every school day morning, she chased us out of our beds, made us dress, and fed us breakfast. Then we'd load ourselves into the car for the mile ride to the local elementary school. School started at 8:00 A.M., but our brood arrived each morning no later than 7:30 A.M.

My brother Jim and I took a break from punctuality during our senior year in high school. The principal contacted our mother with news that we'd been tardy thirteen successive days. The tongue lashing we received changed our ways. A beating would have been more welcome than the long lecture we received. The main point of the speech was that being late is a sinful act that neither of us should practice. We were told to go and sin no more.

All the harping on not being late finally seeped to my core. As a freshman in college, I constantly worried about not being able to find my classes on campus. The thoughts of arriving late and being verbally chastised by a professor kept me in a near panic. I also was concerned about not being prepared for class once I arrived. What if I forgot an assignment? What if I needed to use the restroom? To prevent such disasters, I would find the buildings and rooms for classes at the beginning of each term. Then I would arrive for each session approximately a half-hour early.

The fear of being late turned into a compulsion to be early to all events in my life. This driving force played havoc with married life. My wife Amy is one who believes that arriving for an 8:00 appointment at 8:00 is acceptable. Showing up any earlier is a waste of time to her. On the other hand, I pace the floor, wring my hands, and curse as I wait for her. With every passing moment, my heart rate increases and my blood pressure spikes. Drives to our destinations often include heated arguments as I throw temper tantrums about being "late" to a function. The tension grows even more if we arrive on time or a couple of minutes early. Amy never says a word, but a smirk is pasted on her face, and her look screams, "I told you so!"

I became so anxious waiting for Amy on Sunday mornings that we finally began driving two cars to church services. I'd leave in time to be the first person there, and Amy and the kids would arrive only a couple of minutes after assembly had started.

The fear of being late carried over into my job as a high school English teacher. Teachers were required to be at work at 8:00 A.M. To me, that meant the correct arrival time was no later than 7:15. During the years that I taught an early morning class at 7:00 A.M., my arrival time was usually 6:30. The reasoning for such early arrival was it gave me time to do some work prior to students arriving. However, I usually spent the time in activities that had nothing at all to do with school. Not being late was what mattered most.

My children are adults now. Unfortunately, they've learned too well from their father. During their years in sports, we arrived at practices or at games before anyone else on the team. In their present lives, both Lacey and Dallas are early arrivers. They, too, have come to believe that being early is the same as being on time. Lacey's husband and Dallas' girlfriends struggle with the compulsion. Perhaps the newest member to the family, grandson Madden, can break the cycle and discover that being late isn't a capital offense.

~Joe Rector

My Beloved Crazy Relatives

Friends are God's apology for relations.
~Hugh Kingsmill

n 1982, my Aunt Melzie passed away. She called me in Florida a few weeks before to tell me she didn't have long. I didn't really believe her. After all, she thought she was dying for many years.

"And if your Aunt Willowdean cries at my funeral, I want you to turn around and slap her. You tell her that if she didn't have time for me when I was alive, turn off those tears. I don't need them."

My mother's family consisted of nine children, all a few cards short of a deck. My mother, Drucella Drakula, was the firstborn. Grandmother must've been on some heavy drugs when she named her. But my mother fit that role. Always the pet of her father, she remained jealous of everyone else throughout her life.

Then came Aunt Melzie, the smart one. Aunt Lenka was next. Poor thing. She looked like my grandfather's sister in Serbia, and he hated her. Whenever he came home drunk, they had to hide her so he didn't shoot her. No kidding. Is it any wonder she turned out a bit loony? She had a kind heart, but was a pathological liar.

Along came Aunt Luva. She married at sixteen to escape the family, but never quite managed to get far enough away from the loose lips of her sisters. "Your husband has been flirting with that Beatty girl for a long time. We think they're, well, you know." He wasn't, of course. But Mother and Aunt Melzie weren't too happy with their mates and hated that Aunt Luva had married such a nice man.

Aunt Aubrey was shy and rather quiet. It really ticked her off when she picked a fight with her husband and he'd walk away instead of fighting back. She was used to an argumentative family. He smiled a lot. Died from ulcers. That's what happens when you hold it all in.

Uncle Elwood was drafted into the Army, than later joined the Marines. He served in two wars. He relived the war every night in his sleep, screaming and fighting. Is it any wonder he turned into an alcoholic? Well, then again, that was a family trait. He became an English teacher and loved it. Married in his fifties while drunk. Divorced after two years and her taking what little bit he had saved up.

Then there was Aunt Willowdean—the one who wasn't supposed to cry at the funeral, but did. I didn't have the heart to slap her. After all, she was very insecure. She always suffered from women's stuff. No one ever felt sorry for her, though, except me. When she was a teenager and babysat for me, I really hated her. She made me go to bed at six so she could spend time talking on the telephone. I learned to like her when we were older. I felt sorry for her when her husband talked about how he planned to "dump the old broad" when the kids grew up. He never did.

Aunt Darice came along and was spoiled rotten. She was the pretty one. Of course, she grew up to be a barmaid and let's just say was a bit on the loose side. Darice got involved with two married men who said they loved her and wanted to marry her. It's a little hard to marry men who are already married, which she later learned. She finally did marry a man she didn't really love. She was pretty. He was not. She drank too much—that family trait—and became a trophy wife. But you couldn't help but love her, unless you were Aunt Willowdean, who resented her. Funny, but when Aunt Darice went through chemo, it was Aunt Willowdean, who had passed over several years before, who would tell her it would all be okay. But it wasn't.

The baby of the family was Uncle Delmer. Good-looking, smart, talented, but he didn't escape the family flaws. He married a woman just to be married because his sisters were all married, and then his nieces started getting married so he just decided that's what he should do. It didn't take long for him to discover his mistake. When he said he wanted a divorce, his wife ran into the street screaming and tearing off her clothes. He was so embarrassed he stayed drunk throughout his forty-year marriage. I thought it was rather cute to learn that in the midst of having a heart attack, he washed his hair while waiting for the ambulance to arrive. He always liked his thick wavy hair. He died at the age of sixty-three with clean hair.

Let's get back to Aunt Melzie's funeral. She was the first of the nine siblings to pass over. I had promised Aunt Melzie that I would come to her funeral only if the weather was good in Ohio. She passed away on Mother's Day night, the flowers in bloom. Her children said she did that on purpose, to make them feel guilty for spending part of the day with their in-laws. She was an expert at guilt trips, bless her heart.

My mother, Drucella, didn't fly in from Arizona. Why? How could she be the center of attention when she wasn't the corpse?

Later that night, Uncle Elwood stopped by Aunt Melzie's house. We were talking in the kitchen, and he said his soon-to-be ex-wife was an idiot. I couldn't help it, but it just slipped out: "Who else do you think would marry you?" Let me tell you, my mouth cut me right out of his will, especially when I told him to leave his money to a cat. I "sweetly" talked to him like that for the next hour until he looked at me like Drucella had given birth to the devil's child, and then he left.

Aunt Darice and I heard Cousin Doyle laughing hysterically. We went into the living room to see what was wrong with the man who had just lost his mother. "All my life, I wanted to tell Uncle Elwood what I thought of him, but Mother wouldn't let me. And you so sweetly told him to more or less stick it where the sun doesn't shine."

"Well, bless your heart, Doyle. Glad I could make you so happy on this sad occasion."

After the funeral was over, we all went to the cemetery to see Aunt Melzie laid to rest. After the priest finished his eulogy, we sent Aunt Melzie to her afterlife with bottles of Blatz beer and packs of Camel non-filtered cigarettes. She always liked her beer and cigarettes. Probably what made her leave us at the age of sixty-five. I loved that woman and all her quirky ways.

You'd think the next generation of family would've learned something from the previous one, but we didn't. We still have the pathological liars and those who like to imbibe a bit too much. Hey, at least none of us has ended up in jail. What more could you ask in a family?

~Nori Thomas

Call Me Crazy

There are no pockets in a shroud.
~Author Unknown

I've started hiding money around my house. Not a lot. Just ones and fives. Maybe an occasional ten.

Nobody's going to get rich if they find it, but when I'm doing a really thorough housecleaning (which believe me, isn't all that often) and I'm climbing on ladders to dust the hidden nooks and crannies, I've started putting money up there out of sight.

It's not just in the obvious places, like stuffed inside the antique kitchen implements that are arranged in Cracker Barrel restaurant-style on the shelves over my kitchen cabinets. I've also pushed some bills through the slats of the air conditioning vents and even removed an electrical outlet here or there to poke in a few bills.

I don't do it so that I'll have a secret stash if I ever get in a financial bind. My memory is so bad, it wouldn't be worth the effort to try to find it if I needed it. I do it because when I die, I want people to find it and say, "That Betsy. She sure was a crazy old broad."

When I was young, I remember hearing stories about my crazy Aunt Sally. People say that when she died, they found money stashed all over her house. They also found a dead coyote in her freezer.

Now, to me, that doesn't seem all that crazy. I'm sure Aunt Sally (whom I never met) had a perfectly logical explanation for the coyote. Maybe times were hard and she was keeping it in case she ran out of food. Maybe she killed it in the winter and couldn't bury it because the ground was frozen. Maybe she just wanted a dead coyote.

I do know that everyone loved the stories of "Crazy" Aunt Sally, and because of those stories, she has been remembered far longer than anyone else in that generation of our family.

Recently, I was filling out an application for a passport. One of the bits of information I was supposed to provide was my father's birth date and place of birth. I didn't know the answer. I asked my sisters, but they didn't know the answer either. Somewhere in Pennsylvania and sometime in November 1918, they thought. I knew that much myself, but none of us remember much more. Not just about his birthday, but about the man in general.

Granted, it's been some time since my father died. Thirty-two years, to be exact. But there is almost nothing left of him. Not even memories. His brother and parents are all gone. Because of Alzheimer's, my mother's memory of him is gone. He was a good, sweet man, but just an ordinary man. He wasn't extreme in any aspect of his being. He wasn't eccentric. There was nothing about him that made him really stand out.

He did have five children to carry on his genes, but genes do not a legend make. We do not sit around at family gatherings and share belly laughs or colorful tales about the man who did his part to create us and rear us. The memories, like the man, are functional—almost utilitarian. There were no crazy quirks to add color to the memories. No eccentricities to recall. He lived. He worked. He raised some kids. He died.

Thinking about all of that is what made me decide to start hiding the money.

I don't have any children of my own, which makes the likelihood of my memory lasting very long after I die somewhat limited at best. But I think if I make a real effort, I might still have enough time left to make myself into a memorable oddball. I do have nieces and nephews, so there is still hope that tales of Crazy Aunt Betsy might survive. I could probably do it the easy way and buy a nice pleasant memory from each of them. I have some money saved up, and I could give them all a nice hefty sum when I go. Certainly getting them all a new car would give them something to remember me by. Maybe. But remembering my money isn't really the same as remembering me. And although a nice gift like that might elicit a smile, it probably wouldn't result in a laugh when they are sitting around a big bonfire at a family reunion. A new car doesn't get anywhere near the same reaction as a dead coyote.

I wish I could do something really dramatic when I go, like lying inside an open casket at my memorial service, wearing one of those pairs of fake glasses with a big nose and mustache. But I kind of doubt that I can get a funeral home to fulfill that wish for me.

So I'm starting with little things like hiding the money.

Oh, I'll have a will, of course. I'll leave each of my heirs a long detailed list of my assets, which I'm sure will be several million dollars by then. But I won't just be boring and write them each a tidy little check. I'll let them know it's out there for them somewhere, if they can find it. If any of them remember my stories about Crazy Aunt Sally, eventually one of them might check the freezer.

~Betsy S. Franz

9
The Family Collection

You can never get enough
of what you don't need
to make you happy.
~Eric Hoffer

When you really get right down to it, there are two kinds of people: those who take hotel bathroom minis. And those who don't but secretly want to.

Since I come from a family of packrats, I'm a collector, and naturally see any hotel room as a place of opportunity. A small sewing kit with a button? Not just one, but two little bottles of shampoo? A couple of tea bags? You name it, they are all scooped up and put into my suitcase, hidden among clothes should the maid decide to go snooping and not refill what is rightfully mine for the next day.

I go so far as to come back to a hotel room after a day of work or sightseeing and be personally offended if the maid has not replaced all the little freebies in a plentiful fashion because then I'll have to go through my suitcase and use yesterday's new bar of soap. The horror.

But it goes both ways. If everything's been restocked, you can't imagine my excitement as I do a clean sweep and dump even more of the little goodies—lotions, bath gels, and soaps—into my suitcase.

"Stealing the soap again, are we?" my husband says condescendingly, actually wanting to use the soap instead of taking it home to admire for decades.

"We paid for these," I'll say, stressing the word "paid." But he'll just grumble and groan, imagining hundreds of little bottles falling into the sink as he opens our already bursting bathroom cabinet looking for his razor.

The thing is, I haven't figured out why I take this stuff. It just pleases me to see the bottles pile up at home. But I have figured out that my collections can only result from one of two things: learned behavior or gene inheritance.

After all, my mother doesn't just limit herself to hotel freebies, but also covets restaurant ones. If there's a big bowl of mints near the register, my mother excitedly takes one or two handfuls and throws them in her purse.

"I love sucking on one of these after teaching my class," she'll say, as if that somehow excuses her for being so greedy.

But since she's talking to one of her own, I'll grab an extra heap and give them to her.

"Oh my gosh, thank you," she'll say, like it's the best gift on earth. And then I'll just smile, knowing that, to her, it is.

If the freebie gene isn't inherited, then the most notorious collector of the family—my grandmother—trained me at a young age. Every time we went to a restaurant, my grandmother would hide her menu in her gigantic Art Institute of Chicago purse, pretending innocently to the waiter that she didn't get one. She took napkins, little sugar packets, and once, even a cup and saucer from a fancy Paris restaurant.

Most of these items were stored in drawers in the family room. You name it, and there was a drawer for it. A drawer of napkins. A drawer of menus. Even a drawer of paper placemats with coffee stains on them.

As I child, I would look at these items in wonder, imagining all the different places they came from. When I visited my grandparents, I would play tea room and set the different napkins and placemats on a blanket that masqueraded as a fine tablecloth, using my grandmother's many menus as inspiration to create my own.

Since my grandma passed away four years ago, my grandpa has

inherited her collection. He doesn't know what to do with it all, but he goes over each piece, remembering where it came from and the joy it brought Grandma, while examining the amazingly low prices on menus from the 1970s.

"It was only fifty cents for a cup of coffee back then. Can you imagine?" he'll say, the vinyl brown menu shaking in his hands, his words choking him.

Even though he is on a mission to clean out the house they lived in together for fifty-three years, he cannot rid himself of any of her "collections"—not even the napkins. As treasured as the piles of photographs that surround him, these simple freebies have become priceless. They are the stuff of memories—of the places they came from, of the person who took them.

Maybe someday my husband will understand.

~Chantal Panozzo

All in the Family

Chapter 2

In-Laws and Outlaws

*Happiness is having a large,
loving, caring, close-knit family —
in another city.*

~George Burns

The Blue Cooler

Never rely on the glory of the morning
nor the smiles of your mother-in-law.
~Japanese Proverb

On a clear, perfectly cool day in August, our family and friends gathered to honor my daughter on her graduation from high school.

Plans had been in the making for months, and the yard looked more elegant than we would have thought possible, with splashes of color in flowers, pictures, and tablecloths. The setting was perfect, the caterer was excellent, and everything was in place.

For once, I was out of bed before my mother-in-law, so her phone greeting, "Did I wake you?" didn't require a fib this time.

"Listen!" she demanded. "I just made porketta sandwiches—120 of them—and they're so good, I want only family to have them. They're too good for the others. We're not going to give them out—just to family."

"Okay," I said, hoping there was more to the story and keeping the questions forming in my mind from creeping into my voice.

"I'll pack them into the cooler. Remember—nobody but the family...." And she hung up. She was never one for slow, warm goodbyes.

"Okay," I said again to myself, with a bit higher pitch to my voice.

"Okay," I said, turning on my husband, rapidly moving into

attack mode. There was no time for nonsense today as I "calmly" explained to him, my voice rising.

"Your mother doesn't want anyone but family to have her porketta sandwiches, so we're going to give little tickets to family members. They need a ticket to get into the cellar. Once they're in, they'll get one sandwich each, but they have to eat it in the cellar, so no one — except the family — knows where the porketta is. And I'm pretty sure this doesn't include anyone who married into the family. You know how she feels about us," I finished as my hands rose into the air, a hopeless "I give up" gesture.

"What???" questioned my husband, his face tightening up in irritation at my obvious sarcasm. A brief glare in my direction, then his hands in the air in the same gesture, followed by a new expression learned from my daughters, "Whatever!" he said as he quickly made a break for the yard. He had lived with his mother for thirty years before marrying me. There were no surprises.

"Count to ten, go for fifty... go for 100... but this isn't going to ruin your day," I scolded myself as I got back to work. I had learned over a brief eighteen years that logic and cool reasoning were not handy in this family.

Guests arrived, time flew, music played, and conversation was great. She slipped in when I was in the house. I saw her talking with my husband outside as he carried the blue cooler down the driveway. I saw her motion, him motion, her motion, him motion. Still a draw. Then her sharp thrust of her cane to a spot under the small tent showed that she had not accepted defeat. John carried the cooler filled with porketta to the spot, put it down, and then helped his mother lower herself into her new seat on top of the cooler. He had won — the porketta didn't go into the cellar. But she had won, too.

There she sat, reigning like a queen from her perch on the little blue box. It was just a regular-sized beverage holder, built for beer parties, floating in canoes, summer fun, but not built for my mother-in-law. As the family came, they paid homage to her. And so the day went on.

My older brother took me aside, shocked that I would make

my mother-in-law sit on such an uncomfortable accommodation. "What's wrong with you?" he whispered. "That poor old lady." He had no idea.

My younger brother took me aside, too. "Where's the beer? Is it in that cooler that Margaret is sitting on? People are looking for the beer," he stated, also having no idea. "Can't you get her to move?"

"Not with a stick of dynamite," I said, heading off to bring the liquids out of the cellar to keep him content.

And so the day continued, until some of the guests got restless. Ronnie, a neighbor of my mother-in-law, started the problem.

"Margaret, when I was over at your house this morning (Ronnie often dropped in coincidentally right at pancake and bacon time), that porketta you were cooking smelled great. Where is Anne hiding it? I'd love a few porketta sandwiches."

She smiled, gave her "I can't hear you—I'm deaf…" look and didn't say a word—a sin of omission.

So Ronnie moved away, but he started the crowd thinking. You can't have a Maroni party without the Maroni porketta, rumored to be the best in town. Where was it? The buzz about the golden pork spread through the party, like the telephone game that kids play sometimes, laughing at the message that finally arrives at the end.

This end message wasn't any better. About a half-hour later, serving desserts, I heard the end version. Anne didn't want anybody but family to have the porketta, and she was making Margaret sit on the cooler to guard it.

Ironic, yes. Surprising, no. I was the reason my kids were on the skinny side, my sheets weren't pure white, the hems came down on my family's pants too soon, so why not be the Porketta Grinch? It suited me.

But I could not and would not fight Delmo, Ronnie, Quinto and the rest of the boys who wouldn't go home until they had had their sandwiches, plus two to go each.

I put my plan into action. Margaret had been sitting there for two hours. "Get your mother some nice iced tea," I ordered my husband.

Not long after, I again gave him the command. "Get her another glass. It's hot today. You know how thirsty she gets."

It wasn't long before my plan worked.

"John, Gene, somebody help me up. I need to go into the house," she said, looking around for me. Spotting me, she pointed her cane at me, banged on the poor little sagging cooler, then shook the cane at me again, not needing any words to get her message across. As he helped her into the house, my husband's glance told me, "Please don't. Please." But I had had it.

My nephew was the first to raise the lid. He got his hands in, and then the pillaging started. Porketta sandwiches were passed hand to hand and flew through the air with Ronnie yelling, "Go long, Delmo," thereby satisfying their need for the sandwiches and to relive their old football days all in one action. The air became filled with the redolent, heavy garlic odor. Faces became filled with "Wow! This is good porketta!" smiles.

It took her a while to return, but it took her no time to see the lay of the land. Her first clue was my nephew, who had two sandwiches in each pocket and one halfway to his mouth when she spotted him. Standing by the cooler and standing my ground, I could only say, "Everyone really loves your cooking, Margaret."

As parties do, this one ended soon afterward. My mother-in-law went home early, beaming with pride over everyone's praise of her food, but burning with irritation that her treasures were used up by the unworthy.

Margaret passed away just a few months after that. She never said a word to me about the flying sandwiches. It was my first open act of rebellion in eighteen years, and I'm not sure she knew how to handle me. But every once in a while, I would find her looking at me, her eyes clenched together. And if I looked back, she silently shook her cane at me. She was willing to let me have her son, but taking food was another story.

The cooler still sits in the garage, never used again. Those two or three hours in the summer, as the poor thing sat stuffed with 120 porketta sandwiches, had given it an aroma that was not good for other uses.

I don't believe that people who have gone from this world can still have much to do with us down here. I don't believe that my mother-in-law left this world with any malice in her heart toward me. But I have gained twenty-five pounds in the two years since her death. No matter what diets, exercises or mind controls I try, that weight just won't come off.

I wonder — maybe she does bear a grudge. Maybe she has a little control from up there. But those pounds aren't from eating porketta. I hate porketta. If I didn't, the sandwiches would have been brought out a lot earlier that day.

~Anne Crawley

Trickster-in-Law

It is the ability to take a joke,
not make one,
that proves you have a sense of humor.
~Max Eastman

At a gathering of my husband's family a few weeks before our wedding, a good-hearted uncle warned, "You still have time, you know. But once you marry into this family, you're done for!" He smiled, but there was something serious behind the joke. While I had no doubts about marrying Bill, his family was a different story, especially my future father-in-law.

As I warned my parents before they met him for the first time, it's difficult to know when he's serious and when he's joking, for he's usually deadpan regardless of what he's saying. The only advice I could give my parents is this: when in doubt, assume he's joking. I imagined being married for years and still sitting across the table from my father-in-law, unprepared for his next practical joke or humorous comment.

When I first met him, he was unloading groceries into his refrigerator. "I just picked up some Yuengling," he said. "Ever hear of it?"

Not being from Pennsylvania, I hadn't heard of that brand of beer. "No," I admitted.

"It's Chinese," he lied. "It doesn't taste like American beer. It tastes very strange, actually. Here, try some."

"I guess it sounds Chinese," I said, taking a sip. "But it tastes like other American beers."

He dismissed me with the wave of his hand. "You don't have a very discriminating palate," he said. "How can you think that tastes like other beers?"

I frowned, and looked at Bill, feeling that I had made a bad first impression with his dad.

Bill just smiled, and then he and his dad broke out in laughter, finally explaining the joke.

"I guess I forgot to warn you about my dad," Bill told me later. "He's a trickster."

From that moment on, I put up my guard. Still, it wasn't enough to anticipate the many pranks my trickster father-in-law would play.

One time, close to Halloween, he sat at the table upstairs. "I'm so tired," he told me, "but I sure could use a soda from downstairs. Would you mind grabbing me one?"

I nodded, glad he felt comfortable enough with me to ask for a favor.

"The light switch to the basement is right near the door. It's the middle switch."

I nodded and followed his instructions, creeping down into the darkened basement. I felt around for the switch. When I turned it on, a huge, bulbous, and furry spider dropped from the ceiling and practically landed on me. I screamed, of course, and behind me — peeking down over the stairway — was my father-in-law, laughing hysterically. I turned back to see the spider — a Halloween prop — retreat back into the basement rafters, ready for its next victim.

You'd think I would have learned my lesson, but he pulled a similar prank a few Christmases later, this time rigging the basement with a light-activated singing Christmas tree that scared the jingle bells out of me!

When we would go out to eat, he would often torment the waitresses — in his lighthearted but deadpan way, of course. Once in a while, when the waitress brought our food, he'd grab his plate while her back was turned and place it on his lap. When she turned around again, she'd say, "I could have sworn I brought your food." And the trickster would just shrug, letting her lose her mind for a few more moments before revealing his prank. He was never mean-spirited about his pranks, and with the waitresses, he usually left a large tip to compensate.

Still, seeing his trickster ways, I should have been prepared. One night, he came to my house with a bottle of "cleaning solution" for my engagement ring. He poured some of the solution into a small glass, then gave me a stiff paintbrush and showed me how to apply the solution to the ring to make it sparkle. He demonstrated using his wife's ring and watched as I cleaned my own.

"Now," he said, "you've been doing well so far, but let's see if you have the guts to go all the way." He looked at me and smiled, then drank his small glass of cleaning solution.

I didn't know how to react. My first thought was to call poison control.

"Bill!" I yelled.

Was my father-in-law going senile? Should I try to induce vomiting?

Bill came into the room.

"Your dad just drank the cleaning solution!" I screamed.

Bill just smiled. I knew instantly I'd been duped.

"Come clean," I said to both of them, and they explained that we'd been cleaning the rings with vodka.

Yes, my father-in-law is a trickster, and I don't think I'll ever be able to predict all his pranks. Each time I visit his home, there are new gadgets sitting on the shelf: singing rats, remote-controlled bats, flashing alarms—you name it, he has it. And I'm sure one day they'll each get me in one way or another.

But underneath his prankster exterior is a sweet man who cares only about bringing joy to others, even if it's in the form of laughter. He listens carefully to everyone he cares about—though whether he uses what we say for or against us is left to his devices.

When I mentioned on the phone that I liked the way the neighbor's clematis plants were growing up their lamppost, he seemed quite interested, asking me specifics about size and color. I knew he was planning something, but I wasn't sure if he'd show up with a singing clematis plant, or a real one! This time, it was real. But whenever I walk past my new plant, I still keep up my guard, for I never know what to expect. After all, I'm married to the son of a trickster!

~Pat Maloney

On Esther Time

How long a minute is,
depends on which side of the bathroom door you're on.
~Zall's Second Law

My mother-in-law was always late. Something always happened at the last minute: a slip strap broke and had to be pinned, the hem of her skirt or pants unraveled, the heel of her shoe broke, or something equally drastic occurred, like spilling coffee, tea, or food down the front of her blouse. It never failed. She was accident-prone, but only when it was time to go somewhere. When Esther was diagnosed with pancreatic cancer and undergoing chemotherapy, she was even late for her treatments.

Esther's habitual lateness wore down everyone's nerves and patience.

"You'll be late to your own funeral," my father-in-law Bill said with a wink and a smile at his sweetheart.

"I'll get there when I get there," Esther said as she took her time getting ready to go. "The Lord gives us plenty of time." She smiled and patted Bill's arm. "Plenty of time."

"There's not enough time in the Lord's day for you. You always try to get a little more," Bill said as he kissed his wife.

There was never any argument, just the calm give and take of a well-worn discussion that no one ever won—no one but Esther. She always had the last word—with a little help.

Bill couldn't handle even a little pepper. He couldn't taste it, but he felt it. Over the years, Esther had determined exactly how much pepper it took to send him running to the bathroom moaning, as it did its fiery work. The moments passed with Bill in the bathroom and Esther quietly smiling while she did the dishes. Life went on in this way until they found out Esther had cancer.

Esther was determined not to let it change her or her life. Bill tiptoed around the house and Esther until she peppered his food one night. He ran to the bathroom moaning and holding his stomach while Esther placidly cleared the table and did the dishes. My husband Nick and his brother Larry snickered, forgetting their fear and grief as their father raced up the stairs.

"Don't you two have something better to do? Take out the trash? Get ready for work tomorrow?" Esther jiggled the pepper mill in her hand.

Nick and Larry beat a hasty retreat — Larry to the garbage and Nick to his room to lay out his work clothes. Neither of them wanted to be present for the confrontation they knew was coming.

When Bill came back down the stairs, Esther was putting the dried dishes into the cabinet. He watched her from the doorway as she moved about the kitchen, occasionally stopping to catch her breath from the pain. She closed the cabinet doors and picked up the broom from the basement stairwell, walked over to Bill and handed it to him. "It's about time you started helping around the house," she said.

Bill took the broom and, under Esther's eagle eye, swept the kitchen linoleum to her satisfaction. She took great pleasure in directing him to get under the edges of the cabinets and between the stove and refrigerator, ordering him here and there until each speck of dust or a cobweb, invisible to Bill, was thoroughly removed. Bill knew Esther wasn't going to allow her family to treat her like an invalid; she'd had enough of that, taking care of her mother before they could marry. They both knew she wouldn't be around long, but what time they had left together would be shared the way they shared everything in their life — in Esther's own time.

When Esther finally gave in to the cancer and died, the family was grief-stricken, but none more so than Bill. He had lived every moment of his life for Esther. She was his sun, his moon, and his heart.

On the day of Esther's funeral, the family gathered at the funeral home for the last time. Everyone waited for Esther's casket to appear. It didn't. The clock ticked on. People shifted in their seats and talked quietly. Bill checked his watch. Five minutes. Ten. Fifteen. Twenty minutes late. The funeral director asked Bill to follow him.

"I'm so sorry about the delay, but something has gone wrong," the funeral director said.

"What?" Bill asked.

"Well, it seems the cart's wheels are stuck. We have to get one from storage. The spare is being used for another funeral."

"Mr. Southwick," one of the funeral home attendants said to the director, "we got it fixed. Should I tell Jerry not to get the other cart?"

Bill laughed and shook his head, checking his watch. Twenty-five minutes. Esther was always thirty minutes late. She would arrive on time, her time.

The funeral director looked like he thought Bill had lost his mind.

Bill smiled. "I always said Esther would be late to her own funeral." He chuckled as he went back to the parlor.

Bill sat down and put his arms around his children. I watched in surprise as he smiled and looked at his children. My husband was stunned, trying to hold back his tears.

"Check your watches," Bill said as Esther's casket rolled into the parlor. One by one, Esther's children smiled. I didn't understand. I checked my watch; it was 1:30. Then Nick laughed.

His brothers and sisters soon laughed with him. The rest of the grieving family looked on in horror. Standing and turning toward the assembled aunts, uncles, cousins, and friends, Bill tapped his watch. Each of them checked their watches, some through tears. One by one, they smiled and nodded. I had only heard the stories, but they all knew Esther very well. She loved making an entrance and controlling time just a little.

Bill walked up to the coffin as the attendants raised the lid. "You just had to have the last word." He leaned over and kissed Esther's lips one last time. "I love you, my darling," he whispered, "but I pray there's no pepper in heaven."

~J.M. Cornwell

Sharpening the Pointy Hat

We don't see things as they are; we see them as we are.

~Anaïs Nin

Think of any mother-in-law horror story you've heard. I've probably lived it. Yes, my mother-in-law and I had a rocky start.

My mother-in-law and I are in many ways opposites. She grew up in a small town—a town so small it doesn't have traffic lights. I grew up in a city. She's lived in the same place her entire life. I've moved around. Understandably, our perspectives differ greatly.

At first, Maggie's old-fashioned perspective was a refreshing change from the hustle of the city. Tommy's mom is a great cook, making everything from scratch. And she pays such attention to detail! Snowman serving ware in the winter. Harvest wreaths in the fall.

But it wasn't long before I noticed sour spots below the too-sugary exterior. What follows are just a few of the more lighthearted clashes we've had.

One summer, I invited the in-laws to dinner: burgers and corn on the cob. Impossible to spoil, right? Not according to Maggie. When everything was cooked and set on plates, Maggie helped get fixings from the refrigerator.

"Oh…" she said in that voice I'd grown accustomed to. It was a voice that encompassed displeasure, criticism, and a hint of self-righteousness.

"Oh?" I asked.

"Margarine..." she muttered.

"Margarine? Are we out?"

"No, there's plenty here. It's just..."

"It's just what?" I asked.

My father-in-law walked in.

"Honey," Maggie said to her husband, "they have MAR-garine." She said it like we were concealing drugs.

"Oh, no," her husband whispered.

"Guess we'll be going to the store," she said, shoving the unholy margarine back into the refrigerator.

I eyed the steaming dinner.

"Why?"

She was already out the door.

"Margarine just doesn't melt on the corn. There's just no substitute for honest-to-goodness butter," my father-in-law managed to say before he, too, disappeared.

I looked at my husband in frustration. I'd been proud of my low-cholesterol cooking.

But it didn't stop there. On the phone later, my mother-in-law brought up the subject of mashed potatoes, of all things. "You know," she said, "there are some people so lazy that they buy mashed potatoes in boxes. They're powder, and you just add water. What is the world coming to?!"

I tried to be as ambiguous as possible in the sigh that escaped my lips. Being busy, I often came home from work glad for the easy-to-make boxed potatoes. But did she already know that? Had she searched my pantry while she was here for dinner? I felt like she was an inquisitor demanding a confession. I changed the subject quickly, for I knew enough not to get on her bad side.

She often told stories of her job, relishing in the power she held over co-workers. During one particular visit, Maggie had just been promoted and was soaking up the limelight. She had her husband cook dinner, as she had worked late that day.

"I'm getting so busy I don't even have time to cook," she said, looking to me for a reaction. I felt like telling her to make a box of powdered mashed potatoes, but I held my tongue. My lack of response annoyed her, so she continued the story—speaking louder.

"At work today, the secretary left a check on the copy machine. She must have been making copies for her records, but she forgot to take the original from the machine."

"So did you give it back to her?" my husband asked.

"No!" Maggie said indignantly, surprised that such a thought would cross her son's mind. "I put it in my desk drawer."

"What? Why?"

"Why? Because..." Her eyes lit up, and her manicured nails tapped the kitchen table authoritatively until I looked up from the floor. "Because I'm going to wait until she realizes something's off about the books. It's irresponsible to leave a check on the copier like that. I can't wait to see the look on her face, and boy do I have a mouthful for her!"

I was waiting for her to accuse the secretary of cooking mashed potatoes from powder! But, as usual, I held my tongue.

In another episode, shopping downtown, we came across the new-age store that Maggie refers to as "the witch store that Ali likes." Her tone of voice makes it sound like all they sell is margarine and powdered mashed potatoes. I enjoy the store's unique items—browsing the tarot card sets, smelling the candles, and seeing if there are any distinctive necklaces to buy. This time, Maggie insisted on accompanying me into the store. As we walked past each display, she loudly questioned everything at a volume that ensured everyone could hear.

Maggie looked at a woman wearing a maxi dress and colorful bandana. "My, I wonder if anyone in here wears this stuff at church!" she half-shouted. A woman giving a tarot reading looked up with a snarl. "No," she said loudly to me. "I guess not."

We perused the jewelry section. "I wonder if they have any crosses here. Nope, doesn't seem like it."

I shook my head at her self-righteous tone.

It was nearly Halloween, and the shop had a small display of costumes. One of them was a pink, pointed witch hat with a matching cape. A few thoughts crossed my mind involving my mother-in-law and certain infamous wicked witches, but I pushed them back, hesitant to even entertain them in the privacy of my mind lest Maggie read my face. I turned away to compose myself.

To my surprise, Maggie tugged at my sleeve. When I turned to her, I couldn't stop laughing. She was wearing the pink witch hat.

"What do you think, Ali?" she asked. "Does it fit my personality? The wicked witch of the town? I could wear it to work. I'm the wicked witch of the office, you know. I could come to your house and be the wicked witch of your kitchen. And when I get to be too nice, I'll just sharpen the tip of the hat a little bit, and I'll be back to my old witchy self."

Part of her was kidding, but partly this was her lighthearted way of explaining herself to me. Her way of making peace.

After that day, I saw her in a new light. Something about her recognizing her flaws made her human. As I looked at her with impartial eyes, I learned that we weren't so different after all. Sure, we went about things in different ways, but our core personalities we shared. Maybe there was something to the saying about men looking for their mothers in their wives.

Both of us like to do things our own way—in stubbornness, we are equal. Both prefer being in charge rather than being told what to do. And while I would never have hidden a missing check, there are instances I can recall where my vengeance button was pushed, and I did things I regretted later.

I knew things were fine when she turned to me one day and said, "Ali, if I get too witchy, you'd better let me know. But, likewise, if I get too nice, you'd better tell me, 'Maggie, it's time to sharpen your pointed hat!'"

~Ali Monroe

"Of course I can insult you.
We're family."

Spring Cleaning

*Traditions are group efforts
to keep the unexpected from happening.*
~Mignon McLaughlin, The Neurotic's Notebook

I've always been led to believe that the devil is in the details, not lurking in the closet. So one spring when my Italian-American mother-in-law invited me to participate in her annual ritual to chase out the devil, I paused to consider.

Throughout my long marriage, she had taught me the correct way to hand over a knife so as not to cut a friendship and how to throw salt over my right shoulder when someone gave me the evil eye. I had learned how to pull out Holy Water at the slightest hint of trouble, and I wouldn't dream of preparing eggplant without first placing the raw, salted slices between two dinner plates. (I never knew why, but it worked!) After twenty-eight years of marriage, I thought I'd seen it all—until that Saturday.

It was the day before Easter, and we were visiting my mother-in-law and other family back in the West Virginia hills. My husband was still asleep downstairs, my mother-in-law was chopping carrots, celery and potatoes for a stew, and my nine-year-old niece Jean and I played with dolls at a nearby table. Suddenly, my mother-in-law yelled.

"Quick! Grab a towel or a flyswatter! It's a quarter till noon."

"Why?" I asked. I jumped into motion and opened the

kitchen drawer to pull out some dry, clean towels. "Is there a fly somewhere?"

"Open all the windows," she directed. As I cranked open the window, my mother-in-law explained that, in just a few minutes, she would carry out a Sicilian custom, a family tradition she had practiced for more than seven decades. At noon, on Holy Saturday, the day Jesus rose from the tomb, the women of the family stopped their work to chase out the devil. Her Sicilian mother had brought the custom to America when she immigrated in the 1920s, using brooms or sticks to beat the walls and force the devil out the window. Since the house we were staying in was newer and had freshly painted walls, my mother-in-law would improvise with towels and flyswatters. She asked me to join her, but said it was okay if I chose not to participate. In a devil-may-care instant, I said yes.

My niece, a veteran at this devil-chasing business it seemed, motioned me to follow her upstairs. There we ran in and out of various rooms rapidly cranking open windows. She laughed and called out to me, reporting her progress as she flew through the house.

"I got my room! You get Grandma's," she said.

"What about the closets?" I asked.

"Yes, open them," she answered, her voice rising in excitement as high noon neared. After we finished the upstairs, we rushed to the basement, but not before my mother-in-law cautioned, "Don't open the windows down there. The spiders will get in."

Couldn't the devil be in the basement? And if so, how would he leave if we didn't open the windows? Were spiders a more tangible threat on this day? And there was the question of whether to disturb my husband from his sleep. I don't think the devil would want to tangle with my husband before his first cup of coffee. I know I don't. I let him be.

We returned to the kitchen to wait under the clock with tools in hand, my niece and I armed with dishtowels and my mother-in-law with a flyswatter. Vegetables simmered on the stove, and steam drifted up to the ceiling. My mother-in-law gave us further instructions.

"Devil be gone, *levati di cca diavulu*," she said. "Repeat this as you run through the rooms waving the dishtowels. I'll get this area with the flyswatter."

"It's time!" my niece shouted, pointing to the clock's straight-up hands. We took off and darted through the rooms of the house like hellions, waving and flapping towels.

"Devil be gone, devil be gone" and "*levati di cca diavulu*," we chanted to the swooshing of the flyswatter and the crisp snap of towels. After ten minutes or so, my niece and I reunited with my mother-in-law in the kitchen. We were breathing hard with faces pink from all the running and shouting. I felt exhilarated.

The clean spring air drifted in through the open windows. I looked out toward the white blossoms of an apple tree resting upon an expanse of emerald lawn. Not a devil in sight. I do not know if my mother-in-law's custom had succeeded in ridding the house of any demons, but as my niece's warm laughter filled the room and I saw the satisfied smile on my mother-in-law's face, the devil if I cared.

~Janie Dempsey Watts

The Power of Pasta

Conscience is less an inner voice than the memory of a mother's glance.
~Robert Brault

On the day that I was married, I took the usual "love, honor, sickness, health, etc." vows out loud. I made a few other vows to myself, one of which was to stay calm and understanding about the incredibly close bond between John and his mother. After all, he was thirty-three when I married him, and he had lived with this mother that whole time, so a few precedents had been set. The dating years had taught me that, in the choice between her and me, I might get a sheepish look followed by an apology in private later, but he would never take my side against her in front of her or others. My mother-in-law, in her own way, is a wonderful woman, and I could give her some unflattering labels such as "quirky" or "difficult," but what comes to mind most is "very loving," in a unique way.

So I vowed to stay calm whenever he took her side, knowing that the results of hurting her were far worse than the results of letting me down. Or at least I hoped so.

And so it went for many years, smoothly as can be expected. My teeth are shorter from grinding them down, and the neighbors have become accustomed to my running out in the backyard to scream from time to time, but, overall, it has been smooth, except for a random holiday here and there.

As in all families, we had holiday "traditions," unwritten rules set in concrete, never to be changed. Christmas Eve was at my sister-in-law's because she knows how to do that seven-course fish thing so well. So Christmas Eve was his family's. Each Christmas Day, we attended church and spent the morning at home. Around noon, all presents opened, we headed to his mother's for homemade cappelletti and ravioli. Around four, we went to my mother's, pretending we were hungry because she had worked all day preparing a turkey or ham dinner. These endearing, if fattening, traditions were embedded in our lives.

As fate would have it, one year we just couldn't follow that routine. It had snowed, snowed and snowed, leaving us buried in feet of white powder. Our home is situated in a large natural wind tunnel between a sizeable lake and a pond, giving us a double lake effect, plus a wind chill factor worthy of the Arctic. We could barely open the door that day and had to force the dog to go outside to do his duty. No one was traveling; the roads were barely plowed, and TV announcers urged everyone to stay put. We almost did.

I knew there would be trouble. My mother-in-law began calling at 9:00 A.M. Those bags of cappelletti and ravioli that she had created were bursting out of her freezer. It was Christmas. They had to be eaten that day. Weather had no influence on her schedule or her cooking. I said no. She called at 10:00, 10:30, 11:00, 11:30 and 12:00, frantic by 1:00.

It was Christmas! There were ravioli! About 12:00, John had started to pace. From 1:00 to 2:00, we all shoveled, trying to move at least two feet of snow off the house roof, as it was leaking more than usual. Of course, this made him even hungrier. Thoughts of ravioli obsessed his genetically-driven mind. I said no. Then I watched in amazement as his primal instinct took over. He became crazed. Christmas and ravioli had to be honored! I said no—we would not go out in that storm just for pasta. At 3:00, he lost all control. "Get into the truck! Everybody!" he screamed as he grabbed for the phone, dialed and yelled, "Put the water on. We're on our way!"

It certainly was an exciting trip. We live at the top of a one-mile hill, followed by a bit of level road, followed by a two-mile downhill fondly known as The Wildcat, then a two-mile uphill stretch. There was no "over the river and through the woods to Grandmother's house we go" because nothing could be seen but snow, waist-deep snow that sprayed out on both sides of the truck as we plowed our own path. We were on the road, off the road, in a ditch, in the opposite ditch, but my husband is a veteran of driving on roads like this, and his truck is built for this challenge. The girls were having a great time in their car seats, whooping at all the white spray. I had confidence in John and very little fear, although I realized that my mother-in-law's wishes were dominant again. In the true Christmas spirit (and because I just LOVE her pasta), I hung on and enjoyed being the only family out in that untouched winter wonderland.

We did not pass a single vehicle the whole way down, and the twelve-mile journey took more than forty-five minutes. The bleak, beautiful snow had brought the Valley to a halt—except for one blue Chevy avalanche on an "emergency" ravioli run.

She complained as we walked in. "What took so long? The pasta is getting cold!" Unbelievable. I almost decided not to eat at all when she nagged like that, but even I could not hold out against Margaret's homemade ravioli and sauce. I felt thankful and peaceful that we could spend Christmas together—at least our branch of the family. John's two sisters and one brother never made it, thereby proving to their mother—neglected on Christmas—that their love for her was nowhere near as strong as John's. John beamed.

My mother lived nearby, but we didn't stop in. She would have been shocked, appalled, furious, unbelieving that we had left the house in such weather. The ride home was faster, the road almost hidden in the night. Our tracks were the only ones through the snow. John once again made it seem like a Sunday drive in the park, even though he was working hard to keep the truck in line. By the time we got home, we all knew this had been a Christmas to remember.

Someday, I hope I have a child who loves me, or at least my cooking, as much as John loves his mother and her ravioli. But I will insist that they stay home until the roads have been plowed.

~Anne Crawley

The Puzzle

Great minds think alike.
~English Proverb

"Hahaha!" Dad screamed maniacally, sounding scarily like a B-movie monster as he clutched the jigsaw puzzle to his chest. "She'll hate this! Hahaha!" Dad had to clutch his sides he was laughing so hard.

It was the early 1960s, and our family was Christmas shopping. Mom had taken my little sister to the other side of the small department store, which left my brother, sister and I standing with jaws dropped, wondering what on earth had gotten into Dad for him to be acting so strangely over a 1,000-piece, non-interlocking jigsaw puzzle. The picture on the cover of the box showed mostly variant shades of a blue sky and a few small green slashes for trees.

"Who is that present for, Dad?" I hesitantly asked. He was acting really weird.

The adults in the extended family drew names to get each other presents and had a five-dollar spending limit. I knew Dad had drawn Grandma's name, and Grandma had drawn Dad's name. Even at a young age, I knew that Dad and his mother-in-law, my grandma, had "issues" with each other. Maybe it was the two-hour rant Dad went on after we left Grandma's house and were driving home that gave this away to me. They barely tolerated being in the same room together. So, it was somewhat ironic that they were the only two family members who refused to work on the jigsaw puzzle my Aunt Mary set up on a card table at Christmas time. They each made no secret of the fact that doing jigsaw puzzles drove them crazy. That was how I positively knew the puzzle couldn't be for Grandma.

Dad paused for a moment and then admitted a little defensively, "This is for Grandma. I know she doesn't normally like jigsaw puzzles, but she'll have hours and hours AND HOURS of fun putting together this great, big…" He couldn't go on as hysterical laughter overtook him again.

Back in those days, you didn't argue with your father, so I just kept quiet and watched as the clerk rang up the sale and we left the store. I was pretty sure Grandma would get Dad something not great but not bad either, possibly a box of handkerchiefs. Grandma was sure going to be disappointed.

I didn't see the puzzle again until Christmas morning. My aunt, uncle, cousins, Mom, Dad, brother, sisters, Grandpa and Grandma were all crowded into Grandma's living room amid a ton of discarded wrapping paper and ribbon. We had all enjoyed opening our presents, but the gift-opening was winding down. There were only two brightly wrapped gifts left under the small Christmas tree that Grandpa had set up in the corner. It was Grandma's turn, so she opened the next-to-last gift and pulled out her jigsaw puzzle. Everyone got a big laugh out of the gag gift, even Grandma, who giggled so hard that tears ran down her cheeks.

We found out what caused Grandma's hilarity a few seconds later when Dad opened his present from Grandma. She had the last laugh after all. We all roared as Dad took the wrappings off his present and, instead of a box of handkerchiefs, he stared at a box with a huge picture of beige sandy pyramids on the outside and 2,000 non-interlocking pieces on the inside!

~Cynthia Morningstar

Better or Worse

We find comfort among those who agree with us —
growth among those who don't.
~Frank A. Clark

Knowing our wedding would be a headache, Ted and I wanted to elope.

"We'll get married at City Hall," I told my parents.

"Hmmm," my dad considered. "I'd like a ceremony and reception. It's been a while since we've gotten the whole family together."

When Ted told his parents we wanted to elope, their reaction was even more adverse. "A secular wedding?" his mom, Erica, asked, flabbergasted. "You won't be married in the eyes of God!"

So we agreed to have a ceremony and reception, more for our families than for ourselves. "Just one thing," we told them. "Keep it small."

Months later, we discussed details.

"I don't really have a preference for wedding favors," I said.

"Me neither," agreed Ted.

Erica smiled. "I saw these beautiful favors at the last wedding I attended: candles wrapped in tulle. We could do them in lavender!"

"Why lavender?" Ted asked.

"That's your wedding color!"

"It is?" he asked.

They both looked at me.

"We haven't decided," I told Erica.

"Well, I just assumed you'd agree on lavender."

"Yuck," said Ted.

"Then what color?" she snipped.

"Since we're getting married over Fourth of July weekend, why not red and blue?"

"How gaudy," Erica said.

Both looked at me.

"I don't mind either one," I said. "Or getting married in City Hall," I mumbled.

We finally compromised on a deep blue and burgundy theme. But over the next few weeks, Erica wouldn't stop asking about the candle favors, which she wanted to make herself. The thing was, she never offered to pay for them, and we weren't sure whether she was expecting my parents to pay, although we assumed she was.

"We'd better get Mom the materials to make these favors before she busts a gut," Ted said one day.

"I agree," I said. "But is she paying?"

"I wouldn't count on it. My parents are very traditional. Parents of the bride pay for the wedding."

"Then I'd better buy the candles, right?" We laughed.

Ted's mom has expensive tastes. Very expensive. Once, when we asked to go "somewhere nice" for a graduation dinner, she took us to a $60-per-plate restaurant. We had nightmarish visions of her buying crystal candle holders for every wedding guest, then passing the bill on to my parents in the name of tradition.

"Yes," Ted said. "We should buy the candles."

My mom volunteered to bring Erica the candles, seeing it as an opportunity to visit Ted's parents and discuss the wedding. She and I picked out some nice votives in clear glass holders.

On the appointed day, my mom drove an hour to Ted's parents' house with a box of candles in hand.

When Erica opened the door, her face turned to scorn. "What are THOSE?"

"Candles," Mom said.

"But those aren't the right ones. They're supposed to be in champagne glasses!"

This was the first my mother had heard of this. Erica had never mentioned champagne glasses. My mom said so.

Erica drew up her face. "I guess I'll make do," she said. "Would you like to come in?"

After driving an hour to be met with scorn, my mom made an excuse. This prompted another phone call to Ted about my mom's rudeness.

A week later, we were summoned to Ted's parents' house.

"Ted," his parents said, "we wanted to talk to you about this 'nondenominational' thing."

Ted and I sighed. My own parents were two different religions, and though they were accepting and tolerant, I had no religious affiliation. Ted's parents had been so strict with Ted that he turned away from organized religion. Ted and I were perfect for each other, but Ted's traditional parents weren't happy.

"We want you to be married in the eyes of God," they said.

"Nondenominational isn't atheist," Ted insisted.

His parents exchanged troubled glances. "We don't like it. We'd like to be traditional."

Then, as if things couldn't get worse, we sent out the invitations. To please Ted's parents, we decided to be as traditional as possible. We researched traditional wedding invitations and then printed them ourselves. We couldn't wait until Ted's parents saw them.

Days later, I heard Ted cursing into the phone. The last thing he said was, "This is exactly why we wanted to get married in City Hall!" Apparently, his parents were irate that my parents' names, but not theirs, had been put on the invitations. Ted calmly tried to explain our desire to please them by being traditional, but they didn't see it that way at all.

Our conflicts were never resolved. At the rehearsal dinner, our families didn't talk.

The final straw came in the form of a phone call the night before the wedding as I was packing for the hotel.

"Aggie," Erica cackled into the receiver, "I'd like to know why my relatives are at table 13, and your high school friends are seated at table 2. That's just not right."

Luckily, the laws of physics prevented me from reaching through the phone. I tried, calmly, to explain that the tables started in the back corner, so table 2 was actually in the corner near the door. Table 13 was right in the middle of the room.

She snickered into the phone.

I said nothing.

She handed the phone to Ted.

"Aggie," Ted said, "I was thinking about the name tags."

"Yes?"

"Well, are we alphabetizing them on the center table?"

"Yes," I explained. "Each name tag is printed with a table number."

"That's a bad idea."

"Why?" The conversation was suspect: Ted didn't even know we had name tags!

"We should put the name tags on the individual tables. Then people can just walk around until they find their name."

"It's a big room. There are lots of older relatives. They'd get confused."

"Thanks for understanding and making that change."

"What?" I asked. "I didn't agree to anything!"

"I know. Thanks for agreeing."

"Ted, what's wrong with you? Are you saying this because your mother's in the room?"

"Yes," he admitted.

"Is she making you do this?"

"Yes."

"Do you even care about the name tags, Ted?"

"Honestly, no." He paused, then said, "Thanks again," and hung up.

I called him back a few minutes later. His mother was no longer in the room.

"They're already alphabetized in my suitcase," I explained, "and they'll be on the center table tomorrow. You can't let your mom boss us around."

I heard Ted's dad in the background. He had been quiet the whole time, but now, driven insane by Erica's incessant nagging, snapped: "Ted, you tell your future wife how it's gonna be and show her who wears the pants in the relationship."

"It'll blow over," Ted said, talking over his dad.

"We should have eloped," I joked. The situation was ridiculous, but at least Ted was on my side, and we weren't fighting with each other.

After all that, the wedding went well, with friends and family reuniting, though my parents stayed away from Ted's.

But as I recount the story, everyone tells me the same thing: at least Ted and I stuck together through all the turmoil, as we've done since. That is the test of a true relationship, and proof that Ted and I were meant to be.

~Aggie Welsh

"...AND YOU SAY THE ROMANCE HAS GONE OUT OF YOUR MARRIAGE?!"

To Each Her Own

Technology presumes there's just one right way to do things and there never is.
~Robert M. Pirsig

My mother-in-law, Helen, grew up on a homestead out in Kimball County in western Nebraska, six miles from the nearest small town. Her family climbed out of their Model-T Ford on a bleak day in February 1917 and stood on a prairie so barren that nine-year-old Helen could not even imagine it green with the wheat that her father hoped to raise.

But that had to wait for spring, and she, her parents and her three sisters lived in a rented house in town to finish the school year. By the time the days had lengthened and warmed, her father had built a barn and a granary, a simple wooden building about the size of a single garage that stood ready to hold their first crop of wheat. This dirt-floored, plank-walled rectangle was the family home that summer and the next winter.

The spring of 1918, her father dug by hand half of the basement for what would eventually become their home. The next year, they lived in this dirt-walled, dirt-floored subterranean space. A tarp served as a roof. It was the summer of 1919 before they could finally move into their new house. Of course, it was without running water, plumbing or electricity, but they felt like it was a castle. They stayed there out on the farm as Helen finished high school and took summer school at the University of Wyoming so she could begin her teaching career.

By the time electricity came to the farm after World War II, Helen was married, had three children, and was comfortably settled in a larger small town forty-five miles east. She had a green lawn, electric lights, natural gas heat and, of course, running water and indoor plumbing. What she did not have, and what she really needed, her grown children decided, was a dishwasher.

This was a woman who, at five feet two and maybe 110 pounds, could turn out two pies with one hand tied up in her apron. She was one of the best-organized, most efficient people I ever knew. It goes without saying that she cooked special dinners for her extended family. She fixed food for shut-ins. She cooked meals for church events, weddings, anniversaries and funerals. She even fixed dishes for potluck suppers for at least six lodges and clubs.

Through all those years, she washed dishes by hand in the sink. We children had all moved into the modern age and had dishwashers. We loved our dishwashers, so we tried to sell her on easing her labors by installing one.

She would not hear of it. "Too much trouble," she said. "You have to handle every dish twice — put it in, wait while it washes, take it out, put it away. I can be all done in a tenth of the time. What's the point?"

We argued about the work reduced, the time saved, the sanitary factor, bidding farewell to greasy water and dishwater hands. We got nowhere.

When the time came for her and my father-in-law to give up their house and move into an apartment, we children were delighted to learn the kitchen was equipped with a dishwasher. At last she would learn she could take it easy, get off her feet, relax and let the machine do the work.

A few weeks went by. They talked about liking the apartment. The storage space was good. It was nice and sunny. Close to church. The neighbors were nice. Not one word about the dishwasher.

Finally, I asked her if she was using her new appliance. There was a pause. Then, "Yes." Another pause. "I'm finding it handy."

Not wanting to say "I told you so," I merely smiled with satisfaction and let the subject drop.

Then one of our boys had a birthday, and we gathered in the apartment for the customary family dinner. When we were all satisfactorily stuffed, we began carrying dishes into the kitchen.

"Oh, good," someone said. "We can use the dishwasher."

"Oh, no," Helen said. She seemed flustered. "Not now. It's full."

"What do you mean, Mom?" her daughter asked as she bent to open it. "It can't be full."

She was wrong. We all stood staring at a full dishwasher. Full of paper sacks. Big tan grocery sacks. Square white bakery sacks. Large shiny sacks imprinted with stores' names. Small flat sacks from the variety store. All carefully separated by sizes, folded where necessary, and neatly filed between the dishwashers' dividers.

Helen stared at us defiantly, hands on hips, daring each of us to comment.

One by one, we closed our dropped jaws. One by one, we swallowed our smart-mouthed comments. What was the point?

She was, after all, using the dishwasher. Her way. And finding it handy.

Helen went to her well-earned rest some years ago, and when we cleared out the apartment, I finished up the kitchen. I packed away her dishes, wiped out the cupboards, and then thought, "Oh, the dishwasher." Smiling, I pulled open the door, intent on emptying it of its unusual burden. Then I stopped.

I could not bring myself to dismantle this last concrete evidence of Helen's unique, spunky personality. Why not leave it alone? A surprise for the new tenant. Something to puzzle over. Something to laugh about. And, just maybe, if the new lady of the house needed a sack, she'd smile to find one handy.

~Nancy M. Peterson

Chapter
3

Family Vacations
and Reunions

No vacation goes unpunished.

~Karl Hakkarainen

Judith Who?

If you don't believe in ghosts,
you've never been to a family reunion.
~Ashleigh Brilliant

I come from a long line of people who haven't spoken to each other for years. When they do make contact at family reunions, they can't even remember each other's names. After not talking with my cousin Jan, I phoned her to discuss our upcoming reunion, an event that occurs once every decade.

"Hello Jan," I said. "It's your cousin Judith."

"Judith who?" came the response.

"Your cousin from Connecticut."

"Do I have a cousin from Connecticut?"

"I moved to Connecticut thirty-four years ago."

"I once had a cousin Judy from New Jersey," Jan said.

"I was once Judy from New Jersey. Now I'm Judith from Connecticut."

"What happened to Judy?"

"She reinvented herself," I said.

There was a long pause on the other end after which Jan said, "Well, I don't know any Judiths."

And that about sums up our family dynamics. We are stuck in a time warp where everyone is treated according to the last memory we have of each other.

After several phone calls and a grueling amount of planning, most of which was assigned to me, we agreed to meet at my Aunt Ray's house for an official family reunion with all those people with whom, under normal circumstances, we would never associate.

Aunt Ray, who for years I thought was an uncle, suffers from terminal carsickness. She cannot travel for more than twenty minutes at a stretch. Thus, we all agreed to travel to her. This meant getting up at the crack of dawn and driving a few hundred miles to a remote part of upstate New York that makes Afghanistan look like a resort area. The "catering" was to be a smorgasbord of everyone's worst culinary efforts. To make matters worse, Aunt Ray, who wanted to be accommodating, prepared most of the food herself. I kept a bottle of Pepto-Bismol in the glove compartment... just in case.

The first person to arrive was my Uncle Max, who was still chomping on the same cigar I could have sworn he was smoking at our last reunion. I greeted him while simultaneously trying not to inhale the smoke that curled around my head and wafted into my nasal passages. Uncle Max was never my favorite person. That's because he always took special delight in using me as a target for his unique brand of humor.

"So, it's little Judy," Max said, joined by my Cousin Elaine-from-Parsippany. Cousin Elaine has never answered a direct question in her entire life.

"Hello, Elaine," I said. "How are you?"

"How are you is the question," Elaine said. "And is it true what I've heard about you?"

"What did you hear?"

"Do you really want to know?"

"Is there something I should know, Elaine?"

"Don't ask me," she said. "If you don't know what I'm talking about, it's better off left alone. I'm not one to repeat gossip."

My cousin Elaine and I have been having these kinds of conversations since we were twelve.

Also included among this familial cast of characters were my chubby aunts who were still sporting their mink stoles. They pinched my cheeks and answered all questions with "Don't ask!" These are the women who have never experienced a day of perfect health in their lives. Hypochondria runs rampant in our family. Occasionally, someone acquires a real illness from which they derive several years' worth of conversation.

"My hip is still killing me," Aunt Marsha complained.

"Never mind your hip," Uncle Henry interrupted. "At least you have another hip. I have only one gall bladder, and it aches me every day. Let me tell you about my last attack."

The thought of Uncle Henry regaling me with stories of his internal organs was more than I could bear. I walked away just as Uncle Ben, the veterinarian, appeared to make a definitive diagnosis based purely on his medical intuition.

"I once had a monkey that had the same symptoms as you," Ben told Henry. "He died a year later of complications from ingesting a banana. If I were you, I'd stay away from fruit."

"And cashew nuts," Uncle Henry said. "The last nut I ate went through my system like a porcupine quill."

The two uncles rambled on like this for the next hour while I moved on to the more exciting among us: Aunt Sylvia.

"Have you tried my prune whip lasagna, darling?" Aunt Sylvia asked me. "It's your Uncle Phil's favorite. It keeps him regular, if you catch my drift."

"It's to-die-for," I said literally, as Aunt Sylvia fork-fed me a taste.

"I would give you the recipe, sweetheart," she said, "but your Aunt Pauline said it's a secret."

"Not to worry," I burped. "I can always ask Aunt Pauline myself."

"No, you can't. Aunt Pauline died five years ago. She choked on one of her turkey meatballs. Uncle Sam couldn't revive her because he never learned the Heimlich maneuver."

Such conversations are the meat of our reunions. They allow me to remember, in case I forget, that my family consists of a wide range of weirdos. And yet, reunions are necessary evils. They allow us to discover the most amazing facts: who has had the most operations and the most expensive dental work, who made the most money and whose children married the most inappropriate people. It's a little like a three-ring circus, except these animals are for real.

Reunions always leave a lasting impression. I learned that my fifty-six-year-old cousin, Eve, has taken a thirty-five-year-old lover. My niece, Francine, has had three facelifts in ten years, and my Uncle James-the-banker broke his nose in the automatic teller. But the one thought that plagued me all the way home was what kind of petty gossip my Cousin Elaine had on me. Was it true? And how many relatives did she manage to tell before the day was over? In the end, though, it doesn't really matter. I won't be seeing these folks for another ten years. By that time, and with a little luck, they might not remember who I am.

~Judith Marks-White

"For us to have a good family reunion, we'd have to run off and join the circus."

Reprinted by permission of Jonny Hawkins
©2009

A Class Act

Insanity is hereditary — you get it from your kids.
~Sam Levenson

There are certain hard truths you must face as you get older. You will never be a movie star, for example. You are not as nice or as smart as you would like to think. That pear-shaped lump following you around is actually your tush. Here is the hard truth I have had to face recently: My family will never be a class act. I had always expected that my family would be elegant, charming, and witty. Somehow, I had this idea that my child would be wise and knowing and mature, and that we'd have lovely, quiet evenings playing cribbage or discussing foreign films. It has occurred to me that I have landed in a different country altogether.

This fact was brought home to me during a trip that my husband, son, and I took a while ago to Washington, D.C. with my sister and her family. I envisioned inspiring visits to museums and government buildings, enlightening discussions during which the face of my precious son, Levi, then five years old, would light up with the excitement of discovery. Yeah, yeah, I know — what was I thinking?

At our first stop, the Capitol, we run into an old friend. Her son is well-scrubbed, polite, and funny. He eats a chocolate ice-cream cone without getting a drop on him. His shirt stays tucked in. He does not yell loudly. In contrast, my son and his six-year-old cousin Dave are rolling all over each other like bear cubs, yelling, "Penis! Wiener!" They grab each other's faces and squeeze in a move they call "oozying." "OOZY! OOZY! OOZY!" reverberates all over the Capitol's rotunda. All attempts to restrain them just bring on louder echoes of words unknown to our Founding Fathers.

We quickly move on to a chi-chi bakery in DuPont Circle, where my son devours a chocolate-chip cookie. He then announces, "My stomach feels all confoozled." I know what that means and immediately shove his head into a nearby garbage can, where he proceeds to vomit noisily. In between heaves, he happily announces the color and texture. A genteel couple next to us who have been leisurely enjoying lattes hurriedly pick up their coats and leave. I am so used to this routine that I don't even stop eating. I have one hand on my son's head, and the other is still shoveling pastry into my mouth. In between bites—okay, even during bites—I do make sympathetic "there, there" noises.

Cribbage? Backgammon? I'd be happy just to spend a day in which I'm not dealing with body fluids. I'd be happy to have a conversation that actually made sensible progress from one thought to another. Instead, our conversations have that disjointed quality usually associated with bad cell-phone connections. "Levi, you are reading so beautifully. Can you take that fork out of your ear?"

Back at the hotel room, both boys are given apples to eat in a vain attempt to keep them away from the minibar. They grasp their apples in ice tongs that the hotel has thoughtfully provided and then try to eat the apples from the tongs while marching across the beds. Levi's apple ends up under a bed. Dave's apple somehow falls into the toilet. The apple in the toilet isn't discovered, of course, until someone desperately needs a fruitless bowl. Returning home on the train, my sister and I agree, "This trip was a disaster."

"This trip was the best trip EVER," Levi and Dave announce.

"It was?" I ask, astounded. We had made it to one museum and spent the rest of the time looking for bathrooms and places to eat. My sister and I look at each other. At the same time, we both conjure up the looks on the faces of that classy couple in the bakery as they bid a hasty retreat from Levi's explosion, and of my husband as he hopped on one foot while attempts were made to defruit the facilities.

"Yeah, I guess it was," I admit. I know these images will enter the family lore and become embellished and exaggerated and retold. They will never fail to make me laugh.

It hits me that my family will never be what I expected because what I expected is not what I want. I don't play cribbage because I don't want to play cribbage. When I let myself admit it, I realize I'd much rather spend the day having a good "oozy." I pictured control and elegance, but I've found that what gives life its juice is the gracelessness of the unexpected: the wrestling bear cubs, the bobbing for apples, the non sequiturs, the insanity. You see, down here among the classless is where life really rocks and rolls.

~Beth Levine

We'll Have Fun Yet

Call it a clan,
call it a network,
call it a tribe,
call it a family.
Whatever you call it,
whoever you are,
you need one.
~Jane Howard

My family reunions take place in hotel rooms and restaurant lobbies. We meet in towns like Cedar Rapids, Iowa, where my grandmother lived until last year, and more recently in Downer's Grove, Illinois, where motels advertise "extended stay" business suites, and low-flying jets roar overhead every few seconds.

We are a small family by American standards: my father and his third wife; my brother and his fourth wife and two children; and me with my second wife and one daughter. My mother, who holds a quarter-century hurt against my father, keeps her distance. Although we are veterans of many emotional outbursts, we do not need a scene. In all, the four original members of my family married twelve times. Seven of those unions ended in divorce, one in death. Perhaps that's why transitory anonymous places do not bother us—we have lost so many homes.

I have missed most of these reunions. When I chose a life

Out West at the age of seventeen, I knew I would come back to the Midwest infrequently, if at all. Youth creates an illusion of absolute truths. I easily bought into my own: I didn't need family. Instead, I relied on craggy mountain peaks, big skies, crimson sunsets, and magical swaths of desert. Truth is, I probably read too many Carlos Castaneda books and listened to one too many John Denver songs about a Rocky Mountain high.

The migration of Illinois high school graduates to Colorado and beyond in the 1970s must have rivaled the numbers attempting the Oregon Trail a century before. We were a ragtag bunch of Boomers armed with dog-eared copies of *Walden* and *On the Road*. Slung over our shoulders were new backpacks and acoustic guitars. College towns and cities like Missoula, Boulder, Tucson, and Durango took us in with the hope that we would only stay four years. But many of us never left. We graduated, found jobs, married, became parents, divorced, remarried. Twenty-five years quickly passed. Suddenly, all those absolute truths that were black and white — the ones we stayed up all night to debate — were now gray. So was our hair.

When I was almost forty, I finally met my Iowa grandmother, Mary, in the unlikely setting of Brooklyn. As the two of us sat alone in my father's living room, she took my hand, squeezed it, and said, "We'll have fun yet." Perhaps she sensed my feeling of loss at meeting her so late in my life, long after the usual familial bonding of grandchild to grandparent. Taking my hand was a way of closing those years, of taking us to the present tense where we could begin.

Grandmother Mary died last year. In my adult life, I had only been around her twice, and we exchanged just a few notes and cards. But her greatest gift was yet to come. A large manila envelope arrived shortly after Mary's death. Inside were letters, charts, journal pages, and copies of small town histories. These were the voluminous results of her life's passion — our family.

I learned that my earliest known relative in America was David Lyons, born in 1788 in Virginia, who served in the War of 1812, where he was paid thirty-nine dollars and ninety-six cents for six months of duty. Among all the pages in my family's history, among all the underlined passages and Mary's carefully written margin notes, one passage stands out: "David's father came to Virginia from England. He returned to England to claim an inheritance and was never heard from again. David, being left in Virginia and underage, was 'bound out' for a period of time." Two hundred years ago, my family was off to a shaky start.

My newest stepmother, Robbie, says it's never too late for family. At the age of forty-three, I crave family. The setting is secondary to the substance. Although there are not a lot of "remember whens," and "whatever happened tos," something vital happens. The three cousins create their own sense of family, one we hope lasts forever. My brother and I can finally practice the role of uncles and, more importantly, the role of sons. Simply standing next to my brother and father in a hotel foyer takes on a heightened importance because decades have passed since we have stood together.

The photographs from our last summer's reunion just arrived. If you saw the images, you would never know the effort it took to reach that moment. In one picture, we are standing in the parking lot of a suburban restaurant that I would be hard-pressed to ever locate again. We have our arms around each other. Our smiles are bright and winning. But the best part is we look like a family. Mary was right. We'll have fun yet.

~Stephen J. Lyons

22

$\mathcal{A}l$ $\mathcal{F}resco$

*The trouble with eating Italian food is that
five or six days later you're hungry again.*
~George Miller

Every few years, my entire family gets together for a huge reunion. Relatives come from everywhere to hug, kiss and eat. It's an Italian fiasco.

We begin cooking weeks before the gathering. It's a "picnic" of sorts, but if you're Italian, you know there's no such animal. Normally, picnics consist of hot dogs, burgers, etc. We Italians are incapable of eating such foods unless accompanied by staples such as antipasto with assorted home-cured meats, shrimp and fried calamari, olives, polenta, soup (regardless of weather... it can be ninety-five degrees, but gotta have soup), greens and beans, sauce and about eighteen pounds of assorted pasta cooked al dente, along with meatballs, sausage and bracciole, wine, roasted chicken and potatoes, about a hundred loaves of hot Italian bread, and more wine and beer (has to be Molson; one uncle is from Canada). Add to this a few ears of corn on the cob and salt potatoes—after all, it is a picnic! And then the desserts follow: about seventy-five pounds of assorted homemade Italian cookies, fruited Jell-O with heavy cream (for the uncles with no teeth), ricotta pies, cannoli, biscotti, pasticciotto and sfogliatelle. Then comes the coffee, sambuca, anisette and Galliano, just in case you haven't had enough wine or beer.

The hardest part is getting all this food to the designated picnic spot. Each family is responsible for lugging their own prepared food, and you MUST bring ice and a cooler. There are no paper plates or plastic utensils allowed at this shindig, so we all bring our own china, silverware and linen napkins. (Paper anything is wasteful.)

On the day of the reunion, we start gathering about 7:00 A.M. We bring banquet tables and folding chairs (Uncle Rocky borrows them from the funeral home), and the men start unloading. This takes roughly three hours. Meanwhile, the women are getting the grills ready. The sauce is already simmering, and the cousins start arriving in droves. Breakfast is served: frittatas made to order.

Since no one believes in birth control, large numbers of children run wild, and there is more hair-pulling and hand-biting than you can possibly imagine. My grandmother and grandfather are immediately seated in "lounge chairs" in a shady spot and remain there for the duration of the gathering. They are asleep in five minutes and don't awaken until they smell the fried calamari.

Each family is thoroughly cross-examined by the others, and the stories run wild. There are at least fifteen family members with a back problem, and another twenty-five or so with hemorrhoids. Three or four of the older aunts have dementia, and a large majority of the day is spent re-orienting them. They each carry a purse that weighs about forty-seven pounds, an umbrella and rosary beads. Aunt Palma carries a shopping bag full of other shopping bags. No one questions her; she's the oldest.

Uncle Richard is a bookie, so he's taking bets on what time the cousins from Utica will arrive. Every obscene Italian gesture and cuss word is used in voices that could wake the dead. Uncle Vito brings his keyboard and does a poor impression of Pavarotti. Uncle Nunzio joins him on the accordion. Laurie's daughter is choking on a quarter, and Nicole's kids are running through the park buck naked. At this point, we pretend to "not be related to anyone near the sauce pots." My sisters and I stare at the aunts' mustaches and pray we don't follow in this horrible hormonal tradition. Our eyes are burning from the cigar smoke, so we decide to take a walk by the water.

We bump into Patty Anne on the path. She was recently divorced (an unforgivable sin) and has taken up with her butcher. They are, as my aunts so astutely put it, "living in sin right under God's face." She and Shawn, a non-Italian, are sucking face like a couple of dogs in heat. Aunt Nunni is telling everyone that Patty Anne has shamed the entire family, and that if her mother were still alive, this would have finished her off. It's bad enough they're living together, but he's not even Italian. I pick this moment to tell everyone that his last name is Murphy. Aunt Nancy faints. (I decide this is not a good time to tell them that Cousin Concetta is pregnant with Jake Goldstein's kid. They'll find out soon enough. Concetta is knitting mohair yarmulkes.)

Uncle Louie says grace, and dinner is finally served. We eat for what seems like hours, and my legs hurt from walking up and down the hill to bring food to my grandparents. Other picnickers are looking at us as if we are aliens. While they enjoy hot dogs on paper plates, we are sweating from the steam of the minestrone soup. Heads are being slapped everywhere, and cousins Gino and Michelle are missing. By this time, I am more than ready for alcohol. I start drinking Uncle Tony's homemade grappa. This is no easy task since it tastes like kerosene, but it grows on you. After two glasses, it goes down like champagne. No women drink the homemade red wine because it permanently stains the teeth a deep shade of maroon.

We take the china and silverware to the lake for a quick rinse before dessert is served. The coffee and after-dinner drinks are passed around, and Aunt Nancy starts telling stories about the "Old Country." Everyone starts laughing like crazy. This hilarity doesn't last too long because someone inevitably speaks of Uncle John and Uncle Mikey, who were killed in a train wreck right after arriving in America. The laughter turns to tears, and the novenas flow. The older relatives are making the sign of the cross and looking upward when one of the aunts spots Gino and Michelle. Gino is grinning like the Cheshire cat, and Michelle's hair looks as if it were caught in a monsoon. Uncle Vito slaps Gino in the head, and then hugs him. Aunt Ida bites her hand and asks Michelle if she wants to end up like Patty Anne. Michelle sees Patty Anne and Shawn still locking lips and nods yes.

My aunts have now infiltrated the entire park by "passing the cookie trays," and strangers of every nationality are joining us. It's starting to get dark, so they figure it's time to re-heat everything. Now the crowd gets even bigger.

At about midnight (or when I have about thirty-six mosquito bites), the party breaks up. Dishes are washed and packed along with the cleaned and polished silverware. Promises are made to keep in touch, and kisses fly everywhere. Of course, we won't see half of them for another four or five years. (This is NOT a bad thing.)

In bed later that night, I think of the next reunion. My sisters and I will be considered "The Aunts" by then. I wonder if we'll be sporting any facial hair. Oh, well. In a few years, Pops and I will be sitting in the "Lounge Chairs" on the hill. Life is good.

~Marianne LaValle-Vincent

Braving Vacation

And that's the wonderful thing about family travel:
it provides you with experiences that will remain locked forever
in the scar tissue of your mind.
~Dave Barry

"Hey, lady! Don't let go!" The man coming down the escalator yelled across the airport concourse directly at my Aunt Bobby going up the other side, her purse swinging wildly on her arm. She was hanging on to my Great Aunt Sheila, whose purse was also gyrating madly as they ascended the other escalator to the second floor. Great Aunt Sheila, in turn, was hanging onto Great Aunt Edna, who, as it happened, had a death grip on the stationary rail of the offending escalator. They were only about a quarter of the way up to the second floor, but they were already upside down.

Great Aunt Edna was a beloved, albeit interesting character in our family. Her beginnings were never quite clear, as she never spoke, stemming from deafness during childhood. Some said it was because of birth trauma; others said fever or childhood illness. Whatever the case, we do know that her parents kept her at home and taught her themselves as best they could. She was rather isolated in many things, except from the family, but this was not necessarily a bad thing in her day. The preferred social norm in her youth was placement in an institution, with medical guardianship given to administrators, regardless of the child's personal abilities.

Great Aunt Edna didn't let her disability get in her way, though, despite conventional attitudes. She was quite a force in the family. I met her once in her last few years, but she made an impression on me then. She had a habit of correcting naughty behavior with a finger wag. That finger was a pretty disconcerting but rather effective phenomenon. But the story I remember the most about this remarkable woman, perhaps because of its continued reappearance at the family dinner table, was of one summer when she decided to visit my mother. She and her sister, Great Aunt Sheila, and Sheila's daughter were to fly from Pennsylvania to Texas and tour the Southwest.

Mom was on her own at the time, trying to hold a household together with three young children, while her husband was away overseas in the military. She also had in her possession a cantankerous car with no air conditioning, a dog, and a cat.

Meanwhile, Great Aunt Edna had never really been out of town, let alone out of state. She certainly had never been on an airplane before, and this was the first time she'd seen an escalator. But she was strong-willed, and instead of asking for help, she studied the other passengers and took a flying leap before anyone knew what she was up to.

But in her rush, she grabbed the wrong rail. She grabbed the stationary one, and immediately she began to head up the escalator. Or at least her feet did. Her grip, though, refused to let go.

This is the image we have of Great Aunt Edna embarking on the trip of her lifetime. And this was just the beginning.

Throughout the rest of the trip, my mother drove her irritable station wagon, with Great Aunt Sheila and Great Aunt Edna in the front, three preteen girls and one teenage boy in the back seat, a dog and all the luggage in the rear, and a petrified cat clenched in the arms of Great Aunt Edna. Nearly every photo of this great American family trip consists of a broken-down station wagon waiting on the side of the road in the desert with its hood up, Great Aunt Sheila looking exhausted in the front seat, and every car door wide open with no other soul to be found.

Throughout this journey, Great Aunt Edna wanted to discover

everything she could, and yet she had little patience for waiting on anyone. She wanted to experience things on her own terms, and as such, she discovered that cacti have spikes (and one really shouldn't lean against them), that caverns are large (and that it's a good idea to stay with the guide), and that not all cowboys are gallant and suave (or sober). Great Aunt Edna's finger got a good workout.

By the end of the vacation, Mom had a few more gray hairs, the kids were thoroughly sick of each other, the dog was sick, Great Aunt Sheila was overjoyed to be going home, the car needed replacing, and the cat was never quite the same. Great Aunt Edna went home with a sigh of relief.

Two weeks later, Great Aunt Sheila went to visit her sister and saw a set of suitcases resting at the foot of the stairs. Great Aunt Edna signed, "I'm ready! When can we go again?!"

~Amanda Eaker

Reprinted by permission of Off the Mark
and Mark Parisi ©2001

The Lost Shoe

No excellent soul is exempt from a mixture of madness.
~Aristotle

If any of you are planning to be on Interstate 95 this summer, and you see a poor guy's sanity lying there, could you please let me know? It's mine.

I lost it somewhere between Reno and Las Vegas when my son said, "I think my shoe fell out the window."

"What do you mean your shoe flew out the window?!" I asked, unable to see the road behind me through the rearview mirror because the back window was blocked by a huge stack of camping gear. "Didn't your mother tell you to keep that window closed?"

"I had to throw out my peach pit," he explained.

"Your mom told you not to do that."

"It was sticky."

"Your sister managed to keep her pit inside," I pointed out.

"She stuck it to the ceiling of your car."

"It's a Christmas decoration," my daughter announced.

"Which shoe was it?" I asked.

"My high-tops."

"Your Desert Storm Action shoes?"

"Uh-huh."

My shoulders sagged. "So how did the shoe fall out?!"

"I don't know. My window was up," he assured me.

"Before or after the shoe fell out?"

"Before," he explained. "Maybe God did it."

"God probably did it because he kicked me this morning with that shoe," my daughter interjected.

"That wasn't my fault."

Now, my wife had been staring at me throughout this conversation, so I finally had to ask: "What?"

"Aren't you turning around?" she said.

"Around where?"

"Back to look for the shoe?"

"Yeah, right," I scoffed. "We're going to find a shoe that not only is designed to be camouflaged in a desert, but also has been called by God, and is right this moment finding holy reconciliation in the desert?"

"That shoe cost forty-five dollars," my wife explained. "I worked overtime to buy that."

Arguing about money with my wife is a lost cause. We went back. We searched fruitlessly for thirty minutes until I had a third-degree sunburn on my bald spot. Back on the road, it was dead silent in the car. I assumed everyone was reflecting on the events of the previous hour.

Finally, my son announced, "I found my shoe!"

"That's not funny," I exclaimed.

"No, really. I guess it didn't fall out of the car after all. Look! My peach pit is inside it, too."

Sanity is a funny thing. Once you've lost it, it's very difficult to get it back.

~Ken Swarner

Reprinted by permission of Mort Gerberg
©2009

Who Are All These Strange People?

*Most things in life are moments of pleasure
and a lifetime of embarrassment;
photography is a moment of embarrassment
and a lifetime of pleasure.*
~Tony Benn

When my husband received a letter from his sister telling him there was going to be a Stafford Family Reunion in Southern Missouri, she said she'd drive there from Ohio and meet us.

My husband, Bill, was not excited about the reunion with his mother's family.

"I haven't seen any of these people in thirty years. I wouldn't know them if we passed on the street," he said.

"All the more reason to go," I insisted. "Besides, it will be good for our kids to meet their aunts and uncles, and they'll have fun playing with their cousins."

We loaded our four grumpy teenagers into the back seat of the car and began the 200-mile drive.

Every thirty minutes, Travis, Troy, Peter or Spring would ask when we were going to stop and get something to eat.

"You don't eat before you go to a reunion," I said. "Those women have been cooking for days. When we get there, they will have a feast prepared."

We drove deep into the Ozarks, getting lost twice, and finally found a sign on a fencepost that said, "If your name is Stafford, this is the right place. Welcome!"

We parked the car next to twenty other cars in the yard and joined the rest of the family just as they were cleaning off the picnic tables. We'd missed the picnic, and there was very little food left. The children did get some chicken wings, Bill found a deviled egg and a piece of cake, and I ended up with a biscuit and a handful of carrots.

My husband phoned his sister and found out she'd decided she didn't want to drive to Missouri in the July heat and wasn't coming.

We spent the next hour introducing ourselves to everyone and wondering why we couldn't make a connection with anyone.

"Are you John and Thelma's boy?" an old man asked my husband.

"No, my parents were Marge and John. My father's parents were Rebecca and Ben," he answered. "They all lived in Kansas."

"Never heard of them," the old man said.

As hard as we tried, we couldn't find our branch on the family tree.

"I think we are at the wrong family reunion," Bill said. "All we have in common is our last name."

"I'm sorry," I said. "I just wanted our kids to play with their cousins."

"There is no one here under the age of seventy. I don't think their cousins feel like playing," he said.

"I guess we should just leave and go get something to eat and head home." I knew when I'd lost.

We said our goodbyes and got into the car. The car wouldn't start. Bill looked under the hood and wiggled and jiggled some things and slammed the hood closed.

"The alternator has gone out. We can't go anyplace until I can buy a new one," he said.

"Oh, that's bad luck. The only garage in the area is closed on

Sunday. You'll have to spend the night here, and one of us will give you a ride to the garage in the morning," an old man said.

There were no extra beds. In fact, the dozens of Staffords had rolled out wall-to-wall quilts on the floor of the living room, and people were sleeping nose to toes. Since we didn't know these people anyway, we decided we'd take our chances outside.

Spring took the back seat of the car, and I lay down in the front seat. Bill and the three boys threw jackets on the ground as beds.

"Mom, I'm starving to death!" Spring said, near tears.

"I know. I'm so sorry," I said. Then I remembered I had a package of M&Ms in my purse. I dug them out and handed them to her. She generously shared some of them with me, but I dropped some of them onto the front seat and couldn't find them.

Somehow, we survived an endless night. At the crack of dawn, an old woman pounded on the car window and woke us up.

"Get up! Some of the people have to leave, and we want to get pictures of everyone before they all go home!" she said.

"But I don't think we are related," I said.

"We can't risk it. We'll take pictures of everyone and sort it out later."

My right foot was tangled in the steering wheel, and I was completely numb. My neck was so stiff I couldn't move my head.

"Mom! What happened to you?" Spring asked when she saw me.

I'd slept on the M&Ms I'd dropped in the seat and now my face had green, orange and yellow spots all over it.

Bill and the boys were covered with mosquito bites, and Travis had slept on the zipper of his jacket and looked like he had a huge, crooked scar across his face.

All of us had slept in our clothes, so we were wrinkled and our hair wasn't combed.

We were pushed into a line of washed, combed, clean and well-dressed people. Cameras clicked, and dozens of photos were taken. Photographs of this Stafford reunion would be hung on walls and put into albums. A hundred years from now, other generations of Staffords would look at the photographs of all the nice-looking people. Then they would point to our family and ask, "Who are those dirty, spotty people in the wrinkled clothes? What are those colored spots on that woman's face, and why is her head crooked? Those strange-looking people surely can't be related to us!"

And they would be right. We weren't related to any of them, but our family at its ugliest, dirtiest, worst-dressed and most miserable will be included in the family album forever.

~April Knight

Hitching behind a Hearse

A lot of people like snow. I find it to be an unnecessary freezing of water.
~Carl Reiner

There's nothing more fun than an Italian funeral. People who make a conscious effort not to communicate with each other under normal circumstances come together and sink to a new low in human behavior.

Such was the case when my grandmother, Rose, lost her younger sister, Netty. Now it's important to note that Netty hadn't spoken to my own mother since her divorce from my father fifteen years prior. We'll pass over the fact that Netty herself was divorced three times and currently had a boyfriend more than twenty years her junior whom she kept a secret for the past twenty years! This was decades before Demi and Ashton. No, she and her oldest sister, Marion, frowned upon divorce as a mortal sin. This made my mother the black sheep of the family and made me, by association, the little black lamb.

We were shunned from family gatherings—funerals were exempted—probably not so much for the divorce, but for the rant my mother went on when she told all the relatives exactly what she thought of them. Trust me, I put that nicely. My mother had a colorful way with words that never left people wondering what she was really thinking.

Now of course when you have someone to shun, it's always a good idea to have shining examples of virtue to exemplify all that is good, so enter stage right my mother's younger sister and Marion's only daughter. These fine women would be the ones to offer support to their mothers during these trying days, leaving my mother and I to fend for ourselves. Not that we minded much; we were kind of used to it.

A blizzard was brewing on the morning of my Aunt Netty's funeral, which in hindsight was probably Mother Nature's way of telling us to stay home and mind our own business. Out of respect for Rosie, however, we donned our best black frocks and made our way through the steadily falling snow to the funeral home.

Now if you've never been to an Italian funeral, it's important to note two things: 1) Everyone is dressed in black, and 2) there's always drama.

It's also customary for friends and family to wait in their cars while the immediate family — in this case, the two sisters, their two favorite daughters, and the forty-something boy toy — bid their farewells in private. This is why my mother and I were sitting in my new bright yellow Firebird while the snow rapidly accumulated around us.

"What's taking so long?" I asked, as my mother hit my hand for turning on the radio.

"You know Aunt Marion," she replied. "She's probably trying to crawl into the coffin."

"This car is terrible in snow. I hope I don't get stuck."

"Not to worry. It's a funeral procession. What do you think… they're going to leave you in the snow?"

Aunt Marion was really doing her thing in there. This was a woman who never passed a funeral home without saying, "I wonder who's there." She once went to a wake, ran to the coffin crying and wailing, threw herself on the floor, and then realized she didn't know who it was. She didn't recognize one person in the room. No problem. She picked herself up, brushed herself off, and went into the next room to do an encore performance. So it was no surprise when the funeral director ran out and told us to turn off our engines as it would be awhile.

Finally, they loaded Aunt Netty into the hearse and dragged Aunt Marion into the limo, and we were ready to roll. The snow was now almost a foot high, but I didn't have to worry about getting stuck because my engine wouldn't start. I left on my lights when I turned off my engine, and now I had a dead battery.

The hearse was leaving. The limo was leaving. The Firebird should have been leaving…

"Just leave it!" yelled my mother. "We'll get a ride in another car."

Easier said than done. The next car in line was a big sedan with only two men, the husbands of the good daughters, inside. We ran to jump into their empty back seat, but they locked their doors and laughed as they drove away!

Now my mother and I were running through the snow in high heels trying to find a ride.

The next car contained friendlier faces, just too many of them. That car was packed tighter than a can of sardines, as were the next several cars in the procession.

A kind of giddy hysteria came over us as we realized that we were running through a blizzard chasing a funeral procession that was leaving without us. Everyone was going to be eating ziti at the repast, and we were going to freeze to death in a parking lot.

We finally got to the last car, which was being driven by a little old man whom neither of us had ever seen before.

"Get in!" screamed my mother.

"Ma, we don't even know him."

What choice did we have? There went the "never get in a car with a stranger" rule. Turns out he was a distant cousin of my grandmother and a very nice man. We sat with him at the repast. At least we had someone to talk to. He even seemed to enjoy our company, as we did his.

Don't think we suffered in silence. We squealed to Rosie about what happened in the parking lot. But the two men denied everything, claiming they didn't know we needed a ride or they would most certainly have helped.

Right.

Yes, there's nothing more fun than an Italian funeral.

~Lynn Maddalena Menna

27

A Sweet Family Secret

Life expectancy would grow by leaps and bounds
if green vegetables smelled as good as bacon.
~Doug Larson

There wasn't much to do on the street where I grew up. For one thing, there weren't many kids around. There was Lester Pearbottom, who lived just up the street, but his idea of a good time was beating you up.

The only other kid on our street was my cousin, Cletus Hagood, but he didn't count. Being seen in the company of Cletus was, on a scale of 1 to 10, a decimal point above coming down with the swine flu.

Over the years, an abyss had stretched between our family and the Hagoods. My pop detested them with a hatred keen as a knife blade. He thought my mom's side of the family was nothing but a bunch of lazy, inbred, degenerate hillbillies.

He warned me about them constantly. "If I catch you talking to a Hagood, you're going to be up to your neck in a kettle of boiling manure, and I'll be the one underneath stoking the fire."

I wasn't deaf to my pop's implied threats. I never went anywhere near their place. But I did observe them from a distance. Uncle Howard was a long, bony man with a face that looked as if it had taken hundreds of invisible hooks and jabs in an anything-goes brawl with time itself.

Aunt Mabel was a short, powerful-looking woman. Her meaty arms swung like pendulums, and her feed-sack dress stretched and relaxed over a bosom that went way beyond the boundaries of ample.

The Hagoods were white trash, I suppose. Especially Cletus. He had a pasty white complexion, dark, windowless eyes, and clothes that looked as if they had come off the damaged goods shelf of a disreputable secondhand store. Cletus spent the majority of his time throwing rocks or sitting cross-legged in the dirt with a lighter, burning the wings off flies.

Pop made our family take an oath. None of us were to talk, gesture, or communicate with a Hagood. Their name had become an unspeakable word under our roof.

Unbeknownst to Pop, I broke that vow. It was a Friday afternoon, and I was walking down the street, thinking about supper. That evening's repast was liver and onions, which is not one of those dishes that makes a kid's mouth water with anticipation. I always got the cold creeps on liver and onions night, knowing this dreaded delicacy would be put before me and I'd be told, "Just have a little."

Eating "a little" liver and onions was like vomiting "a little." My stomach lurched sideways at the mere thought of it.

Cletus was standing in his yard, quietly picking his nose, when I walked by. "What ya doin'?" he asked, companionable enough.

"Nothin' much," I said. "And I ain't supposed to talk to you." He gave his nose a short rest, reached into his pocket and came out with something. "Want a Pixy Stix?"

Suddenly, Cletus had my undivided attention. My parents wouldn't allow me to have candy.

"Your folks let you eat candy?" I said, amazed. He smiled. The gaps between his teeth looked grouted.

"Sure do," he replied. "We even eat it fer supper."

"Candy? For supper?" Unbelievable! A miracle! I had heard nothing like it since Sunday school and the tale of the loaves and fishes.

"Yep," he said. "Come on in an' I'll show ya."

Checking over my shoulder several times to ensure I wasn't

being watched, I crept onto the Hagoods' property and headed for the house.

Up close, the place was as ugly as something glimpsed through a rip in the canvas of a freak show tent. There was a dilapidated garage attached to one end of the house and a nest of bony, side-scuttling cur dogs chained to the front porch. Penned wash, gray in the wind, hung on a tilting clothes line, and liberated chickens scratched the ground or squatted inert like swollen feather dusters. On top of all this (or should I say underfoot?) were junk cars, slick tires, soup cans, a dead battery, broken chairs, a hairless doll, bed springs, scraps of paper, and dirty diapers. Indescribable garbage everywhere.

I followed Cletus into the house, which was a helter-skelter mess of old furniture, rummage sale stuff, moldy walls, cats, cobwebs and rolls of flypaper hanging from the ceiling, looking like horror party decorations.

But when I glanced across the kitchen table, my whole impression of the Hagoods underwent a quick and magical change. Before me was pork and beans with cocktail hot dogs, Kit Kat bars, corn dogs, Necco wafers, and nacho cheese the color of a school bus. A feast! And all this time I had thought the Hagoods had been living on boiled bone soup.

"Gol' dang," I croaked. Mabel Hagood was still bringing items from the kitchen: Twinkies in hot Log Cabin syrup. Potato chips. Kool-Aid! With the appearance of each new course, I oohed and aahed as if watching a Fourth of July fireworks display.

It kept coming: Ding Dongs. Mountain Dew. Pork rinds.

"Have you et yet?" Mabel asked, shuffling up to the dinner table.

"No, ma'am," I said.

"Are you hungry?" I nodded with everything I had. I was as hungry as a wild dog. Cletus gestured for me to have a seat. I sat down, and Mabel handed me a plate, which I loaded with ice cream and powdered donuts. Two mouthfuls later, I was in the most complete throes of ecstasy I had ever known. Delicious! I tore into the barbecue chips and washed them down with a bolt of Pepsi.

For the next hour, Mabel kept carting out the fine-tasting

victuals: cheese balls and dip, fudge bars, French fries, 7-Up. Each item mixed amid my cries such as might have greeted a Turkish belly dancer or the Messiah.

I thought of my father. It would have made him angry to see me at that moment, dining with the enemy. The thought gave me goose bumps. But angst or no angst, it wasn't hurting my appetite any. I was gorging myself on Dr. Pepper and SweeTarts as though I had just been plucked from the edge of critical starvation. I chowed on yummy peanut brittle that would stick to my teeth for at least twenty-five days and actually fight decay while wrapped around my molars like wax Halloween teeth.

I felt closer and closer to this wonderful family with each mouthful, and did not stop wolfing down food until I had eaten myself nearly sick. By the time I stepped outside, I had a completely different impression of my relatives. The Hagoods had taught me a very important lesson: It's never good to judge people prematurely. You should always wait until you find out what kind of food they eat.

~Timothy Martin

All in the Family

Chapter 4

Forgiveness

Forgiveness is the fragrance the violet sheds
on the heel that has crushed it.

~Mark Twain

Meeting the Man Inside

Resentment is like taking poison and waiting for the other person to die.
~Malachy McCourt

As a child, my father was the scariest living creature ever to walk the planet. When he would lose his temper, thick smoke would curl from his hands and cloak his body, creating wafting ribbons that would trail down a dark hallway behind him. One would never guess it came from a tiny cigarette cradled between his fingers. His footsteps fell hard on the creaky wooden floor, and his deep voice boomed, echoing only a hint of Texas drawl that even a trained ear would have difficulty detecting. In my youth, I believed he was the tallest, most handsome fire-breathing dragon the world had ever seen.

The awe, enchantment and blind love I'd given him so freely turned to anger as I grew from a little girl to a young woman. He would never physically hurt me or my sisters, but his intimidation method fell short when dealing with three rebellious teenaged daughters, which in turn fueled his hot temper. For ten long years, resentment sat in our house like an uninvited guest.

When my dad was hospitalized during my senior year of high school, a wave of mixed emotions flooded my brain like a tsunami. A blood clot in his left leg had become so severe that a case of life-threatening gangrene had formed, forcing the doctors to amputate.

At seventeen years old, I saw my father vulnerable for the very first time, and it frightened me more than any of his intimidation tactics.

We all recognized the day he came home from the hospital as the gift that it was—a second chance from above. We were a bit more appreciative for a while, but it didn't take long for things to end up exactly where they'd left off. Anger, hostility and resentment clouded our everyday life after only a few weeks.

Time passed, and I moved out, thinking I knew everything. I moved back in, with my tail between my legs, when I realized that I didn't. I was saving every spare penny for an apartment away from the chaos when my father's mother, who lived in the next town over, became very ill. For weeks, he would refuse to see her, and we could never understand why. Finally, after being hounded by my own mother day after day, he went to visit for the last time, with a Catholic priest in tow.

Funerals are never really "good," but this one had all the earmarks of a catastrophe. As we walked into the funeral parlor, my father couldn't make it up the single stair in the lobby without my help, thanks to a night of binge drinking. Drowning his pain, he'd figured, was enough to get him through the early morning service. Part of me wished I'd had the foresight to do the same when I realized before the procession to the cemetery that, in my absentminded grief, I'd accidently locked my parents' keys in their car. After a few attempts to unlock the car with a coat hanger, we simply decided to catch a ride with somebody else and worry about the keys later.

The graveside service was poignant, beautiful, and blessedly brief, and as our small crowd cleared from the site, we quickly made arrangements on what to do about the car. My mother agreed to go back to the funeral home and wait for help, while I went with my sister.

"Are we going to wait for Dad?" she asked as she wiped a few stray tears from her eyes.

"No, he's going with Mom."

"Are you sure?"

"I don't see why he wouldn't," I replied. "It's his car."

We made the forty-five-minute journey back to the house in silence. I was dreading the confrontation that was sure to occur when my father finally arrived home with his keys, and the bitterness I knew would be cast my way for the next few decades.

Instead, when we walked in the door, we received a phone call from my very frantic mother.

"You left your father at the cemetery!"

I felt the blood drain from my face. "I thought he was with you."

"No, he was supposed to be with you girls. We just got a call at the funeral parlor saying a few workmen spotted him. He's catching a ride with them back here in the bed of their truck. You'd better get over here and pick him up."

If I'd thought confronting him about the keys was going to be bad, this was much, much worse. I'd abandoned my father, a man with one leg, at a cemetery the day of his own mother's funeral. He was going to kill me. I hopped in my car and defied a few traffic laws as I sped across town to the funeral parlor, figuring the less time he had to stew, the less painful my death would be.

What I saw when I got there took me by surprise. Instead of an angry, bitter man ready to tear off my head, he was sitting next to my mother patiently.

"It was your mother's doing, Frank," I heard her say to him. "She wanted to spend some time with you, and darned if she didn't make you stay there with her."

For the first time in years, I heard my father laugh. Actually laugh. I'd forgotten what a great sound it was. "You're right. That's the feeling I got, too. It's what she wanted."

I apologized profusely for the duration of the car ride home, but my sincerity fell on deaf ears. He didn't say much to me for days after the incident, but his silence was different this time. It wasn't fueled by resentment or anger; it was powered by deep thought.

That was when a miracle happened. As he pulled out of his shell, he began to talk to us—not with screams and shouts, which was our usual form of communication—but actually sitting down and talking. He was having conversations, telling jokes, and laughing. It was a side of him my sisters and I had never seen before. In his endless stories, we found out who he'd been before settling down with a family, and we got the chance to see who he was as a human being instead of the intimidating dragon we'd envisioned in our youth. He even made the decision to start going to church every weekend, and for the past five years he hasn't missed a single sermon.

When the Lord closes a door, he always opens a window. We may have buried my grandmother that cool, dreary morning, but I'll be forever grateful that we somehow managed to unearth my dad.

~R.D.

The Trashcan Incident

*Speak when you are angry and you will make the best
speech you will ever regret.*
~Ambrose Bierce

People aren't kidding when they say dead folk look like wax. It's true, they do. There's sort of an unwholesome sheen to the forehead; maybe it's the make-up they put on them. My uncle's forehead was unexpectedly cold and waxy when my lips pressed against it. I guess his body must have been in some freezer.

Everyone feels something similar when someone they love dies. Even a pet. You think back and say, "God, I hope they know how much I loved them." Then, sadistically, you think about all the bad things you ever said or did to them, all the evidence stacked up against their knowledge that you loved them. You don't mean to, but the mind is sick.

Standing over my uncle's chestnut-brown coffin, I was thinking about the day I was suspended from the ninth grade. I'd lived with my aunt and uncle at the time. I was getting ready to go to high school, where my uncle was a janitor. I was sitting on my bed, watching my breath in the cold air. The heat had been turned off the day before because we couldn't pay the bill. My uncle stopped in my doorway.

"Thought you told your aunt you were gonna clean your room last night?" He was always ascribing things to my aunt.

I looked up. "I didn't have time. I was doing my homework." But my eyes glanced over at the Nintendo. He looked, too.

He stepped into the room. "Homework, huh? My ass. Listen, if you're gonna live here, you've gotta live by my rules."

"Why?"

"'Cause I pay the bills around here!" he roared.

I raised my eyebrows superciliously. "You do?"

His bushy eyebrows met menacingly as his face registered what had just been said to it. "Yes, I do pay the damn bills around here!" he hollered. He brought up his hand as if to slap me, then turned and split my bedroom door with a crack. The hallway steps sounded like they'd rattle apart beneath his banging boots.

I probably hold the world record for the most "I'm sorrys" in a minute. I followed him right up to the front door as he was going out, but the ground was covered in snow and I did not follow him. He trudged up the street through the wind-slanted snow on his way to work at the school I was going to soon. I thought I was so clever. I'd been rehearsing that line to use on my uncle. That's how vindictive I was. But the second it was out of my mouth, I wished I could reel it back in.

I got off the freezing bus and followed the shivering line of backpacks toward the brick fortress that was the high school and through the double doors. Downstairs, his office was empty. I turned and saw the office lady hurrying by. I asked her, "Have you seen my uncle?"

"He's not here," she shot at me without turning her head.

Well, I'd done it. He'd left. See, he was from California, and he had hitchhiked barefoot all the way to New Hampshire in the 1970s. It wasn't all that uncommon back then, from what I hear. Barefoot hippies everywhere. There was even a Polaroid of my uncle riding a snowmobile barefoot, with a big, bushy Afro and a big smile to match.

He always talked about California and how he wanted to go

back. When he and my aunt had just had a fight, especially if he'd been drinking a bit, he'd say to me, "I might just end up back in California some day. I just might."

And now he was gone. He was dressed for work, but he didn't show up. I probably don't have to tell you I felt awful. And it was Winter Carnival, too, the one week where every day is supposed to be fun. No classes, no boring lectures. Just games and working on the stupid float that nobody really cared about.

The first-period bell rang, and the halls were empty. I was late, but I didn't care. My uncle was nowhere to be found. Talk about feeling like dirt. Suddenly, down the hall, I saw Jason Kensey emerge from a janitor's closet pushing a trash can on wheels. We didn't hang out anymore, really. It was one of those things where we were best buds in middle school, but when we got to high school we were just doing different things. That, and Jason started smoking a ton of weed and hanging out with some sketchy people.

So Jay called down the hallway, "Hey, Scrawny Ronnie!" I really was scrawny.

"Heya, Jay!" He was just what I needed. My old good-time pal, the first person I ever got drunk with. Also the first and only person to convince me to swallow chewing tobacco 'cause that's how you did it he told me. That wasn't good. But, anyway, Jason got this idea.

"Get in the trash can, Ronnie, and I'll push you down the hall. It'll be wicked funny."

We say "wicked" a lot in New Hampshire. Maybe it has something to do with those witch trials next door in Massachusetts. Who knows?

Anyway, I got in the trash can with wheels, my uncle's trash can, and Jason started pushing me down the hallway. It was great. We were laughing just like the old days, singing some song about racing. Seemed appropriate. But then I saw the end of the hallway rushing to meet me. The stairs. It was a pretty short flight of steps, only about five, but five steps is plenty for you to crack your head if you happen to fly down them inside a trash can with wheels. Oh, yeah, I remembered suddenly why I wasn't friends with Jason anymore.

"Jay! Stop!" I yelled, but he didn't. His laughter became hysterical. Great. I thought I'd smelled something. He was stoned.

So, zing! There I went, like a trash bag flung into the sky, arcing over the steps. Only I didn't stay in. Just as the trash can went over, I squatted and sprang straight up. I was captain of the track team, you know. Thing was, I was terrible at the high jump.

I managed to clear the can and was grabbing out wildly for anything I could get a purchase on with my hands so as not to kill myself flying down the steps, but I got something. Up by the ceiling there was this big banner, and I ripped right through it, hands outstretched, like I was coming on to the football field before a big game or something. I came down on my feet. Slam! And I stuck the landing.

I looked up, and there was my uncle! Only he had a party hat on, and he looked small walking next to the monstrous principal, who had one of his enormous mitts on my uncle's shoulder. God, we were scared of him. Something echoed in the back of my mind. I looked behind me at the banner. It said:

"Congratulations Custodian Mark Kelding on Thirty Years of Service to Memorial High School!"

Jason, of course, was nowhere to be found. Probably hyperventilating in the bathroom, laughing himself to death.

The principal grabbed me by the scruff of the shirt and dragged me into the office. My uncle averted his eyes and just walked away, crumpling his party hat.

The principal was matter-of-fact in his office. "I don't have time to deal with you today, Ron. You're going home."

"I'm suspended?"

"Yes, for the rest of the week. No winter carnival for you." He stopped, took off his glasses, and looked at me. "It's terrible for you to do such a thing to your uncle after all he's done for you." Then, glasses on again, he wrote me up, and off I walked, home.

I wish I had remembered. My uncle wasn't at school because he was having a pancake breakfast with the principal and superintendent.

The snow banks were piled high on either side of the sidewalk on the way home, confining me to a narrow corridor, as if I were walking one lone plank to face my aunt and uncle. It's always eerie to be out of school when you're supposed to be in it. You know all your friends are in there, and you always wonder what they're doing right at that moment. A quiz? A test? Not my friends. Everyone at my school was playing games and eating free food. And Jason Kensey was probably telling everybody what an idiot I looked like, tearing a banner in half right in front of the principal.

I walked in the door and kicked my boots against the mat to knock off the snow. My aunt emerged from the living room, and as I opened my mouth to explain why I was home early, she did not stop. She went to the dryer, pulled the clothes out and walked briskly to their bedroom, her brown ponytail a perfect line down her back, and shut the door. I took off my backpack. Her door opened, and she was walking toward me, keys jingling in her hand.

"I'm sorry," I said. She didn't say a thing, just walked out.

I had a whole day off at home alone, and all I could think about was my uncle's face when I insulted him, how his big caterpillar eyebrows contracted together, not in anger, but in humiliation. I felt too guilty even to play Nintendo. I cleaned my disgusting room instead.

Three o'clock rolled around, and I was still alone. Looking up the street for my uncle, the rough wind was still driving big snowflakes almost horizontally, and I could only bear to keep the front door open for a few seconds. We were supposed to get twelve to eighteen inches that night. Figures, it would be a snow day tomorrow, and it wouldn't even be fun because I didn't have to go to school anyway. Yellow headlights came through the storm, and I was out in the snow in my bare feet. But it was just my aunt, and she said she didn't know where my uncle was. She didn't blame him, the way I'd been acting. My face flushed, and I brought in the groceries quietly on feet burning with cold. I noticed a space heater in the corner of the kitchen that I hadn't noticed before. Better than nothing.

The sun dropped later, I suppose. I say this because there was no evidence it had even come out that day, only gray skies all day. The sky turned a darker shade of gray, and as I lay in bed I saw a figure taking shape in the middle of the road in the icy torrent. I darted downstairs and ran up the street barefoot. It was my uncle, and he was carrying two big red cans that read "Kerosene." For the space heater. He smiled when he saw me, his big bushy eyebrows and hair all encrusted with snow and ice. I took one of the cans of kerosene from him and felt the cold steel handle burn my hand, the line of cold that stretches from one side of my palm to the other even now whenever my hand gets cold. A frozen reminder of my crime. I fell into step next to him. My feet were sizzling in the snow, but I didn't show it.

Smiling, he looked down at my feet and said, "Just like your uncle, huh?"

As I finished remembering that long ago day, and looked at my uncle stretched out in that coffin, I broke down. Deep sobs wracked me, making me gulp that funeral air. I laid my arms over him one last time.

Yes, he definitely knew I loved him.

~Ron Kaiser

Brotherly Love

The black moment is the moment when the real message of transformation is going to come. At the darkest moment comes the light.
~Joseph Campbell

"Your brother is dead," my niece said bluntly. It was not unusual for her to call me the day after Christmas, but her pronouncement was not what I'd expected to hear. Stunned by the news, I stared at the twinkling lights on my Christmas tree, trying to absorb her words. Tears stung my eyes as we both sobbed into the phone. Knowing she must be lost in her own grief following her father's unexpected passing, I offered to inform the rest of the family. Strangely enough, Lenny's death opened the door to healing my broken relationship with my other brother, Daniel.

On Christmas Eve, many years earlier, Daniel lay dying in a military hospital in San Diego. My mother received a call from his doctor informing her that he was not expected to live through the night. Though she did not tell me, out of a misguided idea that she was "sheltering" her ten-year-old daughter from the truth, I knew. My child-like faith was confirmed as I prayed in my bedroom, asking God to spare Daniel's life. He was home within two weeks.

But five years later, Daniel was caught in a downward spiral. The vortex of his alcoholism, combat fatigue, and depression affected us all as he played games of Russian Roulette with his .45 in our living room. On his birthday, Daniel's suicidal thoughts turned outward. After making his favorite dinner, I sliced the homemade blueberry pie on the stove. Turning to give Daniel his dessert, I was stunned to feel the cold steel barrel of his Saturday Night Special pressed between my eyes. I heard the ominous click as he cocked the revolver. My mouth was suddenly dry as cotton; my hands trembled in fear. The plate I had prepared to serve him crashed to the floor, splintering and coming to rest in gooey blue blobs around my bare feet. Then, staring into my eyes, he pulled the trigger.

Nothing happened.

A look of genuine surprise came over his face as Daniel opened the chamber and confirmed that it was indeed loaded. The gold tone of the bullets shone in the light, contrasted against the black metal of the gun. He spun the chamber, as I had watched him do hundreds of times before. Hearing the familiar sound as it locked into place, I stood, paralyzed by fear, as he raised it up to my forehead once again. My eyes slammed shut as he squeezed the trigger one more time.

Again, it did not go off. In my mind's eye, I had a picture of an angel with his finger stuffed down the barrel of the gun.

Daniel cocked his head sideways as he looked at the gun quizzically, and then looked up at me.

"Your lucky day." These were the only words he said during the entire incident. He turned away, downed another beer, and passed out on the couch.

Minutes later, his snoring helped me regain my composure enough to clean up the chards of broken plate, bits of crust, and blueberry filling from the kitchen floor. I washed the dishes, gathered my courage, and tiptoed into the living room. Gingerly lifting one finger at a time from his clutch on the revolver, I held my breath and prayed that he would not wake up. He didn't.

Curious, I took the .45 out to our backyard. Remembering how much of a kick these guns had, I sat down, put up my knees, and rested my elbows on them. I locked my forearms and closed one eye. Aiming at our massive oak tree, I shot off a round. The wide hole in the trunk testified that, yes, the gun did work.

The angel's image in my mind was no mirage, no figment of my imagination.

The following day, Daniel had no recall of the events of his birthday. Like many alcoholics, the things he did while in a blackout were wiped from his memory like an eraser on a chalkboard. Only the blueberry pie in the refrigerator and the hole in the tree gave any indication that I had not dreamt it.

About a month later, we were preparing to plant a vegetable garden in the backyard. While I raked up leaves, weeds, and other debris, Daniel hacked away at errant bushes with the chainsaw. The annoying noise of the chainsaw rattled my brain as I sweated in the Florida noonday sun. Taking off my gardening gloves, I went inside for a moment, returning minutes later with two glasses of cold lemonade. The screen door slammed behind me as I turned around, and once again I heard the familiar whirrrr of the chainsaw. Daniel stood less than a foot away, swinging the buzzing chainsaw toward me, like one would swing a baseball bat.

When he swung it, another miracle occurred: the chainsaw cut my long, honey-colored hair on both sides, but it never touched my neck. Once again, I had a mental picture of an angel, its protective hands around my throat.

As before, he didn't say a word afterward regarding the incident, but it shook me. Adolescence was hard enough already without having to endure my brother's homicidal blackouts. Two months after the chainsaw incident, Daniel tried to murder me once more.

Fleeing on my bicycle, I stopped at a 7-Eleven and dialed a friend from the pay phone outside. After hearing my story, she put her father on the line. He told me he'd call the police and advised me to go inside the store to wait for them. But Daniel had found me by driving around until he recognized my bike on the curb. He watched me from his car, and I crouched low behind a shelf of Twinkies, hoping that the police would show up before he came after me. Once the black-and-white entered the small parking lot, Daniel drove away. The officer took me down to the station and listened intently as I told him what had transpired. He believed me and took steps to provide protection: I entered foster care that night.

Fast forward thirty years to the next time I saw Daniel. He

and his wife met me and my two older sisters as we gathered for Lenny's funeral. Daniel had changed so much that I almost didn't recognize him. Over waffles and coffee, we got caught up on each others' lives. He had quit drinking decades before, had gone back to school, earned a degree in engineering, and obtained his pilot's license. Daniel's wife, a dear Christian woman who obviously loved him very much, had helped him turned his life around. She giggled as he embraced her and gushed about celebrating their twenty-fifth wedding anniversary.

There was no need to revisit the events that had occurred decades ago. Having forgiven Daniel long before, there was no bitterness or vengeance in my heart toward him. Though the memory remained, the pain was gone, replaced by genuine brotherly love. I had lost one brother through sudden death, but regained another in reconciliation. It was heartwarming to see Daniel, and I was overjoyed at his transformation. Perhaps this was the greatest miracle of all: the miracle of forgiveness.

~C.H.

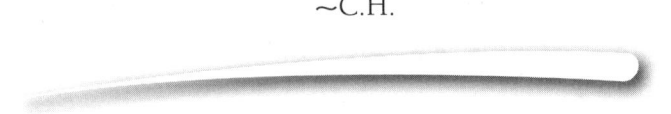

31

Loving Without Words

The one charm of the past is that it is the past.
~Oscar Wilde, The Picture of Dorian Gray

"Are you okay, Grandma? Is this hard for you?"

Leave it to my oldest granddaughter to spot the pain I thought was well-hidden.

As we drove into the dusty little town, I silently reviewed the call that began an inner prompting to revisit my past, and my granddaughter's willingness to leave her job for several days so I did not have to make the visit unaccompanied.

She knew that it had been years since her great-grandmother had stepped out of my life due to the stressful behavior of a disease neither of us had recognized or understood, and she knew about the shocking phone call. After a dinner out celebrating my birthday, I'd preceded my husband into the house as he parked the car, and heard the answering machine in his office beeping that we had a message. Automatically, I stepped into the dark room, pressed "play," and then gasped when I heard the familiar but thready voice singing, "Happy Birthday... dear daughter." That was all. The click and "end of messages" notification from the answering machine left me standing in mute shock. It was as eerie as the scene from a mystery thriller, and I felt like I'd been turned to stone.

Ken came in, alarmed to find me frozen to the spot, staring at the answering machine with my arms wrapped around myself. "What is it? Bad news?" he asked, as he held me.

Mutely, I reached over and hit "play," letting the message repeat. As we listened, his whisper echoed my thoughts. "Why now, after all these years?"

Continuing to hold me, he prayed for me. He'd known my story and married me despite all the baggage I brought into our relationship. He'd been my protective knight through traumatic visits and volatile "episodes." As time slipped by, I thought I'd grown immune to the painful memories, yet here I was years later, trembling in fear from the sound of my past. Still, a feeling grew. I knew I needed to go. Perhaps her call meant there was hope. Ken's prayer relit a faith that believed God would lead me each step of the way.

Her doctor confirmed there had been occasional losses of memory and much consternation over things that appeared to be missing but were later found misplaced in odd locations. The loss of memory problem stirred me. I remembered being doubtful of people who said their past was so traumatic they forgot it. How many times I'd wished I could forget my troubled past. Now, it seemed, Mom had forgotten—at least some of it, some of the time. Was that good, or did it mean it was too late to heal our relationship? Whatever the outcome, I knew the commandment to "honor" my parents, so I armed myself with all the information I could find and prayed for the faith to remember I was not facing this alone.

Now, weeks later, as we passed the familiar sign announcing my hometown, I was disappointed with myself for feeling eleven years old again, and allowing my granddaughter to see memories I thought I had left behind now roaring over me like an emotional Niagara Falls. My chest hurt with the pain of remembrance, and my face must have shown it as well.

"I'm sorry, Aimee, I didn't expect it to hit me like this," I responded truthfully, as I mentally returned to her. Even though I'd spent the last several hours answering her questions about the past, symptoms of the disease, and detailing what subjects might be taboo in case the "deterioration" as the doctor called it made for volatile episodes,

I suddenly felt clueless. Clearly, I needed to "refuel" spiritually before I could make the visit.

We spent the night nearby, and my darling granddaughter distracted me far into the night, sharing funny escapades and future plans until she dozed off and I crept out of bed to pray and think.

The "fixer" in me was clamoring. What should I do? What should I say? I felt so responsible to cleanse all the past, when I didn't even know how much of it she would remember. Like the Apostle Peter, I often spoke without thinking, filling quiet spaces with whatever words came to mind. I grappled now with what I should or shouldn't say or what I might say if I didn't plan every word. My mind was whirling when I grabbed my Bible. As I dropped onto the blue easy chair in the corner, the book fell open to the marker left from a recent Bible study, the yellow highlighting on the page ironically announcing the little phrase without words. I knew instantly that was my answer. I did not have to say anything; I just had to be there. I quietly chuckled at God's sense of humor. Now that would be a miracle! I was stunned at the simplicity, but I was filled with peace because I knew God would enable it to happen. Once the choice was made, I slept peacefully, and morning came quickly.

A gentle touch and a meaningful glance from my granddaughter as we approached the home silently softened in sympathy as the door opened and Aimee's glance moved from my mother to me. Together, we helped an unexpectedly quiet and subdued little woman shuffle behind the walker that we folded into the trunk of the car and began our journey.

I'd purposely planned more than a day would hold, hoping there would be no empty opportunity for an "episode." We visited some new restaurants for meals between little drives across the countryside, ostensibly to show my granddaughter where I grew up and went to school. It was treacherous emotional territory, but Aimee kept up innocuous chatter sprinkled with innocent questions comparing cars, clothing, and school days "back then" with her own recent experiences. There were no life-changing conversations or heavenly reconciliation scenes, but there was a constant opportunity to show honor and love as the memories carried both of us into some good places of our past.

Each time feelings of tension or fear crept in, remembering the little phrase "without words" kept me calm and reminded me that God could work out His plan without any help. How, I wondered throughout the day, would my unusually silent behavior be interpreted? The day's end told all.

"Before you go," my mother asked, "would you help me change to my slippers? It's hard to bend down now."

As I folded one knee down before her and reached to slip off a shoe, she rested her hand on my head like a benediction, noting with surprise that her little girl had silver in her hair. Kneeling there, barely restraining the tears, I swallowed and looked up. Our eyes met and held, and I could not speak for what I heard.

"Thank you," she said, her eyes mirroring a response to words I hadn't had to say. "I love you, too."

~Delores Liesner

Twiddling Thumbs and Drawing Daisies

What art offers is space — a certain breathing room for the spirit.
~John Updike

Dad was often hard on me. When he didn't like the way I did something, said something or just the "look on my face," he would pick me up by the hair and throw me across the room. The hardest part of loving Daddy was not knowing what look on my face angered him or what his mood would be. Still, in all the closets of my mind, the memories I most love about Daddy are from the day he taught me to twiddle my thumbs and draw daisies.

Mom went to work because Daddy couldn't find a job. He'd lost his last job because of substance abuse, and a new one was slow in coming. Daddy was wonderfully creative. Every house we lived in, whether owned or rented, we left more beautiful than when we moved in. He built and rebuilt, painted, added on and planted glorious gardens to make the trip up to the house a delight. He was a good worker when he worked. A perfectionist with a good eye, many contractors sought him out to work with them. When he worked, he made good money, but his binges of drinking sometimes left him jobless, angry and depressed. That meant Mom had to work until someone trusted Dad to stay sober again.

With Mom going to work, though, it was hard for him to set his mind to anything more than chasing after the five children they had together at that time. He would tell us, "Sit on the couch and be quiet so Daddy can think." Then he would begin to pace the floor. Day after day, this was the drill, and we would watch Daddy pace until I imagined the floor would wear away and Daddy would be lost in the basement.

I tried to sit still, really I did. I sat arrow straight and looked into the air, trying very hard to be quiet. Do you know what you see when you are five or six years old and look into the air? You see glorious, sparkling, fairy-like creatures dancing wildly, beckoning you to dance with them. The warm rays of the sun sneaking between the slats of the blinds made the fairies dance feverishly while those in the shadows seemed to float, deliberate and ballerina-graceful through the air.

I couldn't stand it; I had to dance with them. I needed to leap and twirl in the air. I ached to feel the sun stretch the skin on my face and make the freckles pop out on my nose. The fairies summoned me to move, and I could no longer sit still. Though Daddy's wrath would likely be the price I would pay, there was no keeping still when the sun called my name and the fairies crooked their fingers. I danced hard and fast until his shadow loomed ominously over me, and the sun ran away to hide and took the fairies with him.

There was one day, though, when Daddy didn't grab me by the hair. He stood, hands on hips, and sighed deeply as he looked down on me, frozen in mid-pirouette. I began to cry, and my sister, Gayla, cried too because she hated for me to get hurt. Daddy stood silently. When I dared look into his face, I saw something that day I'd never seen before. I saw kindness. I didn't know how to identify it, but I saw compassion in the beautiful blue ocean of my daddy's eyes that day.

"You can't do it, can you?" He smiled at the confusion on my face. "You just can't sit still, can you?"

My face dropped with the shame I felt. "I tried, Daddy." Hot tears ran like a river down a straight line in my face.

"I know you tried." Daddy wiped the tears with his rough finger.

"I couldn't do it either when I was your age. Oh, and my dad would strap me bloody for it!"

He picked me up and carried me back to the couch where my siblings stared wide-eyed.

"Let me show you something you can do to help you control that energy." Daddy spoke softly and sat next to me on the couch. He picked up my hands and clasped them together. "Watch my hands, Jilliann." He clasped his hands together, too, and then made his thumbs dance around each other. "You can make your thumbs dance just like your legs do. Did you know that?" He gently rolled my thumbs over each other to show me how. "Next time you feel like dancing, do this instead, okay?" Smiling reassuringly, he patted my head and began pacing again. I didn't find the thumb dance as invigorating or as lovely as the fairy dance, but I did it because it seemed to make Daddy happy.

Later, as the shadows deepened and our stomachs growled for food, we were still assigned to the couch. His mood had grown quiet, which we later understood would be the prelude to a binge of drinking. His pacing quickened, and his face revealed the inner turmoil of a battle already lost. The rain poured from the sky outside, and thunder crashed on occasion to remind us there is always someone bigger. I began to chatter, as I did when things got too quiet. "Yackety, yackety, yack."

When Daddy's gaze went from the floor to me, I realized I had interrupted his thoughts. I sat stone still, hoping he was not thinking about me with that scowl on his face. He pursed his lips tightly and then ran his hands through his hair. With purpose in his stride, he walked from the living room where we were to the kitchen and back again. In his hand, he held a stenographer's notebook and a pen. "Can you draw Daddy a daisy?" he asked in his most cordial tone as he sat next to me. My siblings and I were leery; we all leaned away from him. "Look," he said as he looped circles around each other to form a flower. "And if you are very clever, you can make it look like a real daisy by never taking the pen off the paper." He showed us how to draw daisies and then handed the notebook to me. "When you feel like you have to talk, draw me a daisy instead, okay?"

I became proficient at drawing daisies. During lectures at school, I drew daisies to keep from interrupting the teacher, especially when the subject excited me. It got me through school without getting thrown out for being a chatterbox. People have asked me if the reason I draw daisies is because I am bored. No, it is because Daddy understood the energy within me that must be used or I feel as though I will burst. He had the same energy. Fortunately, he chose one day to teach me rather than beat me. If my dad were alive, I would thank him for understanding.

~Jilliann McEwen

Right from Wrong

There are some things you learn best in calm, and some in storm.
~Willa Cather

I was the youngest of three boys. We lived in a four-room house with our parents. Dad liked to say we had four rooms and a path. He referred to the well-worn trail to our outhouse. We didn't have hot running water. We heated water in pots on an oil stove, poured it into a bucket, grabbed a facecloth and towel, and washed in the privacy of our rooms. We washed our hair in the kitchen sink. We were poor.

Dad had a job, but he spent most of the money on alcohol. There were many nights when I would wake to loud voices. I'd lie still and listen, aware it was Thursday night, and like every Thursday, Dad had come home drunk.

Thursday was payday for my father. After work, he and his co-workers went to the tavern and drank. It was the start of four days of hell. On Friday, he'd go to work hung over and return in the evening drunk again. For the rest of the weekend, he'd drink with his buddies.

He came home drunk one evening, got out of the car, lost his balance, staggered twenty feet, and smashed his head into the front porch. He was that drunk and somehow drove home.

Dad was nasty when he drank—not violent, just mean. He'd yell at us for the smallest thing. Even though we tried not to disturb him, he'd lash out with complaints about our behavior. There was no pleasing the man. Four days of the week we cowered from him.

I know more about him now and can even understand his bitterness toward the world. He was born out of wedlock and spent many years in an orphanage. The abuse he received there... I don't want to think about it.

As the school week wound down, my stress increased. I knew the weekend was coming. The drinking and arguing were near.

How did Mum tolerate him? It's a mystery to me. She had nowhere to go. Where would she be able to support three boys on her own? She stayed for us. My biggest fear? She'd give up, walk out, and leave us with our father.

I was in the first grade and sitting in my classroom one morning. We had large windows. I could see my house and the store across the street from it. We had a small bus service. It came twice a day and took people to the city and back.

The bus pulled up. A lady with a red jacket boarded. My mom had a red jacket! I started to cry in front of my classmates. Mom was leaving!

The teacher calmed me. "Michael, your Mum wouldn't leave you. She loves you."

I wasn't convinced. The lunch bell rang. I rushed home and found Mum making my lunch. I ran up, clutched her around the waist, and cried.

Mum did everything for Dad. She made his lunches, cleaned, cooked, and took care of us. Dad did little. He worked, and in the evening, he sat.

If I needed his help, I refused to ask for it. If I asked, I knew he would get angry at me for interrupting his TV time. When he came home from work, he expected his dinner waiting and complained about the lunch made for him that day.

I was afraid to ask him for anything. The chain on my bike was loose and would fall off the sprocket. It took me forever to figure out how to tighten it myself, but I did it. I learned to do things myself—the hard way.

My brothers grew older, got their driver's licenses, and were blamed for every mark, dent, or scratch on the car. I got my license and refused to drive Dad's car. I was not going to be blamed for anything that happened. I walked or biked and gave Dad no excuse to yell at me.

Christmas was bad. He'd be drunk on Christmas day and have no patience for small boys enjoying new toys. There would be more fighting than laughter from my parents. When my brothers and I were older and slept late on Christmas morning, Dad would come to our room — drunk as usual — and wake us. He expected us to be the kids he ignored. We'd groan and tell him to go sleep it off. He wanted to make up for what he missed out on when we were younger, but the damage was done.

One night, when I was a teenager, he was sitting drunk at the kitchen table. The look in his eyes was a warning. They were red and evil. "Why don't you go to bed?" he snarled.

I knew best. I went to bed. I tried to sleep, but I heard the distinct sound of his shotgun being loaded. I snuck from my room and saw him going out the door with his gun. I rushed up and grabbed the barrel. "Dad! No! Let me have the gun. Go to bed."

"Son, let me do it," he said. "I'm no good."

"Dad, please! Go to bed."

He loosened his grip on the gun, allowed me to take it from his hands, and staggered to the bedroom.

I learned a lot of things from my dad. I learned how not to treat my wife. I learned to make my own lunch and not expect my wife to make it. I learned it is wrong for a man to complain about cooking and cleaning, which should be team efforts. I learned to give my children love and attention.

Dad didn't teach by example. He taught by making me aware of what is wrong. His drinking caused a lot of trouble, but all three of his boys became better people because of his wrong.

After Dad passed away, our mother, who was a strong and beautiful woman, was freed from his abuse. My brothers and I said, "Now Mum is free to enjoy her life."

I don't hate my dad. He was my father. He gave me life. I can't hate him for that. However, I'm disappointed he never experienced the good things a family can provide.

Dad, I love you. One day, we will be able to meet again. I will hug you and forgive you.

~Michael T. Smith

Stubborn Love

Many are stubborn in pursuit of the path they have chosen,
few in pursuit of the goal.
~Friedrich Wilhelm Nietzsche

My mom used to tell me, "You can pick your friends, but you can't pick your relatives." She'd usually say this after some wayward relative acted in a certain way or pulled a dumb move.

I never imagined the "pick your relatives" part would apply to my father. But after Mom died in 2000, Dad and I struggled to get along. It wasn't that we didn't love each other, but Mom and I had a unique relationship. She was my best friend, confidante, spiritual adviser, sounding board, and the one I turned to for anything. Dad remained quietly in the background, supportive and loving.

Dad and I had to relearn how to relate to each other, and most of the time we did a pitiful job. We grieved for Mom in different ways and were unable to comfort one another. While I went to grief counseling and attended a grief support group, Dad sat at home in his recliner, watching baseball on TV, reading or just being alone. One trait we did share was stubbornness. I had no idea how much this obstinate nature — in both of us — would come out in full force years later.

Dad had always been independent; he didn't want to impose on anyone for anything. In his eighties, he continued to drive, mow his yard, shovel his driveway, buy groceries, do home repairs and take the 350-mile trip several times back to his hometown in South Dakota.

In 2001, he underwent carotid artery surgery, then two months later, quadruple bypass surgery. Five months later, he had gallbladder surgery. A few years after that, he was diagnosed with congestive heart failure and suffered several small strokes. The only one I found out about was when he felt faint while driving. He pulled his car over, waited for it to pass, and then drove himself to the doctor.

That's when the doctor told us that Dad shouldn't live alone. Again, his independent and stubborn nature reared its obstinate head. He didn't want anyone telling him what to do. He also didn't believe that his health was that bad.

But Dad finally relented, put his house on the market, and moved into a wonderful retirement home where he enjoyed three meals a day, laundry and housekeeping services, and plenty of companionship and activities.

Dad seemed happy, and my brother, husband and I were relieved, so much so that my brother and his wife felt comfortable enough to sell their house and move to Texas, more than 1,100 miles away.

Things were good for about seven or eight months. Dad had made a lot of friends and had a full social calendar. Then in early 2006, he called and told me to take him to the emergency room. When I asked him if he had talked to his doctor, he said, "No, I don't like that man. Take me to the hospital."

After sitting in the ER for three hours, the doctor told Dad his condition wasn't an emergency, and he should see his regular doctor. Dad told that doctor the same thing he told me. I got so mad I had to leave the room. I called my husband Randy, and he offered to bring Dad home so I could cool off. When Randy came home, he told me the ER doctor said Dad had congestive heart failure, something his regular doctor had told him countless times before. But Dad refused to believe it, let alone acknowledge it.

As his condition worsened and I got frequent calls from retirement home management about Dad falling or having accidents, Randy and I realized we needed to do something. Dad was adamant about not going to a nursing home. "I'll die if I go there." I wanted to honor his request, but I also wanted to ensure he was cared for.

With a brother in Texas and another in Alabama, Randy and I made the decision to put Dad in hospice. We found one that provided care for Dad where he was, so he didn't have to move, which we knew would please him. But when Randy and I talked to him, he threw a fit. In denial about congestive heart failure, he didn't believe he needed hospice. After the hospice nurse explained everything, he reluctantly gave the go-ahead.

Although hospice workers visited him several times a week, they couldn't be there to monitor him 24/7, and it became clear he needed round-the-clock care. I was there as often as possible, but it took a toll on me physically, emotionally and mentally. I considered quitting my part-time job so I could be with Dad, but then the hospice chaplain suggested twenty-four-hour-a-day care available through a local hospital.

"You can't continue the way you're going. It's wearing you out," she said. "This will give you a break so you can enjoy the time you have left with him."

I knew Dad would object because of the expense, and he didn't disappoint me. When I talked to him, he threw another fit—not because he was a selfish tightwad, but because he wanted to have money left for my brothers and me when he died. I got upset and had to leave the room. I called Randy and asked him to come over as soon as he could. "That man is so stubborn. I just can't stand it!" By the time I returned to Dad's room, Randy and he were having a nice, calm conversation. Dad looked at me and said, "I love you, CJ."

I had been fighting to keep Dad comfortable and well-taken care of while he fought for the last shred of control over his life. Realizing that, my anger faded, and I hugged him and told him I loved him, too.

Even with round-the-clock care and his weakened condition, Dad's stubbornness was as strong as ever. He hid his medication, and when the hospice nurse called him on it, he told her she was "worse than a drill sergeant." He refused to use a walker or wheelchair because he didn't want to admit defeat, then fell trying to get out of bed.

As Dad's bodily functions began to shut down, his breathing became labored, and he wasn't able to swallow, making it impossible to eat or take his meds. The doctor prescribed liquid morphine to ease his pain. I knew it was the beginning of the end. Two days later, I was with Dad as he died quietly in his sleep.

For months, I agonized over feelings of regret, mostly over our head-butting. I also wondered if Dad knew how much I loved him. When I talked to Randy about it, he said, "Who took care of him? You did. Who was there when decisions had to be made? You. Who was there when he died? You. You were there because you loved him, and he knew it."

Yes, my father aggravated and exasperated me, and many times he just plain ticked me off. But when I look at those instances of Dad's stubbornness, I know it's not because he was a cantankerous, mean-spirited old man. His stubbornness was his last shred of control when he was losing control of everything else. My stubbornness was masking my fear of losing him.

It's been more than three years since Dad died, and I miss him terribly. He had his faults and so did I, but we were a perfect match.

I'm glad I can't pick my relatives. That's a job best left up to God, who did it perfectly.

~CJ Hines

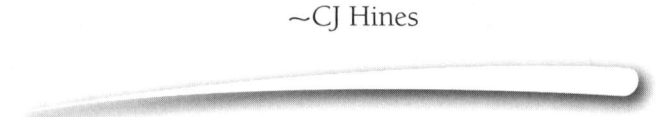

And the
Beat Goes On

He conquers who endures.
~Persius

Before I was born, my dad ran a casino in the Chicago area. He was also a bootlegger and did a little "bookie" business on the side. My mother was a nightclub singer on the Chicago circuit. By the time I was born, she had a severe drinking problem.

My aunt, Dad's sister, tells me that when I was just an infant, on more than one occasion, Dad would get home from work after midnight and find me home alone. Whenever my aunt heard pounding on her door in the middle of the night, it would be Dad, holding me wrapped in a blanket and saying, "She's gone again."

My parents divorced when I was three years old. The court awarded full custody to my dad, but Dad says my mother begged and cried and pleaded to have me. So, he gave me up with the threat that if she were to start drinking at any time, he would take me back.

Dad told me he hired a private detective who reported that my mother had started drinking again, which is why I returned to live with him. I'm not sure if that's true. When I was four years old, I distinctly remember hearing my mother say on the phone, "Come and get her. I don't want her anymore."

That might have been the inception of any insecurity I harbored throughout my childhood. Okay, throughout my life. But there was more…

When I was six, my father married his brother's widow. She had a son who needed a father. Dad had me, and I needed a mother. They entered into a negotiated union. I'm not sure if there was ever any love there or not. But, suddenly, my aunt became my mother, and my cousin became my brother.

As soon as my birth mother sobered up, or maybe it was when she was drinking the most, she wanted me back. She would come to my school, follow me home, jump out of the car, run to me, throw her arms around me and cry, "My baby. My baby. I love you."

This left me a bit confused because my stepmother made it very clear to me. "She is not your mother. She gave you up. She doesn't love you." Of course, I repeated these thoughts to my birth mother. How I must have hurt her. Now add guilt to my psyche!

I tried very hard to love my stepmother, Thelma. Not easy! She was a very cold person. When my birth mother asked her for visitation privileges, she was told, "Either take Kay and raise her alone, or stay out of her life completely." Nice choice for someone with money, but my mother had very little. My father had plenty.

I choose to believe my mother unselfishly walked out of my life to give me financial security. This thought, of course, comes to me now that I am older and know what my stepmother told her. When I was little, it meant I was unlovable.

In an effort to have a normal relationship, like all my friends, I asked Thelma if I could call her Mom. "Call me whatever you want," she sneered. My efforts for normalcy were futile. It was obvious that Thelma did not like me. She just tolerated me and let me know that was the case.

Color me insecure. After all, no one wanted me, and I was ugly! One of my eyes was nearly blind and turned in. I wore thick glasses. Thelma braided my hair and pinned it to the top of my head. And she dressed me in hand-me-downs that were always a little too big for me.

My dad was my lifeline to emotional security. Whenever he went out of town, he bought me little gifts. I don't remember what they were — probably just candy, gum and little things he picked up at the airport — but it meant he loved me!

One night when I was six years old and saying goodnight to Daddy, Thelma barked, "Don't you think you're just a little too old to be kissing your father goodnight?!" That ended the one tiny bit of intimacy to which I clung. Dad, as in all things, conceded to Thelma.

The older I got, the more Thelma judged me. I was too dramatic... I wore my heart on my sleeve... I was boy-crazy. She became suspicious of my every move when it came to boys. (By high school, my looks had improved.) When I was sixteen, she actually accused me of having sex in church.

That did it! As Dad had always gone to his sister in times of crisis, I went running to her for safe harbor until graduation. My aunt said I could stay but that it might help to know a little bit more about my stepmother. It was then I learned that Thelma had grown up in an orphanage and had had a very hard life. I suddenly understood why she had become such an unemotional and calculating person.

Wow! It wasn't me! I wasn't the reason for her bitterness. It was not my shortcomings that set her off. It was her own instability. These were her problems, not mine.

So much for dysfunctional families! Now that I had it all figured out, I would fall in love, get married and finally have a normal life.

I went to college, fell in love and got married. Twelve years and two children later, my husband told me he was gay.

And the beat goes on...

~Kay Conner Pliszka

36

Quality Time

The cure for anything is salt water—
sweat, tears, or the sea.
~Isak Dinesen

I had just been through a rough day at work, and all I really wanted to do was stop by the beach on my way home and spend a few relaxing minutes trying to unwind.

When I got there, it seemed like I had made the perfect choice. The sun and the tide were both low, providing a perfect expanse of hard, moist sand that was out of the intense heat that had plagued most of the day. A cool, light breeze had begun to blow, and the beach was quiet and pleasantly deserted.

I set up a chair on the sand and lowered my work-weary body with a tired sigh, mustering up just enough energy to push off my shoes.

I took a deep breath, filling my lungs with the clean, damp ocean air. And as I exhaled, my eyes slowly closing, all the cares and troubles of my day seemed to float out and get carried away into the sea.

With my eyes closed, the sounds of the sea seemed to grow louder, surrounding me, caressing me, and whispering to me with the smooth, slow-motion rush, crash and murmur of the low summer tide. It was such a peaceful sound, almost hypnotizing. What had I been so tense about only moments before? I couldn't remember. I couldn't think of anything but the sound of the waves.

I realized I was almost dozing when a sound to my left broke my reverie. It was the high-pitched sound of seagulls. And then, mingled with the cries of the gulls, I heard the laughter of a small child.

Who was this coming to disturb the first peaceful moments I'd had all day? I lazily opened my eyes and turned toward the sounds.

Down the beach, a man and a young boy stood, laughing playfully as a dozen or so seagulls hovered above them. They appeared to be feeding the birds something from a paper bag, and all of them — the birds, the boy and the man — seemed to be enjoying it immensely. Man and boy would each thrust his hand deep into the bag, bring out their clinched fists, and fling the contents high into the air. And with each fistful, they would look at the birds, then at each other, and laugh with genuine delight as the birds swooped and called and rose again into the air, hovering there, anxiously waiting for the laughter to stop and the food to start flying again.

A father and child sharing some quality time, no doubt, I thought to myself sarcastically, and then I felt a little depressed by my reaction. Such pleasant father/child scenes always made me a little sad, a little jealous, for what I never had as a child. But I sure didn't need these thoughts now, not after the day I'd had. I closed my eyes tightly again and turned back toward the sea.

But it was too late. Bits and pieces of unhappy childhood memories were already pushing their way into my mind, forming into the mental motion picture that I knew all too well — my mind's well-worn saga of a childhood with an alcoholic father. First came the scene of my father passed out drunk in front of the TV, nearly setting his chair on fire with the lit cigarette in his dangling hand. Then the scenes of angry outbursts, played over and over, sometimes accentuated with slammed doors, knocked-over furniture or squealing tires as he sped away, hurrying to find refuge in some dark , inviting bar.

And then, the grand finale: the time he came home so drunk that he didn't even know that he had just been in a car accident, although blood was running down his face in tiny rivulets. I locked myself in my room that day, afraid of the man with the unknowing stare who was stumbling around in our house. That was the last straw, apparently, for my mother. My father was asked to pack his bags and leave our family, to find another home. It was for the good of us kids, she said. And not long afterward, my father died, alone and hundreds of miles away from us. No, "quality time" was not something I had much of as a child.

I shook my head sharply and opened my eyes, trying to stop this melodrama in my mind. My breathing began to relax as I focused on the sights around me. There were the waves, still crashing. There was the sand, still damp beneath my feet. And down the beach, there was the boy and the man.

The boy was still looking skyward, though the bag was apparently empty now, hanging limply at his side. The seagulls were breaking up, some flying toward the sea, while others landed cautiously nearby. Just as the boy seemed to be losing his interest in the birds, the man began running and flapping his arms, chasing the few brave gulls that had landed on the beach. Squeals of laughter rang out as the boy excitedly followed, laughing and squawking and flapping after the birds.

I laughed to myself now and let my eyes drift shut once more. The child's laughter carried on the wind and drifted into my mind, echoing there, growing louder and louder until it seemed to fill my whole head. Such laughter! Such pure and simple joy.

Slowly, a new image began to form in my mind: a young girl propped up in bed, her pixie haircut framing a face lit up with joy and laughter. The image began to gain clarity, as if being focused by a giant mental lens. I could see a familiar pink bedroom trimmed in lace, stuffed toys long ago forgotten, and a plump, freckled face that I knew had to be mine. The laughter echoed again, and the image drifted back to include a dark-haired, handsome man sitting at the foot of the bed, telling a wonderful made-up bedtime story of friendly creatures, and a prince and princess who lived in a far-off and exciting kingdom. And as the story ended, the child realized that she was the princess and threw her arms around the man's neck and squealed, "And you were my prince, right, Daddy?"

Other memories came flooding back to me now as the man and

the boy on the beach continued to run, laugh, and chase crabs and waves. It was as if the boy's laughter was pushing into the farthest reaches of my mind, discovering memories that had long since been buried.

Very clearly now I could remember my father working for hours in our basement, meticulously setting up tunnels and mountains and trees on a room-sized train set as my brothers and I waited eagerly for the first running of the train.

I remembered the pride in my father's eyes as he taught the teen-age me to drive a stick shift. And though I stalled and stripped and tortured his car, he never got mad at me. He never yelled or got impatient. He had that same loving smile that I saw on the face of the father on the beach. It was a smile that beamed with love and joy and fatherly pride.

The tide was coming in now, but I sat motionless as I saw it catch my shoes and inch them up the sand. I couldn't move. I felt drained from the intensity of the emotions I was feeling.

He was a good father once. I could remember that now. What had happened to him to make him want to escape into a bottle? I stared out into the sea and thought of the things that had sometimes driven me to drink in my adult years. Had he felt the same feelings of loneliness and inadequacy that I sometimes felt? How could I know the challenges he faced, the loneliness he felt from a loveless marriage, the fears he must have felt when he lost his job with a family still to support? I couldn't have known. I was too young to know because he had died many years ago when all I felt for him was resentment and shame and embarrassment. I was still too young to understand his pain and frailties.

On the beach, the man and the boy were nearing me now, their feet splish-splashing in the waves as the setting sun cast their shadows out upon the sea. They were quiet now, holding hands, gently swinging their arms, dragging their feet through ankle-deep water. The fading sunlight seemed to outline them against the sea, and I thought I could almost read their minds—the cluttered, tense, worried adult thoughts of the man and the playful, carefree innocence of the child. And just then, as they passed in front of me, I heard the child's quiet voice as he said, "I love you, Daddy."

I smiled as a feeling of warmth and peace began to grow inside of me—a peace I hadn't felt for many years. And as I closed my eyes once more, I saw my father and me walking hand-in-hand down the beach, swinging our arms and splashing through waves.

"I love you, Daddy," I whispered aloud. And somewhere, carried on the wind and only slightly muffled by the sound of the surf, I'm sure I heard his reply.

~Betsy S. Franz

Chapter 5

Thanks for the Memories

Every man's memory is his private literature.

~Aldous Huxley

Commodious
Memories

It's surprising how much memory is built around things unnoticed at the time.
~Barbara Kingsolver, Animal Dreams

Have you ever experienced a loss so deep it wounded the tapestry of your soul? That's how I felt the day my brothers and I cleaned out my parents' house after their deaths. My mother had died nine months after my father, after sixty-two years of marriage. Having lived through the Great Depression, they were packrats. Nothing was ever thrown away if there was the slightest possibility it could be used for something later.

My childhood home was nothing fancy, but it was certainly better than the converted four-room chicken-coop house I was born in. I was child number five, and Dad knew we needed something larger. He found a seven-room house with five acres of land that he thought would suit our needs, and we moved there in 1954 when I was a mere four years old. It was the first time I'd ever seen an indoor toilet.

As the years went by, my four brothers and I married and moved away, but Dad saw no reason to uproot and find a smaller house. Our old bedrooms became storage bins for sundry treasures and antiques only he and Mom knew existed.

As we cleaned up the house and land, tears of laughter as well as tears for a bygone era could be heard resonating from the deep recesses of our souls. Our biggest laugh came from the commode sitting in the yard. It was the original commode that had been in the house when we moved in. When it finally needed to be replaced due to a cracked base, Dad couldn't part with it. Placing it gingerly underneath the old oak tree just outside the front door, my father beamed with pride as he and Mom planted a small rosebush beside it to commemorate the years of service the commode had given to the family. It was Dad's first indoor toilet, too.

Through the years, we tried to reason with him to move the commode to another location besides the front yard, but Dad stubbornly refused. Once when Dad was hospitalized for an extended period of time, one of my brothers actually had the audacity to move it behind an old building on the property, thinking Dad wouldn't miss it. How wrong he was! The first thing out of Dad's mouth upon returning home from the hospital was, "Who moved my commode?" It had to be quickly retrieved and placed back in its place of honor beside the rosebush.

Those fond childhood memories flooded our minds, but the undercurrent of knowing this would be our last visit to our home was evident as we packed box after box of items to be donated to Goodwill.

When the last box was loaded into the van and the floors had been swept clean, my heart broke. The finality hit me hard as I walked through the empty rooms, tears welling up in my eyes as I faced the fact that this would be the last time I'd ever see the inside of my childhood home. As I walked into the den, I pictured Mom and Dad's recliners as they used to be, facing the TV in the corner. I could almost see them laughing and talking, smiling… enjoying their children and grandchildren.

I had to laugh as I looked at the replacement commode in the bathroom, the one that never seemed to capture Dad's heart.

Just around the corner was their bedroom. I could still see Dad lying in bed as the effects of Alzheimer's took over his brain. I could also see the antique dresser in the corner handed down from my grandmother, which was now resting comfortably in the corner of my own home thirty miles away.

As a plethora of memories flooded my mind, I walked into the back bedroom for one last look around. This bedroom had housed two brothers at a time. When one of them married and moved away, another brother took his place in the "man-cave." I saw the hole one of my brothers had put in the sheetrock when he decided wall climbing was a great form of entertainment.

The empty house echoed with memories. As I turned to leave, I pushed back the door of the back bedroom. That's when I saw it hanging solemnly on a nail, its black button eyes glaring at me, begging me not to leave it behind. It was a brown crocheted teddy bear, my mother's handiwork, placed there long ago for the entertainment of a grandchild. About six inches tall, and no more than four inches wide, it brought me to my knees as I looked at it—the last remaining item in the house, overlooked and almost forgotten by everyone.

Carefully removing it from its nail as I wiped my eyes, I held it to my cheek and felt the softness of the crochet thread against my soul. Of course I won't leave you behind!

Today, that brown teddy bear holds a place of honor on the wall of my kitchen. It's the first thing I see when I walk into the room. It's a constant reminder of a life of love and happiness—of a childhood of pleasant memories—of being thankful for loving parents who taught me right from wrong. On days when my world seems upside down, I find comfort in that brown button-eyed friend.

Eight years have passed, and occasionally I find myself gazing thoughtfully at the commode that now graces my front yard, the spring flowers I planted in it emitting a soothing smell of lavender. After all, I am my father's daughter!

~Carol Huff

Grandma Lillie's Red Cadillac

When in doubt, wear red.
~Bill Blass

Grandma Lillie always drove a red Cadillac. I'm not really sure why except that red was her favorite color. Not just any red, of course, but a gleaming candy-apple red with a hint of metallic that glistened in the sun. Grandma always told me that men "always look twice at a pretty woman in a red car." She did seem to get plenty of glances when she was behind the wheel of her Caddy, but I wasn't sure if they were directed at her in admiration or in anger over her limited driving abilities.

I used to stay with Grandma during the summers, and washing her car once a week was one of my chores. I never dared miss a spot, either inside or out, or I would have to redo the whole task. Grandma was of the school that a job worth doing was worth doing perfectly, so I tried to do it the way she wanted, as best as I could. She would come out and survey my work when I was done, bringing me a glass of ice-cold lemonade or a Coke in a bottle, and if I had done well, a homemade cookie. She would inspect her car and then remark, "Pretty doggone good for an eight-year-old," which made me feel like a queen.

After the car was cleaned up, Grandma and I would ride over to the Navy base to get her hair done and a "man-cure" on her nails. Grandma had long, thick acrylic nails, painted, of course, the same deep red as her car. She vowed you could always tell a real lady by the condition of her hands, and long red nails were another "man magnet."

Paw-Paw was in the Navy, so the base was where Grandma and I did all our shopping. Grandma would get her nails filled in by a nice lady from Barbados, and I would listen to their conversations, enthralled by the topics they discussed—everything from witchcraft to voodoo. Most of it was far above my eight-year-old head, but intoxicating nonetheless. Although Grandma was a devout Catholic, she and Paw-Paw had lived in Barbados for many years, and she had embraced many of the customs of the local people she befriended there. I loved looking at the photos she brought back of the ebony-skinned people and the palm trees waving in the tropical winds, and imagined the most magical place on Earth. Grandma told me that any time a good-looking man was married to an ugly woman, the woman must have "put the voodoo on him." I had no idea what she was talking about, but figured it must be true because Grandma said it was.

Of course, these ideas of Grandma's, along with her salty tongue, were of great concern to my parents. After one of my visits with Grandma, Mama and I were walking through JCPenney when I witnessed a nice-looking man strolling with a most unfortunate-looking lady. Upon seeing them, I commented loudly to Mama, "Look at that man with that dog-faced woman! She must have put the voodoo on him!" Then, after a pause for dramatic effect, I stated, "Either that or poontang." Of course, I had no idea what "poontang" was since Grandma had never explained it to me. I tried to tell Mama that, but she still gave me a butt-whipping all the way back to the car.

Later, I learned that was a slang term Grandma used for lovemaking. She never used the right words for any body part that was "down there," but had her own vocabulary for the "privates," as she called them. The girl part was either a "hoochie mama" or "pocketbook," and the boy part was a "weenie" or a "pecker." Grandma always told me and my cousin Scarlet to keep our pocketbooks closed until we got married. We never really did get why it was bad to open up your purse prior to marriage, but again, if Grandma said it, we thought it was the gospel.

After Grandma would get her nails done, she would usually get her hair dyed jet black and teased up till it looked like cotton candy. I thought it was so pretty and wished I could get my hair dyed or teased. To me, Grandma looked like an older, racier version of Priscilla when she married Elvis. Of course, everyone in the South knew that Mrs. Presley was the most beautiful woman on the planet. Otherwise, Elvis would have never married her.

Grandma usually took me shopping after her hair/nail appointment. She had to show off her freshly done "do," and the first place we always went was the lingerie department at the Navy Exchange. Grandma loved lingerie and bought it in her favorite color as well. She thought black lingerie was only worn by "open-bottom hos," and white was only for your wedding night—if you kept your pocketbook closed and deserved to wear white, that is. She said red lingerie meant a woman was ready to "get down to business." I didn't know what "business" meant either, but I noticed Paw-Paw always seemed real happy the next day after Grandma got her new lingerie. He would wake up smiling, "whisker" us grandkids with his unshaven face, and walk around the kitchen singing, "She's got dimples on her butt, she's perty, she's Lillie Helen Miller, and she's perty!" at the top of his lungs while Grandma fixed his breakfast.

Grandma was a real good "cooker," and I never tired of helping her in the kitchen. Rolling out her yeast rolls and feeling the sticky dough between my fingers, or rolling out homemade noodles for her vegetable soup, began my lifelong love affair with cooking. The smell of the yeast and the fresh-baked bread was the first thing to greet anyone who came to Grandma's house on a Sunday or holiday. Paw-Paw would help out by grilling steaks on an old charcoal grill out back of the house, marinated in a "secret sauce" that only he knew the recipe to, but which made the steaks fork-tender and scrumptious. Grandma would cook us a baked potato to go with our dinner, topped with mounds of freshly made butter and sour cream. "Low-fat" wasn't a word heard in Grandma's kitchen, and all of us grandkids would come home from a visit a little "healthier"—i.e., with about ten extra pounds.

I continued to visit Grandma throughout her life, even after I married and had children of my own. After Paw-Paw passed on, Grandma lived at home for a while, making one of the bedrooms a shrine to him with all his military medals and photos on display. After a while, she had to be put into a nursing home, but continued to be feisty in spirit. Her worn-out body still housed a little fireball. The workers at the home called her "Ms. Froufrou" because of the many demands she placed on them. Even in the home, she wanted to keep up her appearance and gave the staff of the nursing home fits. Still, they loved her and tried to keep her looking pretty whenever anyone would come to visit. However, she was saddened by the fact that she was no longer at home and continually asked about her precious red Cadillac. She was sure she would go back home some day and drive it again.

Grandma died just shy of her ninetieth birthday. When my brother called to tell me she had passed away, I was saddened, but glad that she did not have to live in the nursing home any longer. In my haste to get down to Florida for her funeral, I didn't have time to get a manicure, and I was glad Grandma wouldn't see my ratty-looking hands and un-"mancured" nails.

Her funeral was beautiful and meaningful, and brought back a flood of memories. My cousin Scarlet had written the eulogy, which made all of us laugh and cry. All the things that had made Grandma a unique Southern lady came back to us all that day.

I got up to see Grandma's body and tell her goodbye before the casket was closed. As I looked at her frail little hands, I noticed something that would have made her real happy. Her nails had been painted red—not just any red, but a candy-apple red with a little sparkle that matched the paint on her Cadillac. I smiled, taking comfort in the knowledge that Grandma was finally home, driving her red Cadillac around heaven and scaring the heck out of any angels who might get in her way.

~Melanie Adams Hardy

Keeping the Peas

Kindness is in our power, even when fondness is not.
~Samuel Johnson

Uncle Harry's first wife, Annie, a stylish dark-haired beauty, had always suffered frail health, and when the tuberculosis epidemic struck, she was among the first to be hospitalized for nearly a year until her death at age forty-six. Annie left behind two teenage daughters, and Uncle Harry had no idea how to care for them. One day, without a word to anyone, he married Ruth, ten years his senior and the only spinster in town. Very set in her ways, she had waited nearly a lifetime to become someone's wife, and the role went straight to her head. Her bossy, humorless personality nearly crushed the spirit of the two motherless children and stirred up one storm after another with her two sisters-in-law, who found her crass and meddlesome. For the sake of the two young girls, the two women tried to keep the peace, but Harry's brothers got a daily earful of Ruth's behavior.

Uncle Harry, who sold real estate, busied himself away from home most of the time while Aunt Ruth, inexperienced as both a wife and mother, went on a mission to impress his family. And even though there was no love lost between the sisters-in-law, Aunt Ruth became the annoyance that bound them together. For the next twenty years until Uncle Harry died, they did their "dance of uppity," while Aunt Ruth tortured their sensibilities with her clueless, unrefined behavior. By the age of eighty, both sisters-in-law had died, her stepchildren were long ago estranged, and Aunt Ruth was alone. And over our very loud protests, Mother insisted on inviting her to join us for family holidays "because she is old and alone."

And that started the once-a-week visits. Aunt Ruth, in her bright yellow house dresses, nylons rolled down just below the knee, would march on a mission from her apartment to our house with a big pot of something homemade. Mom graciously praised and thanked her for such a thoughtful and unexpected bounty. Unfortunately, our mother must have raved a little too much about her special pea soup. And whether she really loved Mom that much or just started to forget things, the pea soup deliveries began to come more and more often. The big enamel pots took up the whole refrigerator and were pushed around as we tried to find "normal food." The soup actually wasn't that bad, but how much pea soup could one family eat?

Then one day Aunt Ruth was sighted coming up the driveway with more pea soup while the previously-delivered monster pot still sat in the fridge. In a panic, Mom rushed the pot upstairs to the bathroom, and together we poured it into the toilet. But though the gallant old plumbing did its best, the soup just sat there—except for a little swirl and a couple of gurgles. Mom's cheeks blazed as she frantically jiggled the handle again and again. "Oh, my Lord," she murmured, close to tears. "Quick! Run a bath!" she ordered. "Lock the door and sit in that tub until I tell you to come out!" Then she dashed downstairs to greet Aunt Ruth at the back door while I, giddy from our scheme of deception, turned on the water full blast to fill the huge claw-footed tub. And that's where I sat, soaking in hot water up to my chin for nearly two hours.

Once Mother yelled up to me, "My dear, Aunt Ruth is here. Will you be long?"

"I'm washing my hair!" I lied, and then I heard no more.

It was Dad's voice downstairs about two hours later that Aunt Ruth took as her cue to leave. Mom yelled up the all clear, and when I finally emerged from the steam-filled bathroom, with my hair all frizzy and fingers like prunes, there stood Dad with the plunger, laughing so hard he was holding his sides.

The pea soup stopped coming. I'm not sure what Mom told Aunt Ruth. She was never proud of having to tell a lie, white or otherwise, so she didn't share the details with me. But muffins started to arrive instead, a gift we often shared with the birds and squirrels.

~Avis P. Drucker

The Burial Plots

*Our death is not an end if we can live on in our children
and the younger generation. For they are us,
our bodies are only wilted leaves on the tree of life.*
~Albert Einstein

Reaching into my purse, I finger the pieces of paper. My security blanket. Some folks have lucky pennies, favorite stones, charms... I keep the deeds of my burial plots with me. In an uncanny way, they keep me in the moment—a reminder that the only thing separating me from the next world is entering a dark box.

Fred, my boyfriend, walks into the room. "You want to meet some of my relatives?" I ask.

Fred halts. The family he has met made a lasting impression. "Who's left to meet?"

"Oh, there's a whole bunch waiting to make your acquaintance. It's a perfect day for a ride. I want to visit the burial plots," I say slowly. "I always make a visit in the spring."

"Are you serious? You want me to go to the graveyard?"

"Why not? You haven't met the whole family."

Our conversation has sparked my teenage son's interest. "Mom, you are nuts! You want to show him dead people?"

"They're part of the family. It's our heritage."

Both David and Fred are looking at me as if I am speaking in tongues. "Your parents took us to your family plots from the airport the very first time I met them," I remind Fred.

"That was my parents," Fred counters.

"Well, they emphasized there was an extra space beside your plot."

"That was their way of pressuring us to get married."

"Great incentive. I get to be buried ten feet under if I marry you."

"Dad just plans ahead," Fred states.

"He has ten plots!"

"Yes, one for each child and their spouse… or partner," Fred quickly adds.

"Well, I don't know anyone there."

"You don't have to."

"I'm not even from Michigan."

"That will not matter at the time."

"Of course it will! I need to feel comfortable."

Fred looks bewildered. "My dad already has the headstone in place and markers outlining the four corners of the site."

"You don't think that is odd but my wanting you to see my family's legacy is?"

"You don't like my father's gravesite?"

"It's too neat, too English, and it doesn't have a good view!"

"What? He keeps it well-tended," Fred responds, perplexed.

"He has a pole with a planter coming out of the headstone!"

"That's to keep the bird crap off the grave marker. Oh, all right. We can go visit your plots if it will make you happy," Fred surrenders.

The cemetery has rolling hills, big trees, and well-manicured lawns. "Our burial reservations are for Tipperarey Hill, way up top," I say as we turn into the gate.

"Tipperarey Hill?"

"Yeah, Great-Great-Great-Granddad owned the land this cemetery is built on. He sold it under the condition that Tipperarey Hill remains undisturbed." After a few miles, the paved road is replaced by a dirt one. We continue to bump along.

"Do I dare ask the significance of the name?" Fred inquires.

"It's named after the place in Syracuse with the upside-down streetlight." I have Fred's full attention. "The Irish kept knocking out the red and yellow lights for the green to be first. The officials finally consented to hanging the streetlight upside-down. My parents were both raised there." We've come to the end of the dirt road.

"This is a gravesite?" Fred says, wide-eyed. The hill before us has rocks, weeds and discarded stumps.

"We go on foot from here. It's at the top of the knoll."

"No one maintains it?"

"Not this part. It's supposed to look like Ireland." With difficulty, we begin to climb the steep slope, reaching out to steady ourselves by grasping nature's strongholds.

"I didn't know I'd need hiking boots," Fred pants.

"Just be glad we're not carting a body." I picture a forklift lifting four-hundred-pound Great Aunt Margaret.

Before us stands a rickety, rusted iron gate, partly off its hinges. Holding on to catch our breath, we look back at a magnificent panorama of the valley below. "This is the top of the world," I whisper.

Fred is speechless. Turning around slowly, he faces the family history. The gravesite has weeds with wildflowers running through. The headstones are at awkward angles to each other. Tall oaks provide shade for the residents resting beneath. Hand-made stone fences set off certain groupings.

"Let me introduce you to my relatives," I say with an expansive gesture of my arms. "You're in good company here with the Kennedys, Fitzgeralds, Byrnes and Caldwells," I add.

Fred starts to move between headstones and grave markers. "Some of these date back to the late 1800s," he exclaims.

"Yes, there are four generations here. They came from County Mayo, County Sligo, the Dingal peninsula and Kilkenny. Both sides of the family are napping quietly next to each other without fighting," I reflect.

"They did not like each other?" Fred asks.

"Yes and no. They argued over who was more Irish: the lace-curtain Irish versus the shanty Irish. The funny thing is the first arrivals were all born in shanties." Grabbing Fred by the arm, I lead him to Uncle Fergus's dwelling. The stone reads "Born in Ireland in 1838. Died at 106 years. Highly recommend whiskey to wipe away your fears."

"Family legend said he buried a barrel with him," I confide.

"There's 100-year-old whiskey down there?"

"Yup, Irish whiskey, but don't go running for a shovel. They say he's mean-spirited; probably rigged his coffin."

Walking between the stone fences, Fred points. "Is that an herb garden on that grave?"

"Yeah, that's Great Aunt Katherine. She died in childbirth on Christmas day. Kate loved her garden, so they planted it with her." We spend a moment in silence.

Fred gestures to a grave marker atop a small mound. "What happened there?"

"Oh, that's Bridget Kennedy. She insisted on being buried upright in her refrigerator."

"You're joking!"

"Nope. She said it cost enough that it may as well double for something."

Fred opens and closes his mouth.

"What can I tell you? It's a lively crowd. My great-grandmother Peggy over there was buried with one hundred rolls of toilet paper," I say, pointing to a grouping behind us.

"Why would she do that?"

"They never had any toilet paper as kids. They wiped with pages from the Sears catalog. She wanted to be prepared for wherever they sent her in the next life."

Walking hand in hand, we visit each relative in turn. We come to an enclosure on the far end surrounded by the rock fence on three sides. "We'll be in good company here," I remark, indicating where our burial plots are. The weeds with wild daylilies have overrun the area. "Daylilies remind you to stay in the moment as the bloom will be gone tomorrow," I ponder.

"It's not very tidy," Fred says, surveying the place.

"Oh, just a nip and a tuck, and it will feel like home," I say convincingly.

Starting to leave, Fred notices a gravesite where the markers are in reverse order from the rest of the plots. Hannah is on the left, and her husband Bernard Fitzgerald is on the right.

"Bernard was hard of hearing, and that was his better ear," I explain.

We are silent climbing down the steep slope as I take Fred's hand over the rough patches. After driving a short distance, Fred glances down and sees the burial plot outlines in my hands. He speaks softly, "I don't know what to say."

I reply, "It's okay," placing my hand on his knee. "They're my reminder to be myself, as my spirit will endure. There is strength in family that has no limit in time."

Fred pulls me close.

~Anne Merrigan

Nana, the Passive/Aggressive Baker

The family—
that dear octopus from whose tentacles we never quite escape,
nor, in our inmost hearts,
ever quite wish to.
~Dodie Smith

My dear, departed Nana used to bake for us grandkids. A lot. Sounds wonderful, doesn't it? The first dozen times or so it was. After that, no. No. NO. Every day. Every dang day. It was like the movie, *Groundhog Day*, only with Bundt cakes.

We'd come home from school, the witching hour for kiddie appetites, and she'd appear with a big ring of dry cake. She'd parade right past my mother, who would be preparing dinner, often within reach of sharp kitchen utensils.

"Have some cake," Nana would say to us, which is Gaelic for "If you love me, you will eat this now or I will die and it will be your fault."

She would then sit down and stare at us, waiting for us to eat. Our mom, knife at the ready, would stare daggers at us, then at Nana.

Our stomachs would growl at us. There was no way out without some sort of home-baked Irish angst.

Nana: "I baked you a cake."

Mom (staring icily at us): "What a surprise."

Nana: "Well, I had nothing better to do."

Mom (eyeing the paring knife): "… Thanks."

Nana (heavy sigh): "Guess I'll go home and watch *The Price Is Right*. Alone."

I took up sports just so I wouldn't have to come home right after school and witness this scene.

Nana was born in Brooklyn of Irish immigrants, living there all her life until her husband, my Pop-pop, passed away. Once she moved next door to us in the country, Nana had to learn how to drive. This was mind-boggling to me. How could anyone make it this far through life without driving? I had been driving tractors since I was twelve years old. Those odd city people got by without driving at all. No "D" train in the boondocks, though, so Nana had to buckle up and learn.

I don't recall many details of my grandmother's driver education, just my dad requiring a few extra beers and colorful curses as he tried to instruct the woman who had brought him into this world. I do remember Nana yelling at him in that special voice reserved for special offspring. Her timing was special, too, because at that particular moment they were heading down our precarious driveway. The one with a sharp turn and a cliff.

Somehow, my dad survived teaching his mother how to drive, but when I turned sixteen and could officially take the wheel, Nana was assigned to be my teacher. Not sure who was being punished for what, we somehow both made it through. Nana was quite patient, at least on the surface. When I didn't slow down fast enough for her liking, however, she'd stomp on an imaginary, non-functioning brake pedal, nearly putting her foot through the floor of the passenger side of her car.

Me: "Everything okay, Nana?"

Nana: "Just fine." (Stomp!)

Me: "Want me to slow down?"

Nana: "No, I'm fine." (Stomp!)

Riding with Nana was an experience. She always made the sign of the cross before driving. After riding with her a few times, so did the rest of us.

Eventually, she bought an AMC Gremlin, a car even uglier than its name. Nana's Gremlin was baby blue with white racing stripes, a rolling exhibition of lipstick on a pig. The upside was that it was unique enough that townspeople quickly learned to hide behind sturdy trees and posts when they saw it coming.

As she aged and her eyesight faded, we questioned the sanity of her continuing to drive. "I've thought about that," she replied. "From now on, I'm just going to drive the roads I already know." Unfortunately, this wasn't comforting to anyone in her path. As you may have guessed, "Driving by Braille" was about as successful as "Closed Captioning for the Blind." But in Nana's world, she knew the road, she drove the road, and everyone else had to get the heck off the road.

Like any grandmother, Nana needed help with some things, like crossing icy pavement. Unlike other grandmothers, she had the vice-like grip of a Teamster. "Help me across the street, Ann Frances," she'd say and daintily take my arm. I'd grit my teeth for the pain that was sure to shoot through my bicep as she grabbed hold, her fingerprints later tattooed on my arm in the form of a florid, multi-colored bruise. More payback, perhaps, for not eating all those Bundt cakes.

We would bring our soda and beer cans to her to flatten for recycling. We had to carry the bags of cans for our poor, frail granny, yet I witnessed her crushing the old-style, thick, steel cans with her bare hands. This show of strength made it even tougher to turn down her Bundt offerings. If we didn't eat the cakes, she might flatten us like so many beer cans.

Nana helped out at our church, assisting the teachers with religious education. In other words, she was the bouncer. If a kid didn't behave, he was handed over to Nana, whereupon he very quickly saw God and understood the pain of penance. As the disruptive student was led away to face "Nana the Corrector," other kids stared at me like it was my fault my grandmother was a drill sergeant.

I'm sure she loved us, but she had a unique way of showing it. She babysat for us kids a few times—not that we needed the watching, but it made her feel wanted. A classic Nana babysitting visit went something like this:

Me (watching television): "Hey, Nana, what's up?"

Nana (heavy sigh): "Nothing good on TV, so I thought I'd come over and look at you."

She would then plop herself in a chair right next to the television and literally stare at us. I don't care who you are—you cannot enjoy television with someone sitting next to it staring back at you.

One night when our parents were out, Nana felt the need to use our oven. Our mother had complained that the oven wasn't working right. Perhaps Nana felt compelled to fix it or prove Mom wrong. Whatever the reason, I was watching television in the living room when Nana called for me casually from the kitchen—casually as in, "Whenever you have a moment, meander over here because I'd like you to see something a smidge amusing."

Nana: "Ann Frances, could you come in here?"

Me: "Can it wait until a commercial break?"

Nana: "I don't think so."

Me: "Is something wrong?"

Nana: (No response.)

Something in her odd silence tipped me off. I raced to the kitchen to see flames from the oven licking the ceiling. Nana was frozen in shock, staring at the growing fire. I grabbed the extinguisher and put out the blaze.

Thank goodness Nana was there to take care of us and to tinker with the ornery oven while our parents weren't around. At least now we knew something was definitely wrong with the oven, now known as the large black hole in the kitchen wall. It was burnt to a crisp.

If there was a Bundt cake in there, it was well-done.

~Annie Mannix

"QUIT GRIPING... YOU SAID YOU WANTED A LIGHT TO SEE WHY THE GAS STOVE WASN'T WORKING — WELL, A MATCH IS A LIGHT, IS IT NOT ?!"

Butterfly Kisses

*May the wings of the butterfly kiss the sun
And find your shoulder to light on,
To bring you luck, happiness and riches
Today, tomorrow and beyond.*
~Irish Blessing

I see butterflies everywhere. Funny how something so ordinary can tug at the heart and bring memories flooding back.

We were four the first time we went to live with my grandmother. My twin sister, Diane, and I had been rustled from bed when my father got home from his late shift. We were bundled into the car and driven through the night to his mother in South Carolina. Our mother was not well, but we were not allowed to talk about it. We would wake sometimes during the night to find her standing in the room with a knife to guard against the voices in her head who told her she was not safe and we were in danger. This was not a horror movie; this was our everyday reality.

That morning, Diane and I huddled together, groggy, scared and shivering while we tried to figure out where we were and who the singing lady was. That morning is engraved in my memory, even though most of my childhood is a blur. I can still smell the coffee and tea and see my grandfather sitting at the end of the table reading his paper. My grandmother turned to us with a heaping plate of homemade biscuits, covered in butter, and then asked us if we wanted honey or jam. We just held onto each other, not sure what to do.

"Go on and take one. I made them just for you."

We each reached for a warm biscuit and watched her sit down across from us, her eyes smiling and kind. I wondered if Diane felt like I did. This had to be a dream. Who was this lady? As if she could read our minds, she said, "Don't be scared. I'm your grandmother. You can call me Nannie." When she got up to clear the table, she was singing again — church songs — and slowly we relaxed and began to enjoy the warm kitchen and the feeling of being safe.

At night, Nannie would read us stories and told us about the fairies who lived in the garden. They were magical creatures who looked like butterflies, but they were fairies in disguise. Then she would lean over to kiss us goodnight, flutter her eyelashes on our cheeks and say, "Butterfly kisses!"

Spring faded into summer. We were able to be children for the first time in our lives. Nannie was there to soothe our tears if we skinned our knees, and there was always time for a hug. She sewed us clothes and marched us down to church on Sundays, dressed in our very best. She would stop outside the church and tell us, "Now promise to be good during church. When Moodys make a promise, it is sacred. And if you promise to be good, you can't change your mind!"

Near the end of the summer, we came in from playing to find my grandmother sitting at the table, her face puffy and her eyes red. We knew she had been crying, but we didn't know why. She told us our father was coming for us. We would be going home that weekend. We cried each other to sleep that night. Morning came, and our father stood waiting outside for us. Nannie grabbed the two of us and told us to be good. She promised we would see her again. She told us, "Moody promise."

At home, our mother was quiet. My father sat us down and told us in no uncertain terms that we were not to upset our mother. We were to be quiet, and we could not have friends come over, and we were not to talk about what went on at home. My mom sat at the end of the table, never moving, never looking into our eyes, not even noticing we were there. My father went to work every day, and we were left at home with our mother, trying to stay quiet but dreaming of our grandmother and the life we had had for a very short time.

One day, my mother sat in her nightgown, staring straight ahead. I crawled into my mother's lap, asking, "Mommy, do you love me?" She simply said, "I guess I have to, don't I?" That simple sentence cut me to the core. I slid off her lap and vowed I would never trust her, never ask her that question again. I knew who loved me, and it wasn't my mother.

Mom was in and out of the hospital. We always knew it was coming. Sad to say, we looked forward to those times because it meant we could go back and see our grandmother. Each time we were wrenched away again it became harder and harder to let go. This went on until we were ten.

One year, we went to Nannie's for Easter. We couldn't understand why Nannie was so upset. Easter was special and we were going to get our pictures taken in our pretty new clothes. Nannie gathered the two of us and said, "I want you to remember Nannie loves you. Never forget that. Even if we are far apart, I will always be here, waiting for you, loving you." It was then our father told us that we were moving to California. He had a job offer in Sacramento. When Nannie hugged us goodbye, I promised her I would come back. I told her, "Moody promise."

Time passed, and my mother got better treatment in California, enough that she didn't have breakdowns as often and the voices were controlled with medication. She was "normal," but there were no highs and lows. She was just there — flat, unable to care about anyone but herself. We always felt like we were in the way.

We struggled to grow up on our own. Both of us married and had children. The marriages failed, but we continued to work and raise our sons. I was at my first good job when my father called to say that my grandmother had passed away. I felt the blood drain from my face. I would never see her again. I had not kept my promise.

Many years later, after both our parents had passed away, Diane and I went back to South Carolina. As I stepped off the plane into the humid heat in Charleston, I felt like I was finally home. The days to follow were filled with meeting cousins and relatives we had not seen in years.

Our final day, we picked out pink roses and drove to the cemetery where Nannie was buried. My sister and I linked arms and stood over my grandmother's grave. I told my grandmother I had made a promise and was here to keep it. I apologized that it had to be this way. I thanked her for saving us so long ago. She gave us something to hold onto when the world was a pretty scary place. As we turned to leave, Diane pulled a small metal butterfly from her pocket and placed it on the headstone. As we walked away, both of us whispered, "Butterfly kisses. Goodnight, Nannie."

Now when I am upset or afraid, I look for butterflies. They always appear, sometimes when I least expect it. I don't know if life transcends death, but I feel my grandmother's spirit with me every day. I know she is still watching out for her little girls.

~Marsha D. Teeling

43

The Sauerkraut Cure

Preserving the health by too strict a regimen is a wearisome malady.
~François Duc de la Rochefoucauld

A recent genealogical expedition into my dad's childhood yielded a folk remedy brought by his grandmother to Brooklyn from her native Alsace. I'd asked my dad to spend a day sharing memories of growing up in New York in the 1930s and 40s, and he had tales to tell, the most colorful of which involved Grandma Fink, the tender-tough matriarch of the extended family that shared her six-unit Brooklyn apartment building.

The close quarters of the Lincoln Avenue tenement were, thought Grandma Fink, a breeding ground for germs, critters and other unpleasantness, so she maintained vigilant guard over her clan's health, administering poultices, plasters, salves and syrups, and occasionally calling in Dr. Hantmann for a twenty-five-cent kitchen table consult. (The patient lay on the table for examination.) And, she did seasonal cleaning, not just of the house, but of her grandsons' insides as well.

Grandma Fink counted tapeworms among the potential threats to her family's well-being, and twice yearly she waged war on any that might have found their way into my father and his two older brothers. Her weapon? Sauerkraut.

"One day each spring and fall, Grandma Fink would call me, Henny and Eddie into the kitchen," recalled my dad. "On the stove was a huge pot of water in which cabbage had been cooking for hours, made into sauerkraut. We knew from the towels and blankets covering the pot that it wasn't for consumption. It was to attract tapeworms."

The boys took turns standing on a stool that Grandma Fink had pulled to the stove. She'd lift the heavy towels that covered the steaming pot and push the boys' little heads into the stinky steam. "We were told to inhale the sauerkraut aroma," my dad explained, "which Grandma said would ward off colds and, most importantly, lure out any tapeworms growing inside us."

Grandma Fink knew that tapeworms loved sauerkraut, especially kraut as delicious as hers, made from an old family recipe. To get some, the parasites would swim up through the intestines to the mouth and try to jump into the sauerkraut pot.

As the boys sniffed the pungent mash, Grandma stood close by, waiting to pull out any tapeworms that might emerge. "Grandma was ready to capture them," said my dad, "and we thought she was very brave because she told us they could be thirty, even up to eighty feet long."

As far as my dad knows, Grandma never did catch a tapeworm. "I cannot recall a single one ever coming out of us," he chuckled. But Grandma never let down her guard, pulling out the pot and firing up the semi-annual sauerkraut boil year after year after year, releasing each grandson from the ritual only when he became a young man and moved, for work, marriage or the military, out of her Brooklyn tenement and into the wide world.

~Lori Hein

Dish Night

Never go to bed mad. Stay up and fight.
~Phyllis Diller

To promote regular and repeat attendance at movie theaters in the 1930s and 1940s, a piece of dinnerware was given with each admission. My fourteen-year-old mama and my twenty-one-year-old daddy were newlyweds in 1940. After being married in the middle of the night by a barefoot preacher in Dalton, Georgia, my mama, a little sharecropper's daughter from Varnell, went with my daddy to his home in Cleveland, Tennessee. My daddy had twenty-one dollars to his name. He paid the preacher two dollars to perform the ceremony. My mama had everything she owned in the world in a brown paper poke: a dress, a comb, and a store-bought toothbrush, as opposed to the frayed sweet gum twig with which she usually brushed.

My Uncle Bo, my daddy's brother, had a 1934 Ford with a rumble seat. He and my granddaddy attended the wedding. Uncle Bo and the preacher's wife were the official witnesses, though the preacher's wife, who had thrown a housecoat over her nightgown, crocheted and cried throughout the ceremony. My mama described her wedding night as a wrestling match. It was not the last fight that my parents had.

My daddy and his brothers were carpenters. Chattanooga was a thriving commercial and industrial center and work was good, so they all loaded up and moved to the big city to make their fortunes.

My daddy made twenty-five cents an hour. He did not have a car. He and my mama rented a tiny two-room house with peeling paint and cold running water and a bare light bulb hanging down in each room. Neither of them had ever known such luxury.

My Uncle Bo picked up my daddy for work each day. Otherwise, my mama and my daddy walked everywhere they went. One night each week they rode the city bus to downtown Chattanooga to catch the latest motion picture straight from Hollywood. They also each received, as an added bonus, a piece of dinnerware as a gift from the management of the theater. Each week was different. They never knew if they would receive a plate, a cup, a bowl, or a saucer. And the patterns never matched from week to week.

But my mama did not care whether or not her dishes matched. She loved having different colors and various patterns and designs to admire. She loved playing house. My mama became attached to a particular plate that she thought was especially beautiful. It had pink flowers on an off-white background, and my mama loved pink.

One night after supper, my daddy was washing dishes, and my mama was drying. Mama's favorite plate slipped out of my daddy's soapy hands, but he caught it before it hit the edge of the porcelain sink and no damage was done.

"You better not break my favorite plate," my mama warned him.

He began to clown around and pretend to let the plate slip from his hands to annoy her. Suddenly, however, the plate actually did slip from his slick, sudsy hands and fell onto the floor, breaking into tiny pieces. At first, my mama was speechless, but then she accused my daddy of breaking her favorite plate on purpose. He assured her that it had been an accident, but my mama was irate.

"How would you like it if I broke your favorite plate?" she cried.

My daddy said later that he did not know that he had a favorite plate, but Mama picked up a plate that was yet to be washed and threw it on the floor. My daddy looked at her for a moment, and then without a word he picked up a bowl and threw it on the floor. Mama picked up a saucer and threw it on the floor. Daddy broke a saucer. Mama broke a cup. They broke up all the dirty dishes, and then reached into the cabinet and broke up all the clean ones as well. That accomplished, they broke up the jelly drinking glasses and the little green bowls that came as premiums in oatmeal boxes, all without a word.

Not only did my mama lose her favorite plate that night, but she also lost every dish in the house, all her beautiful china from Dish Night. Each dish had made her think of a movie that she and my daddy had seen. Movie night was an extraordinary treat for a poor little country girl whose only entertainment prior to her marriage had been listening to the *Grand Ole Opry* on Saturday night on a battery-operated radio.

With the dishes all gone, my mama and daddy had to clean up the china shards and broken glass that literally covered the kitchen floor. By the time they had cleaned up the mess, their tempers had cooled. My parents walked over to my Aunt Essell and Uncle Bo's and borrowed two plates and two cups for breakfast the next morning.

My oldest brother made his debut into the world shortly thereafter. By the age of twenty-one, my mama had given birth to five little babies. Movie night became a thing of the past. My parents did not go to the movie together again until they took their first granddaughter to see Walt Disney's animated re-issue of Uncle Remus in *Song of the South* more than thirty years later.

But my mama always remembered Dish Night. She often recalled her favorite plate and how beautiful it was. She always insisted that the plate that my daddy broke was the prettiest plate she had ever seen in her life. The mention of Dish Night always brings to my mind, not free dinnerware, but my teenage mama and daddy breaking all the dishes in the house. To me, that was the real Dish Night.

~Judy Lee Green

45

Wedding Adventures

The course of true anything never does run smooth.
~Samuel Butler

In my family, the word "wedding" brings a certain reaction. There is always that moment of intense joy when you discover a brother or a daughter is about to tie the knot. That moment is almost immediately followed by a feeling of dread. Not because my family doesn't like weddings. We think they're wonderful: the sacred vows, the singing and dancing, the visiting with friends and family. What scares us is the fact that it's a family wedding because, for our family, weddings tend to be disasters waiting to happen.

A case in point is our daughter's wedding. It was a beautiful affair, held at a small chapel where our family and a few close friends could attend. To save money, they held the reception at the house of friends who had the magic touch at hosting such events. And instead of a professional videographer, my brother volunteered to videotape the wedding. The day of the ceremony, everything seemed to be going smoothly.

Then, minutes before the wedding was to begin, my brother got his hand slammed in the door of a car. The best man got lost on the way to the chapel. The wedding had to be delayed because the priest was finishing another wedding that went long. Some of the older members of the family had trouble sitting on the hard pews for such a long length of time and discussed leaving. Our daughter began to fear the wedding might have to be called off.

But then the best man finally found the chapel, pillows for the elderly patrons and refreshments helped revive the sagging guests, and my brother figured out a way to videotape the wedding with a bandaged hand. The bride and groom made a beautiful couple as they joined hands at the altar.

My son's wedding, on the other hand, went off without a hitch. It was performed in a beautiful garden amidst swaying roses and sculpted topiary. The bride and her maids of honor were elegantly attired, and the groom and his groomsmen made a handsome group. My wife and I flew out to Ohio on a clear blue day, and the weather held throughout the wedding. Watching our son and new daughter-in-law exchange vows was a wonderful experience. My wife cried with joy at the sight.

Then we left for the reception. The bride and groom had rented a hall at a local park for the reception, and it was beautifully decorated with flowers and tablecloths and delicate glassware and silverware. The mood was festive. Adults and children ate and laughed. The bride and groom cut their respective cakes and fed them to each other. They had their first dance together as man and wife under a glittering dance floor. It was a great reception where we met the bride's family and discovered just where her wonderful personality came from.

But just as the reception wound into the night, one of the kids discovered the smoke machine that had been set to produce a thin layer of dreamlike smoke on the dance floor. He accidentally set the smoke production for high. In a matter of moments, the hall was filled with billowing clouds of smoke. The bride and groom had friends open windows and tried to carry on. Unfortunately, the smoke set off the fire alarm, and no one could figure out how to turn it off. Amidst the glittering lights, the blinding smoke, and the screeching fire alarm, the festive mood began to suffer. Things got worse. Within a few minutes, the fire department showed up.

This was our family, however, and we persevered despite the chaos. The groom talked to the fire chief, who shook his head and reset the fire alarm. The wedding party moved outside under the star-filled sky, and the reception carried on. Everyone laughed at the experience and blessed the happy couple with many fun moments to come in their life together.

Then there was my wedding. It was a wonderful affair. The ceremony took place in a little grotto attached to rolling green grounds and an open hall where our guests could sit and eat and enjoy the beautiful surroundings. The first sign of trouble came when my bride and I toured the grounds days before the wedding. By an idyllic river near a quaint wooden bridge, we spied some geese that the owner assured us would add to the festivities. They demonstrated their talents by honking and chasing wildly after my bride and nipping her on the arm.

The day of the wedding, everyone got to the grotto on time, save for the groom. Just as I was about to drive down with my family, I got a call from the florist telling me they couldn't deliver the flowers because their truck had broken down. So, dressed in my wedding tuxedo, I rushed down to the florist's shop, stuffed bunches of peach-colored roses and bridal bouquets in among my family in the car, and rushed to the wedding. Luckily, I managed to get there only a few minutes late.

Things seemed to have settled into the right rhythm, and there didn't seem time for any more calamities when the music started to play, and my beautiful bride began to make her way into the grotto. I stood and watched her slowly walk toward me, a smile on her face. The smile disappeared in the next moment, and she stopped in her tracks. We all waited, but the bride wouldn't budge a step. Her hands began to shake.

Finally, I couldn't take it any longer. I walked over to her with all eyes watching and whispered, "Honey, what's the matter? Getting cold feet?"

"Stuck feet is more like it," she whispered back. She pointed down to the cobblestones that lined the grotto. "The heel of my shoe got stuck between two cobblestones. I can't move!"

I bent down and began to wrestle with her shoe. Someone in the crowd laughed. Someone else started the wedding march again to cover the sounds of my struggling with the point of a heel. Finally, the shoe popped loose. My bride-to-be almost lost her balance, but she managed to stay on her feet and, hand in hand, we walked up to the priest ready to exchange our vows. We couldn't help but smile at each other.

So that's what weddings are like for our family. The chaos mixed with the joy. The disaster mixed with the wonderful moments of love, compassion, and laughter. And the one thing that we always keep in mind is this: No matter how mixed-up and messed up the wedding might be, what comes after is always worth the effort.

~John P. Buentello

46

A Wedding to Die For

A man's dying is more the survivors' affair than his own.
~Thomas Mann, The Magic Mountain

We always promised ourselves that when our daughter, Annie, got married, the wedding would begin at the exact time printed on the invitations. It never occurred to us that my father-in-law would inadvertently spoil our plans, let alone that he would do so in such a dramatic way.

Annie's would be the first wedding in our congregation's new church building. We let our creativity soar. My husband, Mike, along with the groom, Greg, and other friends and family members hauled in "marble" pillars belonging to the church's Easter cantata set, and we draped white netting from them as a backdrop for all the flowers and candles. We strung hundreds of tiny white lights across the platform and filled the auditorium with other special decorating touches.

In addition to being the mother of the bride, the matron of honor, and the wedding soloist, I was also in charge of the reception food. Two hours before the ceremony was to begin at 5:00 P.M., I hadn't quite finished instructing the kitchen crew about pasta salad assembly when it was time to join the wedding party for formal photos.

At 4:00, twenty-eight people crowded onto the platform for pictures of the bride and groom with Mike's immediate family members. More photos followed, and by 4:30, the wedding party retired to a side room. Mike's brothers, Wayne and Karl, went over their notes for the ceremony. Since they were ordained ministers, Annie had asked them to assist our pastor. I went to check food preparations. The clock above the kitchen sink indicated it was a few minutes before 5:00.

In the side room, my father-in-law, Edmund, lay down on a row of chairs. Annie's groom, Greg, asked if he'd be more comfortable on the carpeted floor. "I'm okay right here," Edmund replied. "I just want to rest a bit."

About a minute later, my father-in-law began to snore and turn purple. As I entered the room, I saw my brother-in-law Karl shaking his father and shouting, "Wake up, Daddy! Breathe, Daddy, breathe!"

My sister, Jaclyn, and her husband, Lamar, are emergency medical technicians (EMTs), so I raced to the auditorium where my brother-in-law was setting up a video camera. "Lamar!" I shouted. "Edmund has stopped breathing!"

He dropped the camcorder. "Get Jaclyn!"

Still clutching the long-stemmed rose I'd held in the photo shoot, I dashed on high heels to the nursery where Jaclyn was dropping off their baby. "Edmund isn't breathing!" I said. "Lamar's doing CPR alone!"

Jaclyn ran to the room and knelt in her bridesmaid's dress next to Lamar. Together they worked on my father-in-law while we all prayed and waited for paramedics to arrive. Greg took Annie to another room.

It seemed an eternity before an ambulance and fire engines screamed up to the front of the church. The auditorium continued to fill with puzzled guests as five o'clock came and went.

Neither Mike nor I knew what to do. Dismiss everyone and postpone the wedding to another date? Proceed with all the fanfare we'd planned? Find a way to combine the joy of a wedding with the drama of a medical crisis? None of the wedding-planning books we'd consulted covered anything like this.

Finally, Wayne said to me, "We've talked with Annie and Greg and the rest of the family. Since the guests are all here and the paramedics are still working on Daddy, we think we should just explain to everyone what happened, ask for their prayers, and carry on with a low-key ceremony. Can you do that?"

I thought about my matron-of-honor duties and the song I was to sing. "First let me have five minutes for a good cry," I said. I found an empty office where I could give temporary release to my emotions. Then I repaired my make-up, squared my shoulders, and joined the processional.

As Mike escorted Annie up the aisle to the strains of Pachelbel's "Canon in D," everything seemed surreal. Somehow I sang "Sunrise, Sunset" without a quaver until I got to the last line, "One season following another, laden with happiness and tears." At that point, Karl, who had just served communion to the couple, broke down and wept. He was a former EMT himself and knew the paramedics would have taken Edmund to the hospital if there was any hope. From the platform, he could see the ambulance still sitting empty by the front door, and he realized they hadn't been able to save his father.

Not only did our family have the first wedding in the new church building, but we also had the first death. My mother-in-law, Noreen, stayed by her husband's side and missed the entire wedding of her first grandchild to get married. When Annie and Greg took a break from the receiving line to find out Edmund's status, Noreen tried to relieve the tension with a bit of dark humor. "Well, your grandfather sure knows how to ruin a wedding!"

After the coroner left the church, Wayne volunteered to drive his father's remains some three hundred miles home to the other side of the state. The pastor helped load Edmund's body into the back of Wayne's pickup. Halfway to his destination, Wayne realized he should probably keep to the speed limit since he didn't have a death certificate with him. He imagined trying to explain to an officer, "But the corpse back there really is my father. He died today at my niece's wedding."

Once I got home, all I wanted to do was collapse. Instead, we packed our suitcases, loaded the car with leftover wedding food and flowers, and headed across the state for the funeral.

My husband's family was well-known in the region, and news spread as fast as an Internet virus. Just like in the old bridal-shower game of "Gossip," a few details changed along the way. A couple of people got so mixed up that they announced that Edmund had passed away at his granddaughter's funeral.

Our family handled grief the same way many others do. We alternated between laughter and tears as we recalled Edmund's quirky sense of humor and then remembered we would never again have the opportunity to hear him tell his jokes.

After the country-church funeral, mourners drove to a hilltop cemetery and gathered around the freshly dug grave at the family plot. A tree nearby shivered as wind whipped across the rolling ranchland. To my numb mind, it was a scene right out of an old-time Western.

The patriarch of Mike's clan was gone. In the last photograph ever taken of Edmund, he is surrounded by his large family—his wife of fifty-six years, their six adult children, four daughters-in-law, fifteen grandchildren, and one soon-to-be grandson-in-law. When the photographer clicked the shutter, none of us knew the way in which we were about to be tested. But we did what all good families do in crises. We helped each other cope. It's a wonderful legacy for a family to have.

Another legacy from that day is the standard reply Annie now gives to people who inquire about any recent wedding she's attended.

"Well," she says, "nobody died."

~Diana Savage

All in the Family

Chapter 6

Putting the Fun in Dysfunctional

*People talk about "dysfunctional" families;
I've never seen any other kind.*

~Sue Grafton

Riverbed Fever

An imaginary ailment is worse than a disease.
~Yiddish Proverb

It was nearly 6:00 A.M. when I awoke surprised to find the pillow beside me unoccupied. Since retirement, my husband John lived on California time and had at least two more hours before reveille. I decided I'd better investigate his disappearance.

Faint groans, barely audible as I descended the stairs, grew louder. I followed the sounds into the great room and found John shivering under the afghan on the sofa. His six-foot frame filled every inch of the overstuffed couch, and his toes peaked out from under the fringed coverlet.

"What's the matter, sweetheart?" I asked.

"Don't know. I've never had anything like this. I've sweated so much that I had to change pajamas twice," John responded. "My side of the bed is soaked, so I spent the rest of the night here."

I felt his forehead; he was cool to the touch. He settled back and tried to sleep as I obsessed over the litany of recent health warnings. We live on a river bluff surrounded by trees, once thought to be our friends. Now they harbor villains: tick-infested deer, blood-sucking mosquitoes, and West Nile-ravaged crows. Little wonder after a night of wakefulness that my husband's symptoms set off an alarm.

"Wouldn't you be more comfortable back in bed?" I asked John as he flailed against the unyielding sofa.

"But the sheets are drenched," he protested.

"My side's fine," I said. He trudged up the stairs, only to return within the hour.

"I've started sweating again. I can't stop. It must be a really high fever."

The last thermometer had gone off to college with our youngest, but my mothering instincts kicked in. I gently kissed his forehead—the never-fail temperature test developed over the span of three children's parade of maladies.

"Honey, I really don't think you're warm."

"But I'm sweating so much. Could you check one more time?"

If he weren't so sickly-looking, I'd have suspected an ulterior motive. Once again, I bestowed the medicinal kiss.

"Fever-free," I announced. But the beads of moisture on his neck and his saturated hair caused me to doubt my lip reading.

"Maybe your fever has broken," I said.

My mind began computing symptoms. I pored over a four-inch-thick medical encyclopedia and vowed not to share the fatal diseases with my patient.

"Honey, you don't have any small pink spots around your ankles or a headache? No excessive thirst? You can still swallow, can't you?"

John is not one to go to the doctor, but the advantage was mine. I had him itching, twitching and worried. We negotiated a doctor's appointment for the next morning if he didn't improve.

I kept him afloat with ice water, chicken soup, and grape-flavored sports drinks. We were on a mission to replace lost fluids, although he didn't show any signs of dehydration.

"Strange, I'm not even thirsty," he said, and I force-fed him another bubbling glass of soda.

He held court in his recliner, armed with the remote and a refillable 48-ounce tumbler. By supper, he devoured a full plate of macaroni and cheese, his comfort food of choice. With no excessive perspiration since morning, we hoped for a full recovery.

After the day's ordeal, we decided to turn in early, just in case of a relapse. I grabbed a good mystery, propped up my pillows, and flopped on the bed. Immediately, I felt a cool, damp sensation and doubled over with hysterical laughter.

"What's so funny?" John asked.

"Remember how we thought you might have the West Nile Virus?" I asked, gasping for air. "It's definitely not West Nile, but it is water-related."

I stood up and showed him my soaked nightgown.

"Our water bed is leaking."

~Carolyn A. Hall

Shoes, Glorious Shoes

Funny that a pair of really nice shoes make us feel good in our heads—
at the extreme opposite end of our bodies.
~Levende Waters

There is nothing quite like a package sent from relatives, especially from distant ports of call, like New York City. Our relatives had left the family nest in Pennsylvania and went both east and west to seek sanity, away from busybody clan members and from neighbors who acted as if they were actual blood relatives. Communication with these family members, especially Aunt Midge in Arizona and Aunt Mary in New York City, was sporadic at best. Usually, communication was limited to the annual Christmas card or, on rare occasions, when they would mail out a package.

Aunt Mary, who was my father's older sister, sent such a package of goods in the middle of the summer. Her family was doing well, so well that she had to periodically clean out her small New York closet to make room for new clothing. She sent her hand-me-downs to my mother, as she knew Mama Dida had no budget for clothes, what with six kids and all, and would welcome this generous contribution from the Big Apple.

Although Mama Dida was appreciative, Aunt Mary had a style that rather clashed with my mother's idea of practical fashion sense. Principally, my mother looked for clothing with one thing in mind: stain resistance. Her life was simply a whirlwind of cooking, cleaning, and dealing with the six kids, a perfect opportunity that invites dirt, grime, and mildew to an ongoing, twenty-four-hour-a-day party at the Kish household.

We decided that some of the clothing could be adapted to accommodate Mama Dida's wardrobe, and the rest would be given to Aunt Gladys, who owned a secondhand clothing store in downtown Tarentum. After she picked through the box of clothing, my mother placed the leftovers in the upstairs hallway, awaiting delivery to Aunt Gladys. I assisted Mama Dida in her ultimate selection.

Our only disagreement surfaced when she tossed aside some perfectly fine high heels. Although I agreed that these four-inch-high white pumps would not be worn for gardening purposes, I thought the Lord would welcome the heels if they were worn on a Sunday church visit. Mama Dida, however, refused to wear heels that raised her natural height more than two inches.

This perfectly good set of heels begged me to try them on, and since the entire household was on a mid-day excursion, I went for it. I placed the citified pumps on the floor, side by side. I assumed that you placed your feet into each shoe much like you would place your feet carefully on a small kitchen stepladder. So I leaned on the wall for additional support, placed one foot in each shoe, and all of a sudden, I WAS TALL!

But I was not just tall, I was glamorous! My tiny, fat feet were transformed into haute couture. I slowly took one step at a time, and when I found the rhythm of the shoes, I glided across the floor and heard the sounds of high-step clip-clopping. I imagined a fashion show runway in my bedroom, and entered and exited, never tiring of this newly invented game.

Suddenly, I heard the Kish clan pulling into the driveway. I nearly toppled over when I heard the tires crunch over the black jagged stones we called the family parking space. I jumped out of the pumps and tossed them on top of the box of clothing in the hallway.

"Jim, are you upstairs?" Mama Dida called out.

"Yes, I just finished dusting the bedrooms, like you asked me to do," I answered.

Everyone helped unload the car, and I went downstairs to investigate the new purchases.

"Can someone go upstairs and bring down that box of clothing that's in the hallway? Dad and I are going to drive over to Aunt Gladys' shop and give it to her," Mama Dida announced.

"I'll do it," I offered right away.

I brought down the box of used clothing, including the pair of high heels that I had fallen madly in love with. Should I hide them and play fashion show runway later? With insufficient time to find a good hiding place, I packed the shoes inside the box and placed it in the family station wagon for immediate delivery to Aunt Gladys. It felt like one of my favorite toys had been taken away from me.

I sighed; I pouted; I lamented the loss.

Once you get a taste for fashion, you can never stop. It's such a natural high, like that intoxicating smell of real leather. Fashion designers, acutely aware of this addiction, revel in the fact that the constant craving can never be fully satisfied. After just one taste of the furtive delight of wearing four-inch heels, I craved more. I took chances that might eventually out me to my family.

I hungered for any opportunity to sneak into my mother's bedroom and try on her high-heeled shoes. Yes, I realized that Mama Dida's two-inch heels were not fully satisfying, but two inches is better than no inches, as any woman can attest.

"I must be losing weight. My shoes just don't fit like they used to," Mama Dida said after she put on her shoes one Sunday before Mass. (I had obviously widened them by having one too many clandestine fashion parades in her bedroom.)

I knew I had to be more careful in the future. My mother's double A-size shoe was no match-up for my double-Es. Darn, the jig was up. I couldn't continue to jeopardize my high standing in the Kish household. I had to detox, and quickly.

Walking in high heels would just have to wait until I was absolutely safe from scrutiny or innuendo. Who knows? Aunt Mary might send another box of used clothing with other high-heeled pumps—except this time, with my name written all over them. But until then, I would just have to wait it out in a pair of sensible flats.

~Cuauhtémoc Q. Kish

Making a Stink

Of all the animals, the boy is the most unmanageable.
~Plato

I lowered the car window to breathe in the sweet smells of the warm, autumn evening.

"What is that?" I gasped, glancing to my left at my husband driving.

Larry's nose was wrinkled in disgust. Turning around in my seat, I looked at our neighbors. Linda's hand tightly covered her nose and mouth. As we pulled into the driveway, the smell grew stronger.

"Close the window!" barked Linda's husband from the back seat.

As I got out of the car, the intensity of the smell made my eyes water. Light blazed in every window of the house. The garage door was up, my husband's household furnishings stacked high against every wall on display for the whole world to see. We had three pre-teen children from our previous marriages, and we had recently combined two households with the overflow relegated to the garage.

Horrified, the neighbors, my husband and I stood in the driveway, unable to take a step farther as we realized the offending odor was coming from inside the garage. Wave after wave assaulted our senses as the late October breeze carried the odor out of the garage.

"Skunk!" Larry cried out.

At that moment, the front door burst open, and the sitter came running down the steps.

"Don't ever call me again!"

"Wait! I haven't paid you," I gasped, as the sitter began backing down the drive, her car door still flapping.

"Oh, you'll pay," she snarled through her teeth. "You'll pay for my clothes, too."

Then she was gone.

I noticed my daughter standing in the doorway to the house, her shoulders heaving with the silent sobs she was trying so hard to control.

"They didn't hurt it, did they?"

"Where are the boys?" Larry growled as he pushed past her into the house. "Jim! Ted! Get out here now!"

After all the crying, arguing, and finger-pointing culminated in a reasonable grounding sentence for the kids, it turned out I was as much to blame for the incident as anyone.

Earlier that day, I had taken the kids and our neighbor's son to the *First Blood* matinee in town. None of them liked having a sitter, so I was extracting their cooperation by offering up the outing as a bribe.

Sylvester Stallone as Rambo was a strong role model for teen and preteen males in the eighties, but what I didn't realize was the extent of my boys' imaginations. With bandanas tied around their foreheads, T-shirt sleeves trimmed at the shoulders, and armed with lawn care implements, they spent the evening fantasizing and role-playing John Rambo.

It was all quite innocent until a wayward skunk happened to wander into the garage. Down went the garage door. The boys proceeded to chase the skunk, brandishing a rake, hoe, and pitchfork. With bad timing—really bad timing, actually—the sitter entered the garage to break it up. That's when their adversary exacted his revenge.

The skunk ran frantically around the garage, spraying the furniture stored there as it searched for a way out. When the boys and the sitter tried to reach the opener to raise the garage door, the skunk saw them as even more of a threat and focused his disastrous attention on them. Too late, they managed to raise the door, and the skunk bolted into the woods across the street.

Over the next three weeks, boxes and furniture lined both sides of the driveway. The offensive items sat marinating in a variety of solutions, from tomato juice, white vinegar, and bleach to a concoction of hydrogen peroxide, baking soda, and liquid dish soap. All were guaranteed to effectively reduce the lingering odor.

Each day, as I replenished the solutions, my neighbor Linda would come over from next door, shake her head, and give me advice on raising preteen boys. A proven authority on childrearing, she felt her skills were validated by the fact that Tom, her son, had been home studying the night *First Blood* was being played out in my garage.

"This isn't working," she commented with a frown one day. "I can still smell the odor inside my house, and it seems to be getting stronger."

With no other option available, I had to take steps to keep the horrendous smell from infiltrating the neighborhood, especially my neighbor's home. What couldn't be effectively neutralized finally made its way to the curb on trash day.

The following morning, I stopped next door with a peace offering of baked goods to apologize for the inconvenience.

Linda accepted the brownies, took a bite, and then sheepishly confessed, "The smell wasn't coming from your driveway after all. Seems Tom wasn't home studying. He was at your house and got caught in the skunk's crossfire. He was afraid to tell me he had snuck out until I found the foul clothes balled up in the back of his closet."

What can I say? Sometimes, being a parent really stinks.

~Toni L. Martin

"IT'S THE NEW BABYSITTER. SHE SAYS SHE JUST MADE A RESOLUTION NEVER TO SIT FOR OUR KIDS AGAIN."

Reprinted by permission of Bruce Robinson
©2009

Spider Raid

If you want to live and thrive, let the spider run alive.
~American Quaker Saying

The shrieks of the thirty-year-old man alerted me. The ensuing crashing sounds and his screaming demands for the fly swatter confirmed it. A spider. Sighing, I grabbed the jumbo-sized can of Raid (step two in his "system" for spider killing) and headed for the sounds of panic. The thirty-year-old man is an arachnophobe, and he is my husband. "Marty" (I'll try my best to protect his identity) can fell a ten-point buck at one hundred yards without a flinch. He can pick up a snake with his bare hands and change a dirty diaper with barely a grimace. He rode his bicycle twenty-four hours in the Sierra Nevada Mountains for charity. But show him a Daddy Long Legs, and he runs like a little girl, with shrieks that make our three-year-old (who is deaf) leave claw marks on my neck.

I wish I could send him to a Spider Sissies Anonymous meeting. With so many people in the world living in fear of eight-legged creatures, one would think it would be very popular.

"Hello, my name is Marty, and I am terrified of spiders."

"Helloooo, Marty!"

Unfortunately, there isn't such an organization. Our fourteen-year-old, Nick, used to be our Family Spider Killer. But fear must be a learned trait because he is now the quivering mess that my husband is at the sight of anything with eight legs.

I tried to train the three-year-old to kill spiders, but being the quick-minded toddler that he is, he now knows to point, scream and run—in that order.

That leaves my eight-year-old daughter, Maya. Maya is as tough as a Humvee. She once found a Brown Recluse the size of a peach in the shower. Calmly stepping out, she announced, "Someone needs to get that thing." She's tough, but she's not stupid. Half a can of Raid and a shredded fly swatter later, my husband went to our room to lie down and recover while Maya fearlessly finished her shower.

And then there is me. I am a woman. It's expected of me to fear them. Our family lives in Utah, which is home of the Monster Spiders. My first experience with a Wolf Spider (a slightly smaller version of the tarantula) was actually while I was driving sixty-five miles an hour on the freeway. Something moving on the passenger floor of the car caught my eye. Glancing down, I let out a scream that actually froze the spider in place. It was the most horrid, hairy, striped thing I had ever seen. Slamming on my brakes and jetting sideways into the median, I went from sixty-five to zero in less time than it takes to wet yourself.

It just so happened that I had a pile of rocks on the front seat next to me. (They were for my garden, which is probably where the spider came from in the first place.) Snatching one in my trembling hands, I hefted it onto the spider and then repeatedly stomped on it, screaming the entire time. From that point on, I got weak-kneed at the sight of Wolf Spiders—or anything vaguely resembling them.

So, "Marty" (not his real name, I swear), who vowed to love, honor and protect me, is forced to be the exterminator in our home. I run to another room and shut the door until it's over. My favorite part is listening to the sound of furniture being knocked over, pictures falling off the walls, my husband cursing, the kids squealing, and much thumping and crashing in general. I don't want to see it, but it's fun to listen to. And it's the only way to get a spider killed in this house.

~Susan Farr-Fahncke

Stevie and the Outhouse

Humor is emotional chaos remembered in tranquility.
~James Thurber

It was a bright spring afternoon in Vermontville, Michigan and the family had eaten a hearty meal. Most of the old folks were sitting around inside the farmhouse staring at each other and making light conversation. Grandpa Lee asked if I'd like to catch some fly balls. So we went outside by the apple and cherry trees. After several dozen fly balls had been launched, Grandpa's attention was suddenly drawn by something taking place in the direction of the "out" buildings about thirty yards away.

He dropped the bat and started running. Well, actually, it was more like an exaggerated "trot" toward the area between the shop and the storage shed. This was very unusual and a cause for concern to me because I had never seen Grandpa Lee run or trot anywhere for any reason. He was more of an ambling kind of guy. I started running through the tall grass in the same direction. As I drew nearer to the outbuildings, I could hear a faint noise that sounded like someone calling for help. My attention was quickly drawn to the "two-holer" outhouse. For those who are generally uninformed in the layout of old farms many decades ago, an outhouse was the bathroom of its day prior to the invention of indoor plumbing. Even after indoor plumbing was installed, many outhouses were kept around "just in case."

I saw my Grandpa and my father disappear inside the outhouse, and I heard more pronounced coughing and gagging sounds. Newly arrived on the scene were the Aunties: Blanche, Dorothy, Myrna and Dorothea, and the Uncles: Verle, Lloyd, Clarence and Clare, with Grandma Florence and my mother holding up the rear. I could tell that something important, maybe even dangerous, must be happening to get them all out of their seats... but I didn't know what it was just yet.

Moments later, out came my father holding my little brother Stevie by both tiny wrists as far away from his body as his arms would reach. Little Stevie was covered from neck to toe in what could only be referred to politely as... crap. I remember thinking that the poor little guy must have been messing around in the old outhouse and fallen through one of the holes. How long that excrement had been under that old outhouse no one knows, but one thing was for sure... it was still very malodorous. Dad put little Stevie gently down on the grass outside the outhouse.

The other members of the family were just standing around gawking, not knowing whether to snicker or weep. There was an awkward period of silence when no one said or did anything except gape at poor little waste-covered Steve-Boy. Stevie was sobbing profusely, but for some strange reason, no one made any attempt to cuddle this little guy who really needed a hug. The silence soon ended with sounds of "Oh, my God, what happened?" "For Lord sakes" and Uncle Lloyd's famous blasphemy of "Jezuzz... Kay... Riste!" These were, after all, simple country folks who expressed themselves many times in very non-eloquent terms.

But one thing the family had in common was a sense of humor. Soon, hands began covering mouths in a thinly veiled attempt to hide a smile. It was apparently somewhat early in the lifespan of this incident to express outright hilarity, but with the family penchant for bathroom humor, knee-slapping and gut-busting joviality regarding this event would not be far away.

Grandpa trotted back onto the scene with a broom and large pail full of water. Again, another shorter period of awkwardness set in.

Who would scrub Stevie down? After exchanging glances among the group, poor old gagging Dad had to do the duty. Mother just looked disgusted, satisfied to be an observer. There was plenty of bold-faced gawking and not-so-subtle tittering going on by the others while Dad gave Steve-Boy the broom bath.

I always wondered what was going through Steve's mind as he stood there covered in ninety-plus-year-old odoriferous crap, being basted with a wet broom while on display before the covertly amused old folks. I wonder how often thoughts of this moment cross his mind or if he can really remember the event at all. I'm sure some have become mass murderers or at least occasional bed-wetters as a result of less provocative childhood incidents.

Just to make sure this did not become a lost or forgotten family incident, I related this story in Steve's presence at least two dozen times as we passed into adulthood. I always told the story about my brother's misfortune of falling through the "two-holer" and wrote it off as bad luck or bad balance. However, as an adult, Steve finally got around to telling me that he had not fallen through the outhouse hole at all but had let himself down "just to see what was down there in the dark." I always wondered how this incident would have been portrayed if Steve had been six inches shorter or if the pile had been six inches deeper. I can see the local newspaper headlines now… "Vermontville Boy Suffocates in 100-Year-Old Dung Heap."

On the positive side, little Stevie certainly learned the appropriateness of keeping his mouth closed at a very early age.

~Michael Kilpatrick

The Unkindest Cut

*We have war when at least one of the parties to a conflict
wants something more than it wants peace.*
~Jeane J. Kirkpatrick

How can I put this kindly? My parents had... issues.

They both loved me dearly, as I did them, but between each other there were often serious failures to communicate.

Dad was a big believer in "his way or the highway," and Mom could carry a grudge on her shoulder that would make Atlas jealous. They divorced when I was five. And though I'm sure it wasn't solely over my hair, I know it played a part.

Let me explain....

When I was around two years old, I had red-gold ringlets almost to my shoulders. Both my dad, who was of Italian descent, and my mom, a Native American, had brown hair. If not for the fact that I looked exactly like Dad, there might have been some question as to my parentage.

My hair was my mother's "crowning glory" and a constant source of conflict between her and my father. Despite dressing me in overalls and cowboy boots, and outfitting me with toy guns and G.I. Joe action figures, my father was constantly being told what a cute "little girl" he had.

This made him crazy.

My mother, on the other hand, would spend time every morning brushing my hair to a fine, soft sheen. Any talk of a haircut was strictly taboo. Apparently, my grandfather and my uncles took great joy in teasing my father about my hair (when Mom wasn't around) and over his apparent inability to make my mother cut it. Being a family of redneck "manly men," this was intolerable.

One morning, my mother and my aunt went shopping, leaving me and my cousins in the care of the men.

BIG mistake!

Goaded beyond his ability to endure, Dad allowed my grandpa and Uncle Vern to go at my lovely locks with a pair of scissors. (I have pictures.) When their barbering skills proved inadequate to the job, Grandpa broke out his clippers and my head was shorn to a quarter-inch crew cut. Looking at the photographs of that day, I see a chubby-faced baby boy grinning and totally enjoying the attention he was receiving, with little or no idea of the storm that was about to rain down.

The exact details of the conversation that took place when the womenfolk returned home were never shared with me. My mother had been raised in a quiet, old-fashioned, God-fearing home, and may have never uttered a word of profanity in all of her life.

Apparently, she made up for it that afternoon.

In later years, the "incident" was seldom brought up, and then only sheepishly by the menfolk, who had clearly rued the day. Of the infamous hair-cutting, I do know three things: My father spent a month sleeping on the couch at my grandpa's house… my hair grew back mud-brown… and my mother never forgave any of them.

~Perry P. Perkins

Blended by a Snake

You enter into a certain amount of madness
when you marry a person with pets.
~Nora Ephron

He had two sons and I had two sons. We were so smitten that we expected our respective children to love each other upon first sight and our parenting skills to overcome any obstacle thrown in our path.

That was before I saw the snake.

I met thirteen-year-old Josh the same day I met George, the ball python, a recent gift from his mother. Snakes had haunted my dreams since I could walk, hiding under my bed, chasing me through a house, or slithering from under my car seat.

As I entered the apartment with my sons, Stephen, age six, and Matthew, age eight, my eyes darted, expecting the creature to attack from behind every item in the room. My future husband had warned me that Josh had acquired a new pet.

My boys ran to the bedroom. "I want to see the snake!"

Gross! How would I hug my boys with snake ick on them? Mustering courage, I held onto my fiancé's arm, watching the elongated, articulated, twisting animal make itself at home around Josh's neck. Then, cringing, I watched the thing wrap around Matthew's arm. That sweater was going in the washer as soon as I got home.

"Shut the door," I begged. "Wait… don't." My boys would be locked in with George. "Oh, God, I can't stand this."

"They're fine, sweetie," my beau reassured. We closed the door as giggles and little-boy coolness exclamations sifted through the crack. "George makes for a good introduction."

"For who?"

He rubbed my back. "You'll get used to him."

"Can't it stay with your ex?"

"Not if Josh lives with us."

Dang it. My goal to win over Josh competed with my desire to ban the snake. How the heck was I to sleep in the same house with a reptile, turning three decades of nightmares into reality? On the other hand, how did a new stepmother ban a mother's gift to her son?

I visited the apartment a week later, walking by the door, afraid to turn the handle. What if the animal escaped, and all it took was me opening the door for it to slip out? By my third visit, I had washed and folded clothes for Josh and needed to place them on his bed. My shaking hand gripped the knob and eased the door open an inch. Nothing hit the door. Nothing jumped out.

I set down the clothes, noting the sleeping creature basking under a lamp, safely locked in his tank. Backing out, heart pounding, I sealed the room again and leaned against the wall. I'd made it to first base. I could do this.

The next week, I made myself sit in the room. The snake moved. I instinctively jerked back. With only a little heavy breathing, I was fine. By the time we married, I'd become accustomed to seeing George, as long as he remained behind glass. Josh, Matthew and Stephen played with George daily.

"Mom, can you pick up some food for George?"

"What does that mean?" I said, not sure I wanted to know.

Josh walked up as Matthew explained that George needed a mouse from the pet store. "I can go with you," Josh offered, all pumped up. "I'll show you the best ones to pick out."

Of course, I wanted Josh to come along and help. While buying a rodent hadn't been my idea of bonding, I took what I could get. After the evening's education in the proper size of a mouse morsel for George's size, and my feigned, intense interest, I assumed the duty of purchasing the snake's groceries along with our own. But after hearing a tiny mouse squeak during one feeding, I continued to steer clear of the excitement.

Josh respected my fear and kept his pet confined, or so I thought. Arriving home early from work, I found the boys in front of the fireplace, George stretched out beside them.

"Oh, my God," I exclaimed, backing against the front door. "Out of here now. Back in the aquarium!"

Scrambling, Matthew complained, "But he needs exercise, Momma."

"Then let him exercise in Josh's room," I said. "Shut that door!"

I felt like we'd relapsed a bit as I watched Josh scowl in his retreat. As I unloaded groceries, I worried about how to balance my fear and Josh's needs. Suddenly, I heard my name called from the bedroom. As I rushed in, Josh slid George into the tank, then pointed to the bed where the animal had relieved himself on the bedspread.

"I'm sorry," Josh said, a miserable look on his face. "It was an accident. I'll clean it up."

Smiling, I reached for the spread. "Here, let me. George just got excited. He's probably tickled you guys had him out."

Josh smiled in return. A step forward for us, and a little redemption for me.

Josh, Matthew and Stephen thrived. Josh's nineteen-year-old brother, however, moved out after much drama and controversy. Our union worked for everyone but him. I ached at our inability to create a *Brady Bunch* brood, wondering what I'd done wrong. The family seemed to click with the exception of one. I couldn't understand it.

So I threw myself into caring for the three remaining boys, my new husband... and even George.

George adapted so well that mice proved no more than a snack. We graduated to small white rats.

The third rat proved a challenge. George wouldn't... or couldn't... eat the animal that darted and dodged, even nibbled on the snake's tail. I felt sorry for a snake!

By now, both the snake and the rat grew hungry. Our youngest,

Stephen, vowed to save the rat. "Tackle" moved to an aquarium in his room. We weren't a Norman Rockwell family with a terrier or tabby cat. We had to do it with rodents and reptiles.

Life became more complicated with the prodigal older stepson, the loss of a parent, and confrontations with a few distant family members on both sides. We endured our roller coaster rides and leapt hurdles, fought squabbles and cried hot tears.

But George remained a constant. Whatever happened in our topsy-turvy family, we knew that George patiently waited for it to pass. A slithery, silly snake became the consolation, stability and glue for a fragmented family struggling to become whole.

Josh eventually outgrew George and gave him to another snake lover. Stephen's rat outgrew his aquarium, reaching over a foot in size with incisors that could slice off a fingertip. In a united front, the five of us climbed into the family van and carried the rat to a pet store to enjoy life with his kind. Later at home, my husband and I reclined in the living room.

"We're left with plain old cats and dogs, sweetie," I said.

"And you thought you couldn't live with a snake," he kidded. "You managed George quite well."

"No," I smiled. "George managed us."

~C. Hope Clark

"I can't find Fluffy! He's probably so
scared slithering around in the dark!"

What Did You Say?

Most conversations are simply monologues
delivered in the presence of a witness.
~Margaret Millar

My husband has no internal dialogue. He verbalizes every thought that pops into his head, no matter how trivial. Case in point: Here's my husband, David, making himself a sandwich. He walks into the kitchen with, "Where's the bread?" Now, for years, that question launched me into a major attitude zone because I assumed that "Where's the bread?" was his way of saying, "I don't really want to make my own sandwich so I'm going to bug you until you relent and make it for me."

The first few years of our marriage, his sandwich-making looked like this.

David: "Where's the bread?"

Mimi (patiently — NOT!): "The bread is right where you left it the last time you made a sandwich. It's called a bread box."

David (undaunted): "Where's the mayonnaise?"

(Mimi, gritting her teeth, fishes mayo out of the fridge and thrusts it in David's direction.)

David: "Where's the salami?"

You get the picture. By the time he got to "Where's the speckled mustard? Where are the pickles? Where's the lettuce and tomato?" I'd chase him out of the kitchen and slap the sandwich together for him while he wandered off saying, "Where'd I leave my drink?"

I figured Roseanne Barr was right: Men really do think a uterus is a homing device. Then, one day, I was having lunch with my sister. She was complaining about a houseguest who'd overstayed her welcome and pronounced, "I swear, the woman has NO internal dialogue!"

No internal dialogue? What the heck did that mean? Then she went on to describe this friend looking for a pair of shoes. "Now, where'd I leave those red shoes? I wore them to the art opening Wednesday night, came in, got ready for dinner. I could have sworn I left them…"

That's David! I thought. All these years, when I assumed he was trying to shirk his sandwich-making duties, all he was doing when he asked "Where's the Swiss cheese?" was looking for the Swiss cheese!

Hmmm. I thought about the way he plays cards: "Six… seven… eight… darn… no, nine." The way he surfs channels: "ESPN… Discovery… Why do we need twenty-four-hour weather?" And the way he finds a listing in the phonebook: "A… B… C…"

No internal dialogue. That's it! Now I had a diagnosis. I watched him that night preparing his baked potato at the dinner table. "Sour cream, little salt, dab more butter." Absolutely no internal dialogue.

I watched him change the oil in my car. This was particularly funny because he was outside, and I was watching him through the window so I couldn't see his face or hear what he was saying. But I could see his legs jutting out from under my car and our old collie wagging his entire body with excitement because he assumed David was talking to him! In dog language, "Dang, how'd I get this thing off last time?" sounds a lot like, "Good old boy. Wanna go for a walk?" Clearly, the dog loves the whole lack of internal dialogue.

So does our three-year-old. Since he's at an age when he jabbers from sunrise to sunset, it's nice for him to have someone to talk — if not *to* — at least *with*. I watched the two of them this morning as David attempted to pry up some weeds that had crept through the cracks in our front walk. Jonah was talking about alligators, sharks, and bears while David pondered, "You'd think these boogers would just come right up. How deep do these roots go?" They both looked pretty content.

A friend called this morning to gripe about how she and her husband never talk anymore. David was next to me changing the batteries in one of the kids' toys.

"He comes through the door at night, and I'm lucky if he says two words before he walks back out the next morning," my friend complained.

"Where's the Phillips-head screwdriver?" (This from You-Know-Who.)

"When we were first married, we talked for hours. Now I barely remember what his voice sounds like."

"I had it when I was working on the screen door. When was that?"

"Last week, I decided not to speak to him and see how long it took him to realize it. Two days went by, and he never even noticed!"

"How does this darn thing open?"

"I found a book about reviving the communication in your marriage. I'm halfway through it, but I don't know…"

"Counterclockwise. Counterclockwise."

"The big question is: Can I convince him to read it?"

"Plus. Minus. Plus. Minus."

"So, do you ever have problems like that with David? I mean, y'all have been married for twenty years. Does David still talk?"

"Where'd that dang screw roll? I need that screw."

"David? Talk? Oh, yeah, David talks. He definitely talks."

"Ah, there it is. Now, how do you switch this thing on?"

~Mimi Greenwood Knight

My Big Fat Irish Hospitalization

Every baby needs a lap.
~Henry Robin

R ecently, I gave birth to my third son, and it was an emergency C-section. If you've never had one, it's like this: You go to a magic show, and the magician asks for a volunteer. Eager to help, you say, "Pick me! Pick me!"

And he does.

You go up on stage, climb in a box, and wait for him to "cut you in half." Wink, wink. He takes out the saw, and you wave to your husband in the audience. You pretend to shiver with fear. Then… Mother of God… he cuts you in half! Gulp. You look at him with panic.

But the magician pulls something out of his pocket and says, "Not to worry." It's a staple gun. Honest to God. He staples you back together. Then he gives you a Vicodin and an adorable infant and sends you on your merry way.

Okay, so I'm in my hospital bed, feeling some discomfort, as you can imagine, when my family starts calling. I have an Irish Catholic family. If you've never had one of these, it's like this: If somebody doesn't get married, get born, get sick or get dead, we have nothing to do. This is because our happiness lies in eating casseroles, telling stories, and taking turns holding babies. Hospitals are a great place to do all three. You should see what happens when somebody's in intensive care. We sell our homes and move into the waiting room.

First, my aunt plans the buffet. She calls my mom. "Hi, Sheila. It's Patty. Molly's in intensive care... Yes, pray hard. I'm bringing spinach dip and a ham... No, Margaret's bringing the Jell-O salad. You bring a green salad... Don't bother with drinks. I ordered a pony keg...Well, I know Molly's favorite drink is wine, but she's in a coma... Well, then, pick some up and we'll keep it at the nurses' station for when she wakes up. Or they can hold it under her nose. That oughta do the trick."

Now it was my turn to be in the hospital for major surgery.

Aunts, uncles, and cousins called and asked, "How are you feeling?"

"I feel like a magician cut me in half and stapled me back together," I said.

"Is now a good time to visit?" they asked.

Not wanting to disappoint them (because, to my family, hospitals are the Playboy Mansion of party venues), I said, "Come on over."

They asked if I wanted margaritas or beer. When I said, "Neither," they asked if I was pregnant again.

Everybody brought food. Not a full buffet, mind you. I wasn't dying, after all. Just some nachos and chile con carne. It was a Mexican theme.

But the next day, I was in no mood to party. The hospital staff was as nice as ever, but they were trying to kill me. The nurse came to my bedside and said, "Time to stand up." As she helped me to my feet, she added, "Let me know if blood comes gushing out of your incision."

Frankly, if I'd been aware of that possibility, I would have remained seated.

Between standing and walking, the hospital's torturous exercise program left me keeled over. When my family called that evening, I begged them, "Don't come."

"What if I just drop off my daughter to hold the baby?" my aunt asked.

"Don't come," I said.

That night, I had the baby blues. As my husband and I watched a mystery, I felt personally responsible for the crime. It was Catholic guilt at its worst.

The next day, a nurse took out the staples with, you guessed it, a staple remover, and discharged me. Ta da.

Before leaving, I told a delivery nurse how much I hurt and she said, "We're not in the 'no pain' business. We're in the healthy baby business. And that's what you got."

I looked at my baby. He had thick black hair and tan skin. He looked like my husband's side of the family, who are giants. If there's one thing me and my family like more than babies, it's enormous babies. Babies that, by the time they're six months old, can appreciate a good pot of goulash.

My mom called. My aunt was having a little party for me at my house. Just what every postpartum mother wants.

Only, strangely, I did want a party because I realized that I wasn't the victim of a magic trick. I was the mother of a baby. A big, beautiful baby. And no matter how many times that happens in my family—and, trust me, it happens a lot—everybody treats it like a miracle.

My family could have spent their night doing anything. They chose to hold my baby and eat casserole. Now that's magic.

~Hallie Hastings

Family Antics in Fancy Places

Only where children gather is there any real chance of fun.
~Mignon McLaughlin, The Neurotic's Notebook

Some of my fondest family memories are of events that were, at best, embarrassing. These are not the occasions we try to capture in photographs, like birthdays and graduations. They're the times shared as a family when we had to get ourselves out of a jam. They're the times that still bring a smile to our faces and a glow of warmth from the memory of shared crazy family antics in public places. They're the events that my aunt describes as "mortifying"! This is one of those tales.

I was nine and my cousin was four when my aunt and uncle first took us to a fancy restaurant. "Why is it so dark in here?" asked my cousin. "Shhhh!" my aunt whispered. All classy places have the lights low." It was a busy place, and people were lined up to get in. We settled into a booth, ordered our meal, and waited… and waited… and waited… It seemed like years!

"What's taking so long?" I asked. "Shhhhh! Behave now," my aunt gently whispered. While my aunt and uncle were talking, I discovered a sugar container with a top like a volcano. I stuck my pinkie in as far as it would go to reach the sugar, but once it was in there, it wasn't coming out. It was jammed! My aunt and uncle hadn't noticed what I had gotten into yet, so I slowly slid both my hands under the table along with the sugar container that was now a part of my left hand. Maybe I could wiggle my finger out with a little more work, and no one would have to know it had been in there in the first place.

"Why are you jiggling around like that? Sit up straight and put your hands on the table," said my aunt. When I didn't raise my hands from under the table, my aunt became suspicious. "Put your hands up here," my aunt said, tapping on the table. When my hands were still under the table, my little cousin climbed under the booth, took a peek, and reported that my finger was "stuck in the sugar thing." My aunt then leaned over, stuck her head under the table, and saw my predicament. But now my volcano finger was the least of our concerns. My aunt had gotten herself wedged under the booth and couldn't get back up again.

There she sat with her head and shoulders stuck under the table, pleading with my uncle to help her get out. "I'm stuck, for God's sake. Get me out of here and don't make a scene of it." All our pulling couldn't get her loose, and now we had drawn attention to ourselves, which was a bad thing—not as bad as breaking one of the Ten Commandments, but it was right up there with them in importance. My cousin and I both knew that.

The waitress came over and asked if anything was wrong. My uncle pointed to my aunt, hunched under the table like an ostrich hiding its head. Three men came out from the kitchen. One of them climbed under the table with my aunt to unscrew the booth, while the other two lifted the table out of its place, releasing my aunt from the table trap she had gotten into.

By now, everyone in the restaurant was looking at us and chuckling. With my aunt set free, she pointed out the new addition to my fifth digit—a sugar bowl top that none of us could extract by pulling or twisting. I was brought into the kitchen where my finger was subjected to soap, salt, and grease, which finally allowed the sugar top to slip off. Throughout the process, I howled, my cousin cried, and my uncle muttered under his breath.

Thanks to the help of three waitresses, a dishwasher and a cook, I was free at last. And, wouldn't you know it, just as we were all taken care of, our food arrived. "Oh, there's our food!" said my cousin. My aunt and uncle looked around to see all the other patrons staring at us. Somehow, in unison, the people at the other tables started to clap. We got a round of applause from everyone! How nice, I thought.

"Mortifying. How mortifying!" my aunt said to us. My uncle paid the waitress, and we marched single-file to the door with my aunt wearing that look on her face that said, "Don't ask any questions. Just keep walking toward the door and don't look back."

"This is the last time we'll ever eat out at a fancy restaurant!" she told us. And we went next door to the hot dog stand where we laughed and had the best meal ever.

~Sharon L. Andersen

Chapter 7

Family Secrets

Secrets are made to be found out with time.

~Charles Sanford

A New Brother

Words can sting like anything but silence breaks the heart.
~Phyllis McGinley, Ballade of Lost Objects

My family has always been phobic when it comes to expressing feelings. However, that is not to say that we are devoid of all love and compassion. Rather, we tend to be the strong and silent types when it comes to matters of the heart. I am never quite sure what lies beneath the surface. Perhaps, at times, it's best that way.

Since moving away from home nearly twenty years ago, I have only come back to visit at Thanksgiving. The minute I walk through the door, I feel like I have never left at all. Life remains pretty much unchanged in this neck of the woods. Usually, the highlight of the day is when the daily newspaper arrives. The most read section is the society page, which is the "who's who" for the daily snooper. News about the ordinary folk always takes precedence over world events. If you find out other people have skeletons in their closets, too, somehow this ritual all makes sense. We are just human, after all.

On the first morning of my most recent visit, I was up at the crack of dawn to pick up some groceries with my dad. This has become a family tradition for us as we fill the grocery cart with goodies for my two-week visit. Funny thing is, walking up and down the aisles seems to bring out some of my father's most intimate secrets and thoughts. I wondered what shocking news would be revealed this time.

I remembered a few years back when he revealed to me that he had prostate cancer in aisle 6 of the frozen food section. I nearly fell headfirst into bags of frozen peas when I heard the news. At least he assured me that it was caught in time, and for that I was grateful.

This year, his annual revelation did not come until after we left the grocery store and were driving home. "I don't know how to tell you this," he began. Already, I could feel my heart rate speed up as if on command. I bit down so hard on my bottom lip that it began to bleed. "Something bad happened before you were born," he said. All my worst fears began flowing at once. I stared out the window speechlessly as I prepared myself for what was to come next.

Once my dad mustered up the courage, he continued. "Before me and your mom were married, we had a baby out of wedlock." "Is that all?" I thought. "Wow, what a relief!"

However, this happened in the fifties when *Peyton Place* scandals were just a small microcosm mirroring the reality of American life behind closed doors. What is considered the norm today was quite the opposite back then. My parents were confused about what they should do, so they went for advice. The counselors they spoke with thought it best for my mom to go away to a maternity home to have the baby and then give it up for adoption to prevent gossip. So, that is what they did.

I wondered why my dad was telling me this after years of silence. However, the reason soon became clear. Two weeks earlier, Denny, my secret brother, did an Internet search that helps connect adult adoptees with their birth parents. Denny found my dad's contact details and phoned. He was anxious to meet his real parents. Unfortunately, Mom has been deceased for some time.

Dad was afraid of the rift this might cause, especially among my other two brothers, so he thought it best that we just forget the whole matter. However, I did want to meet my brother while I was visiting, so I nervously dialed Denny's phone number later that day. I was not sure what to say. The words "Hi, I'm your little sister" got stuck in my throat. Rather, "Wow, what wonderful news!" sounded better, at least for the initial contact. Denny sounded nervous at first, but soon warmed up after the introductions were made. Anxious to meet in person, Denny asked if later that afternoon would be okay to drop by. After quickly consulting with my dad, we agreed on a time.

After hearing the news, my older brother decided to turn up that afternoon. My younger brother decided to remain anonymous for the time being. Finally, the moment came when we were standing face to face with our oldest sibling. After the initial introductions and nervousness subsided, we began to feel comfortable in each other's presence. Denny told us he has four children, and one of his daughters has four children of her own. It turns out that I am an aunt, and my dad is a great-grandfather!

Discovering I had another brother was a lot to take in during my two-week visit. I think my other two brothers will have a long way to go toward acceptance. However, I kind of like the fact that we have added new members to our family, with stories of their own to tell. As Denny reminded us, "We sure have lots of catching up to do." I can only agree.

~Danielle Rockwell

Off Course

Bless you, my darling, and remember you are always in the heart —
oh tucked so close there is no chance of escape — of your sister.
~Katherine Mansfield

Last week, my dog Sadie and I escaped to an island off the coast of North Carolina. We needed to rest, to reflect, to feel the sea air and let the endless sound of the ocean cover all the thoughts that run through my mind these days. The last several months, my family has suffered. Uncharacteristically, we pulled together in time to confront an out-of-the-blue tragedy, but once again we have all gone our separate ways in an attempt to heal. Our sister, Liz, whom most of us abandoned years ago in order to save some part of ourselves, unexpectedly brought us back together.

Here on the porch, staring at the ocean, I am empty and worn out. Sadie naps under my chair, and I take deep gulps of the sea air, which is like liquid sunshine after the stale hospital air I have breathed since that horrible day. I think of Liz, lying in her hospital bed. I think of where she could be had we listened to the doctors who said she would not live. Those doctors had thought the flip of a switch and the injection of a drug could rid them of a problem patient they didn't know how to cope with. Their contact with her over the years had been to supply prescriptions. She was a drug addict, regularly showing up at the emergency room. But now, faced with a real crisis, they were clueless.

As a family, we had not known how to deal with Liz for years. We were spent ages ago, exhausted with tough love that didn't work, out of solutions, bankrupt of hope, angry and hurt. Finally, we moved on and did our best to forget we even had a sister named Liz. Drugs had dragged us through an unimaginable turmoil, and we had surrendered to defeat and retreated in absolute exhaustion.

I searched for peace here on this lovely barrier island. I called on the healing waters and powers of the sea to send much-needed relief to my entire family. I begged for a respite from the troubled state this had put all of us in. After all the years of separation, Liz was back. We thought she had finally become a victim of her own addiction, and we were helpless to prevent this horrific possibility. But because of our self-imposed exile from her life, we didn't know that, for the past year, she had left the drugs behind. She had been clean and sober and hoped to rejoin our family.

It seems a cruel joke of fate that our sister became the victim of a mysterious illness that had nothing to do with the myriad of drugs she ingested over the years. Silently and without warning, she went even farther away from us than the drugs had ever taken her. And yet, without explanation, it brought us back to her.

She lives. She talks. She feels. And she hopes one day to move like she did before this cruel disease went to battle with her body and almost won. We live. We work. We wonder. If we didn't know our sister before, how will we ever know her now?

We stand by. We can't fight this battle for her any more than we could the one she fought with addiction. We know so little of the past years when she was at war with life on battlegrounds in unknown locations and for causes that were not part of our reality. News came to us of Liz being here or there, with this or that person. We were sometimes hopeful, but always left with a sense of depression and unsettledness.

My sister's life was a mystery to us... to me. Part of me longs for that time to come back. As distressing as it often was, it seems vastly better than right now. Somewhere out there she was larger than life. She moved and walked and functioned as a person. She was vibrant.

And the emotional disabilities that sent her on her quests seem like nothing now compared to being struck down helpless.

I sit on the porch of the ocean house and wait. In our separate parts of the country, her children, her parents, and her siblings also wait, just like the pelicans doing a fly-by in front of the beach house. Eight pelicans in a perfect flying formation, going somewhere, a solid team. But as I watch, one pelican veers off course and takes a direction away from the formation. This pelican decides, for whatever reason, to abandon the group and the flight plan. He goes off alone while the others fly on. My brothers and sisters went on years ago, but Liz flew off course. Our flight plans took us to school and to establish our own families and careers. Out on her own vectors, Liz had brief stints at these things, but nothing lasting.

Now there seems to be something permanent in her life… a malady that is holding on to her with a fierceness greater even than her dependence on drugs. I pray to God that it becomes as fleeting as the many other things that came and went over the years. I search for the tiniest of signs that this disease will pack up and take with it all the horrible effects it brought and disappear forever.

With each small improvement, my hope grows. She feeds herself with her one useful hand. It's a victory. She stands with the aid of three people and a walker for a few seconds. It's cause for celebration. I see these small steps with the highest of expectations—for her and, selfishly, for our splintered family. I pray for a second chance to become eight going in the same direction once more… a chance for Liz to rejoin the flying formation… and maybe for the rest of us to understand where she went and why she left us. Did we abandon her? Did we fly too high and too fast for her to keep up with us? It seems we will have some time now to figure this out if possible. For today, though, she is here. She is coming back. She lives… and we live.

~Patti Lawson

Grandma's Beads

The difficulties of life are intended to make us better, not bitter.
~Author Unknown

Some of us had rosy-cheeked grandmothers who baked cookies and kissed our boo-boos. Some had grandmothers who traveled and sent postcards and little presents. And some had grandmothers who were stringy, hard-bitten women who thought a little "rough discipline," even when undeserved, never did a child any harm.

Such was my grandma.

She rarely had a nice word to say about anybody. If a neighbor got sick, she was fond of claiming it was retribution from God, payment exacted for some unknown sin.

She was quick to condemn and slow to praise. In fact, the only time Grandma even seemed remotely happy was when she indulged in what she called "making her beads."

"Fetch the cornstarch, child," she would say at unexpected intervals to whichever child in our larger brood was near, "so I kin make my beads."

The talent that woman wrought with those beads was remarkable. At eighty-seven, her gnarled fingers were still swift and deft, expertly shaping round, odd-smelling balls of dough to exact size before drying and stringing. Her beads were a huge hit at Christmas, so she was busier, and often more pleasant, during that season—at intervals anyway.

Usually, my sister, Madelin, and I would watch, fascinated, while Grandma dipped this batch of beads into red food coloring or that one into the small bowl of blue color. Somehow, she even mixed colors to produce a kind of orange tint that would literally shine through the clear nail polish she used later for shellac.

Aside from the eye-popping, artful necklaces she created, the whole experience would take on aspects of a small miracle. And it wasn't just due to the holidays. Anytime Grandma was "making her beads," somehow she let go of that frigid, bitter persona that was her usual self and talked, really talked.

Most of the time, she told of experiences growing up—how she had once burned her hand with lye while making soap or how she had held casings while her papa made blood sausage. Her stories, we thought, were marvelous. Unfortunately, these pleasant lulls didn't last long.

Unexpectedly, sometimes in mid-story, Grandma's head would snap up, her wrinkled neck would tighten, her glare would return, and she would ask in that usual shrill, angry voice why we were hanging around and bothering her with "our foolishness."

This was our cue to quickly skulk away, knowing the unpleasant personality of our everyday grandmother had returned.

One night, though, was different.

"Who taught you beading, Grandma?" Madelin asked in the midst of a days-gone-by tale.

Grandma didn't look up as she twisted a small lump of dough into a complicated swirl. "Mama. Before she died. That was just before Papa killed that man."

I stared, startled. "Great-Grandpa Tom killed a man?"

"Shot him." Grandma thumped a piece of shaped dough. "He was trying to break in on Mama and me. Papa took to the hills after that, hiding out. He was in the right. That man breaking in had already murdered one family in the community, but the sheriff in our parts then didn't like Papa, and that sheriff had been looking for an excuse to jail Papa. Mama caught the flu that winter and died soon after Papa took off. We couldn't find Papa to get word, but he happened upon them digging Mama's grave. When he found out who the grave was for, he told the men to make it big enough for two."

Grandma's hands stilled. "When I heard, I ran to find Papa, to try to warn him, but the sheriff got there first. Papa never raised his rifle. The sheriff gunned him down, just like that, and left. In no more than a minute, Papa was gone. It was snowing and there were wild pigs around. I saw it all, and I'll never forget that minute as long as I live.

"I stayed there so the pigs wouldn't try to eat Papa before they could bury him. It seemed like forever, and I thought for a while I might freeze to death myself, out there with my dead Papa and those wild pigs trying their best to get closer, but I guess someone finally showed in half an hour or so."

Neither Madelin nor I could speak at first.

"How old were you, Grandma?" I finally asked.

Grandma began shaping dough anew. She didn't look up.

"I was twelve years old then," she finally answered.

Madelin and I stared at each other.

Twelve?

Four years older than Madelin and only two years older than me.

What would such an ordeal have done to us? Would it have created a cold, hard bitterness that would have become an integral part of our very beings? Would we have even had the strength to carry such a vivid and mental burden, as Grandma obviously had, for so many years?

Grandma's head suddenly snapped up. Her aged and feeble eyes were slightly moist with unshed tears, but that seemed to change instantly as she focused in on Madelin and me. And then her eyes took on that familiar hard brown glint we knew so well.

"What are you young'uns hanging around here and bothering me for?" she demanded harshly. "What a bunch! I swear I've never…!"

I got up to scurry, for Grandma wasn't above punctuating these out-of-the-blue rants with a stinging slap. But Madelin, instead of rushing off with me in our usual procedure, walked over this time and gently kissed Grandma on her leathered right cheek.

It was enough to stop me in my tracks, and for a moment Grandma went rigid. Then her shoulders slumped and, for a second, she leaned her head against Madelin's small chest.

Then, just as suddenly, Grandma straightened and pushed Madelin away.

"Go on and get out of here with your foolishness, child. You're probably just buttering me up, trying to get out of homework or something. I've never seen such a bunch of lazy kids."

Still, the shove was surprisingly gentle, and Grandma's words didn't sound as biting or as mean as usual.

Grandma died the next spring, and the family was asked to speak at the funeral service. It was obvious some siblings were hard-pressed for something good to say.

"She went to church regularly," one sister said.

"She always made sure we washed our hands before meals," a brother added.

However, it was Madelin who offered the most loving and honest tribute. When her turn came to say something, she simply walked up to the open coffin and placed one of Grandma's colorful cornstarch necklaces inside.

"Goodbye, Grandma," she said softly. "You made beautiful beads."

~Marijoyce Porcelli

A Tiny Piece
of Paper

When someone you love becomes a memory, the memory becomes a treasure.
~Author Unknown

It is just a folded piece of paper that lies in a tiny gold box in my jewelry chest. It's underneath my grandmother's wedding ring, my son's baby ring that I wore until the engraved date of his birth had almost worn away, my engagement ring, and a locket with a baby photo of my son and a lock of his hair. Written on lined paper, it doesn't look like it is worth anything, but it is one of the treasures of my life.

Becoming a mother was not something I thought about growing up as a child. I think I survived my childhood by discarding things I did not want to remember, and I held onto only those things that gave me peace and comfort in a very chaotic world. Some of the bad memories remain, but not many. I grew up thinking I would never succeed at anything. I would never marry, never have a child, so why would I think about one day having a son?

I wanted to be a good mother. I wanted my child to have what I didn't have. I wanted my children to know that, beyond all else, I loved them. Where do you learn to be a good parent if not from your own parents? If that experience is not available, you learn from the people around you. I was taught by a loving grandmother who cuddled her two little twin girls and fussed over them. She told them bedtime stories and always tucked them into bed at night. She was the love in my life, and I tried so hard to learn compassion and understanding from her. My mother was incapable of loving anyone, even herself. A child sees mental illness and feels like if she were just a better child, she could fix what is broken. I could never fix it; it could not be mended.

I fled my childhood and entered into a new nightmare. I was ill-equipped to make good decisions, and I married for all the wrong reasons. I felt like I was on one big losing streak and heading fast toward a life of sorrow and grief. How could I find a way out when I didn't know where to start?

The saving grace came when I learned, ready or not, I was going to be a mom. For the first time in my short life, I began to think about taking care of myself because it wasn't just about me anymore. There was another life inside me, and it was a life I wanted to survive and be whole. The moment my son was placed in my arms, I knew the world had changed for me. Survival was about two of us, not just me. A magic wand did not wave. There was no change in the circumstances of my life, except that now I had a reason to fight. My son.

I owe my son my life. I would never have found the courage to leave an abusive marriage had my son not depended on me. I would never have struggled to be more than I thought I could be without my son. I wasn't worth it, but he was.

The night we fled, our world consisted of five dollars, a laundry basket of baby clothes, and nothing else. Where did that twenty-one-year-old girl find the courage? She found it in the eyes of her baby son. My father had not protected me from a mentally ill, abusive mother, but I would protect my son from a life of pain and abuse if it was the last thing I did on Earth. We left and never looked back.

We were close at first. We spent all our time together. I had never loved anything in the world as much as I loved my son. He was a lovely baby, a happy baby, and I thought it would always be that way. There was peace in my life for the very first time. I never thought that in his teenage years he would shut me out and turn away. I've tried to find out what happened. When did the door close? Why won't he talk to me? Why does he hate me? I had been smug in the belief that I had survived and "saved" my son, but something came between us, and there seems to be no way back.

I've tried to talk to my son. I have faced his anger and tried to break through. It has been so painful, but I never give up. There have been moments when I think I see a chink in the armor he has donned. I see him with his children, and I know that at least he is breaking the cycle because he is a loving, caring father. You can see in his eyes the love for his children, how proud he is of them. Do I imagine his desire to have me there, to want me to stay, to want me to talk, but to step lightly? I don't know, but I hope.

Why should I after all these years? It is that little piece of paper, tucked in the golden box, one of my treasures. It was written by an angry sixteen-year-old boy to his mother. It simply reads, "Mom, even though you don't think I love you, I do." When I wonder if it is worth the pain of trying to reach my son, I take out that paper, unfold it, and read it again and again. It gives me the will to continue to struggle, to reach out to my son and try just one more time. That's what mothers do after all.

~Marsha D. Teeling

My Missing Person

To die and part is a less evil;
but to part and live, there, there is the torment.
~George Lansdowne

Every time I make a bed, I think of my brother Logan.

We did almost everything together as children. He was just seventeen months younger than me, and we had no other siblings for many years. When Logan and I were in grade school, our family lived in a neighborhood with few children. All we had was each other, for playing and for fighting.

One Saturday morning when I was seven, Logan strutted into my room and announced he had just made his bed. He made it perfectly, he said, with the blankets and quilt pulled smooth and tight. I went to his room to see. The bed did look pretty good, so I sat on it. He punched me in the gut. I cried loudly, and our parents came to investigate. Though they usually objected to violence between us, they didn't seem to mind that Logan had hit me this time. They told me I deserved it. Forty-five years later, I can see their point.

Forty-five years. It's been more than thirty years since I last saw Logan. Almost twenty-five years since I last spoke to him. And I don't know why.

In June 1978, just after Logan graduated from college in Los Angeles, our family met for dinner. He and I fought then, too. I had asked him to post an Apartment Wanted ad on campus because my husband and I needed summer housing in L.A. Logan ignored my request, saying he was too busy with finals. Maybe he was, but I thought family should count for something, and I told him so. That evening was the last time I saw him. Would I have been so harsh if I had known?

Several years of silence went by. Logan called me out of the blue in May 1985. I was in the hospital after giving birth to my second child. Someone at my house had given him my hospital number. I didn't recognize his voice as it was so unexpected. I wasn't in great shape to talk, and he didn't have much to say beyond "hello." I'm not sure why he called, but that brief conversation was the last time we spoke. Would I have tried harder to talk if I had known?

Occasionally over the years, I have written to Logan. When our grandmother began to lose her memory from Alzheimer's, I wrote to tell him that if he wanted to see her while she still knew who he was, he should do so soon. No response. She died in 2003. When Logan turned fifty, I sent him a greeting card depicting a cute, blond boy with a crew cut who looked a lot like Logan as a child. No response.

About five years ago, I had a surprise letter from Logan. I was excited to find it in my mailbox. I recognized his handwriting on the envelope and opened it immediately. The letter was written in the proper business format we had learned in junior high. His text was only three sentences. He said he was fulfilling our parents' request to keep me informed of his address, so I could contact him in the event of their deaths. It was as formal and cold as if we had never met, signed "Very truly yours," followed by his full name, including his middle initial. The distance in the letter crushed the hopes I'd had of a renewed relationship when I saw the letter.

The only other communications my parents and I have had from Logan were change of address cards when his postal box number changed. And endorsements on the birthday checks my parents send.

My mother wonders if Logan never contacts them because she wouldn't send him a set of dishes during one of his many moves across country. Or, she says, maybe he is gay, and doesn't want to tell us. My father and I believe he is mentally ill. Perhaps he has schizophrenia, which frequently is first diagnosed in a person's early twenties, the age Logan was when he quit contacting our family. But we don't know. We speculate on causes, silly and serious, but we have no way of knowing the truth. We don't know whether his absence is somehow our fault, or if he simply has no need for family in his life.

We've made attempts to locate him, but we have only a box number at a private mail service. We don't have a street address. We don't have a phone number. Private investigators have not found any additional information. Short of staking out the mail service, we have no way of finding him.

He must have some reason for staying away, but how can it be rational? How, I wonder, could he think our parents no longer love him? How could he think his big sister, much as we fought, wouldn't welcome him back?

Doesn't he know he left a hole in our family? My children, now grown, have never met their Uncle Logan. He did not mourn our grandmother with us. He does not worry about our parents aging.

In some ways, I suppose, our family is fortunate. We know Logan is alive. As far as we know, he is independent. We can contact him by mail, though we never get a response. He is not lost. He just chooses not to contact anyone in the family. We don't know why.

Sometimes I am bitter when I think of all he has chosen to miss over the years. But bitterness does not help me cope with the loss now, nor will it help when I ultimately have to deal with Logan in the future. He might choose to return to us some day, and I will have to respond so as not to send him away again. If he does not return sooner, I will have to tell him of our parents' deaths eventually. Some day I could be contacted upon his death as next of kin. Bitterness will not help me handle any of these situations.

And so I remember Logan every time I make a bed. I try to remember his punch to my gut with a smile — the normal reaction of a small boy to a meddling big sister. I try not to grieve at the emotional punch his absence has caused for the last thirty years.

~Mary Thomas

Where's My Baby?

The past is never dead; it is not even past.
~William Faulkner

"Where's my baby? I want my baby."

We stood around the hospital bed amazed, staring at each other as the gray-haired woman continued to cry out, "Where's my baby?" Her two sons, one daughter-in-law, three grandchildren, and their spouses watched and listened. I was one of the spouses.

Grandmother was more than eighty. Her frail body, shaking hands and pale face didn't seem capable of screaming, let alone making sense. Lying in the dimly lit room, she hadn't spoken for days. Doctors said there wasn't anything to do but wait for her to die.

Her two sons were saddened as they bent close to her, one on each side of the bed, whispering verbal love notes and stroking their mother's hair. She was the stalwart of the family. She'd been alone for more than twenty years, since Grandaddy died. She was vibrant and keen until the most recent days. Now, she cried out what seemed like nonsense to all those in the room. That is, all but one.

Uncle Larry knew why she was crying and what she was saying. He remembered the words from years before. The ghosts of his past shone brightly in his mind even though he knew the family secret was his alone; all others were in total darkness. Larry kept his thoughts to himself as he continued to offer comfort to the dying woman. "It's okay, Mother. I understand." They were seemingly logical words to calm and soothe the illogical thoughts of a lost mind.

Larry was the older son, the wayward son, the favorite son. Always getting into trouble, always needing money to get out of a jam, his mother continually rescued him. Married three times, his children were not quite up to the family standards. The rest of the family regularly discussed the unfairness of the situation, but never in front of Grandmother, of course. After all, peace and harmony were most important, especially when millions of dollars in estate money were at stake.

William, the younger son, was the good one. Married four decades, he had raised three decent children, gone to church, worked hard, and invested wisely. Every time Grandmother withdrew savings to "help" Larry, William and his family would get a similar amount. He used it to buy property and occasionally to bail his brother out of some situation. It was expected of him.

The family get-togethers were cordial, social. Discussion revolved around politics or money. Relationship issues were seldom brought up, and things of the past were discussed even less.

Later that evening as we sat around the dining table, I couldn't handle it. I had to know what Grandmother was talking about. Of course, I was the outsider, married to a grandson; Grandmother was mine by marriage. But I had spent many summer days at her beach condo talking and sharing fun things in our lives. I had moved three thousand miles from my grandmother, so my heart was open to her love. This evening, however, did not seem fun. Finally, I blurted out, "Does anyone know why Grandmother was asking where her baby was?"

The cliché "a hush fell over the crowd" does not do justice to the stillness in the air. I felt as if I was in a time warp. Movement stopped. Conversation stopped. Eating stopped. Did I really just ask that question?

William finally broke the silence. "I talked with Larry today. He told me some stuff I never knew." All eyes stared at William. I sat stunned that this jokester of the family had a serious tone in his voice, a solemn look on his face. He continued, "Grandmother and Granddaddy met when she was only seventeen. It was during the war. Larry told me that Grandmother got pregnant, and because money was so scarce, she gave the baby away."

Wow, I couldn't believe we were talking about this. Anyone at the table could feel the tension, the discomfort of the moment. "Two years later, they were married, and ten months later they had me," he continued. "They decided to move from Tennessee to California so Granddaddy could find work. But Grandmother insisted they find her baby—their baby. That baby was your Uncle Larry. They searched and searched. Larry was moved from the original orphanage to one further south. After several months, they finally found him."

The secret lay hidden for more than sixty years. Grandmother had spoken of it only a couple of times with Larry and never with anyone else.

After William finished, I looked at the faces in the room. Some were amazed; a few were processing; one had tears.

"Can we pray about this?" I blurted out with a little more confidence this time. We held hands as I led the family in prayer, asking for Grandmother's comfort and peace. For Larry's healing and our understanding. Suddenly, the reasons for many of the issues over the years became clear. What seemed like unfairness was more like reparation. What appeared as favoritism was more like making up for lost love. If only the family had known all these years.

"You know," I said to my husband as we drove home, "this was a good reminder tonight of why we should not have secrets."

He smiled and rolled his eyes, knowing how I always found a life lesson in every event.

"If we have secrets in our lives, the time will come when we can't keep them anymore. Our minds will not be able to cover up any longer. Our secrets will be told."

The next morning, the phone rang. "Grandmother's gone," Larry said. Fortunately, her secret did not follow her to the grave.

~Jo Rogers

Keeping Secrets

Some secrets are fires so scorching,
the only way to quench the burn is to tell someone.
~Forrest Loremint

When people tell me I'm awful at keeping secrets, I don't mind. In fact, I'm kind of proud of that trait. My family kept secrets. Big ones.

As children, we were taught always to tell the truth. To this day, I remain stymied by how my parents managed to square that lesson with their secrets. How did they tell the truth yet keep so much hidden? Mostly, by not speaking. Mom just glared until we learned to avoid certain topics.

Grandma lived with us, and I shared a room with her when I was little. Grandma came from Ireland, and she'd divorced Grandpa when Mom was ten — a rare occurrence in our Catholic family. My brother and I didn't know why, and we rarely saw our grandpa. It was one of many secrets that we weren't allowed to ask about.

However good our parents were at keeping secrets, they never allowed me to return the favor. Mom was determined that I would have no secrets. As a teenager, the only time I was allowed to close the door to my room was when I was dressing. At all other times, Mom had to be able to see me. Her friends watched me as I walked to and from school and called Mom at work if they saw anything amiss with my dress or attitude. My friends were afraid to visit my house; Mom intimidated everyone.

I loved Mom, but can't deny that she was a stubborn, determined control freak. Her antics drove me crazy. What was Mom's problem? Grandma was the only person with the nerve to face off with her; she even persuaded Mom to back down occasionally. My dad, bless his heart, shrugged and kept out of our confrontations.

After fifty-five years together, Mom and Dad died within a week of each other. My brother and I went through their closets and drawers, and spent months untangling the different threads of the yarns they told us.

That's when I learned that Grandpa had killed himself. I found the suicide note and the police evidence report in an unlocked strongbox. My brother learned that the hunting rifle he'd been given for his twelfth Christmas was probably the same gun that Grandpa had bought at Sears six months earlier and used to shoot himself.

We put our stories together to figure out that Dad had been unemployed for years, even though he'd gotten up at six every morning and left with his lunchbox. He didn't want us to know that he wasn't working. We found letters revealing that Dad's parents were alcoholics, and that Dad had a teenage marriage, quickly annulled.

One last secret came out years later when my sister-in-law Joanne told me about a conversation she'd had with Mom.

Mom was crying when Joanne called her on the phone that day. Oprah's talk show was loud in the background. Joanne had been watching the same show so she knew what the episode was about: girls who'd been molested by their fathers. She asked Mom, "Why are you crying?"

Mom got out a few words. To Joanne, it sounded like she kept repeating that she knew, she knew. Joanne asked, "What do you mean, you know?"

Mom repeated the phrase, so Joanne took a guess. "Do you know someone who was molested?"

The tiniest voice answered: "I was."

Joanne was dumbfounded. "Are you saying," she asked gently, "that you were... molested? Is that what you're telling me?"

"Yes."

Joanne hesitated, but she needed to be clear. "By your father? Is that what you mean?"

Mom sobbed and finally said yes. Then, Joanne said, "She made me promise never to tell."

My sister-in-law kept that secret until Mom died. Then she told my brother. A long time passed before they told me, but I don't hold that against them. How do you share a secret like that, especially when you've promised not to?

An unexplained divorce, estrangement, overprotectiveness to the point of paranoia—suddenly, it made a whole lot more sense than it used to. Sometimes I wonder why I never guessed, but molestation was simply one of the many, many things never discussed in our house.

The worst thing about such secrets is that the truth comes out too late. I understand, but I can never tell Mom that. Keeping such secrets cheats us all of the chance to show compassion, offer help, or make informed decisions.

So I'm glad I'm a lousy secret-keeper.

~V.K. Lamb

64

The Human Spectrum

Choices are the hinges of destiny.
~Pythagoras

"James." A voice invaded my sleep. My eyes opened slightly to see my mother's frowning face.

"James, come to my room now," she said urgently.

I rose from the warmth and comfort of my bed, the usual weekend smell of pancakes absent. The green numbers on the clock glowed 6:00 A.M. while outside the moon still hung sleepily in the air. As I trudged across the hall into the dark expanse of my mom's room, I tried to recall the last time I had awoken at this hour.

"Stay with your sister for a second, James," my mom said as she exited the room silently, the silence in the house accentuating her feather-like footsteps. I retreated to the corner of the bedroom, sitting beside the sleeping bump in the bed.

Silence. Minutes passed, and the feather footsteps disappeared into the soundless space of the far side of my house. Unfamiliar sounds greeted my ears. The slight buzz of the clock in the room echoed in my head, as did the consistent pounding of my heart in my chest.

"BANG! BANG!" A fury of noise erupted inside the house. The feather footsteps became thumping bricks. The peaceful breathing of my sister transformed into a yelping cry for our mother. There was a powerful knocking on the front door of the house.

The slight figure of my mom filled the doorway. A black telephone was grasped tightly in her hand. Her other hand shook frantically.

"Under... the bed." The tone of my mom's voice was weak but still held some conviction. The knocks on the front door stopped abruptly.

Tears ran down my sister's face. Her face flooded with red colour. Depressing, painful sobs thrust up her throat.

"Sarah, stop crying and get under the bed!" I looked at my mom. Her posture had straightened, and the wrinkles in her face had dug in even deeper.

I slipped under my mom's bed with my sister. At times, it had been an imaginary cave or hideout during our childhood games. Now it was a real hiding spot in the real world.

"Mom?" I whispered. "What is going on?"

"Your..." the shattering of glass stopped her. There was only one thing my mom feared.

It wasn't long before the monster that filled my mom's nightmares had entered the long hallway to our bedrooms. Its footsteps made the floor vibrate. Its voice echoed grotesquely along the hallway, so powerful it boomed into the bedroom where we hid. Just like in my mom's nightmares, the beast was in a blind, uncontrollable rage. Fueled by human-created substance, it would not stop its path of destruction until the substance wore off.

"Elise! Where are you?"

Doors were thrust open and closed. The tension inside our bedroom increased as only one more door firmly stood shut, staring bravely at the monster. It knew it would meet the same fate as its other companions along the hall.

Silence. It felt as if the three of us had somehow paused the functioning of our lungs. Just a few feet away from us, behind our last wall of defense, deep breathing could be heard.

The door knob turned.

A man, about six feet in height, his hair a black mop, walked almost elegantly into the room. His hairy sausages of fingers flicked the switch to turn on the light. A slight whimper escaped from my sister's mouth. From my vantage point underneath the bed, I saw the sweat dripping off the man as he trembled, walking awkwardly towards my mom.

"There you are, baby," he said. Vague memories played through my head as the man's voice filled my ears.

"Dave, what are you doing here?" My mom's voice was epic. Every word was spoken with true dignity.

"I am here to take the kids."

"Dave, you stay away from us!" My mom's bravery was something that most kids never see in their parents.

I saw my dad's mouth open, but it was closed by my mom's persistent defense: "The cops are on their way, Dave."

The words that wanted to roll from my father's tongue were frozen by my mom's statement. He stood stupidly, his mouth gaping open, the smell of alcohol piercing my nose. My mother stood just feet away from him, holding her head high.

Then sirens pierced the quiet of the neighborhood. Childhood as I had known it ended. The two figures of my parents standing next to one another represented the two ends of the spectrum of humanity.

In that moment, I chose the person I wanted to be.

~James McMillan

65

Mendacious Miriam

With lies you may get ahead in the world, but you can never go back.
~Russian Proverb

I have a mahogany grandfather clock. This clock was so much a part of my childhood that when my parents were looking to downsize, I immediately took it home. It had been a gift to my parents, but had originally come to my family through a friend of my mother's Aunt Miriam. My mother had been told that the clock was more than 400 years old and had been brought over from England.

Although I was never close to my great-aunt, I was fascinated by her and all she had done. Keeping this clock made me feel just a little closer to her and to my past. For me, the clock held great sentimental value. And being so old and from England, I was sure it held a bit of monetary value as well. So I was greatly upset when it was damaged during my last move. With a heavy heart, I began the process of filling out insurance forms so the moving company could repair it.

I jumped on the Internet to see if I could get a ballpark figure for the value of the clock. There was a name on the face, so I was sure it would be easy enough to find. All of the sites that came up showed "R. Whiting, Winchester" as being made in Winchester, Connecticut by Riley Whiting, most likely in the 1820s. Huh? This couldn't be my clock. My clock was much older and from England. I called my mother to tell her what I had found. Had I misunderstood the story? No. Through much laughter my mother let slip the family secret.

Aunt Miriam was what some would have called colorful. Others may have said she was inventive. She liked to stretch the truth, embellish it or massage it upon occasion. But, if you want to get technical, Aunt Miriam was a liar.

To Aunt Miriam, appearance was everything. She lied about her age. Not only did she shave a few years off in casual conversation, but she went the extra mile and recorded the incorrect year of birth on her marriage license. She did a little modeling in her earlier years, but vehemently denied it later, even though there was photographic evidence. Proper women did not do such things. She had been divorced when divorce was not acceptable, especially when initiated by a woman. Rather than deny it, she simply just pretended the marriage/divorce never happened. For all intents and purposes, Uncle Len became husband number one.

She worked very successfully as a real-estate agent for several years. But rather than flaunt her achievements, she became mortified when my mother brought it up in conversation, public or private. She felt it was more fashionable if people thought that she relied fully on her husband for support.

Aunt Miriam did not stop at changing her own life story; her husband's life was fair game, too. Uncle Len graduated from Northwestern and became a successful podiatrist in southern California. In an effort to gain prestige among family and friends, it was occasionally mentioned that Uncle Len graduated from Stanford. The story then went on to give him a career change from a podiatrist to a surgeon. They were so convincing in their fabrications that my mother's own siblings believed Miriam and Len over my mother and grandmother.

The stories had been told for so long that most people truly accepted my aunt's and uncle's version of their lives as fact. Those who loved my aunt and uncle were reluctant to reveal the truth, even upon their deaths. When Uncle Len died first, my mother and her sister struggled to write the obituary. What version of the truth should they use? They finally set his profession as a surgeon who graduated from Northwestern. Part truth, part fabrication, and all were content with the story. My aunt could face lifelong friends and hold her head up high at the services.

Upon Miriam's death a few years later, it was believed the untruths would come to an end. There was no one left to lie, and as most of the people close to my aunt had already passed, there was no one left to lie to. But Aunt Miriam was nothing if not persistent. So, it came as no surprise that her grave marker even held the incorrect year of her birth. If anyone can massage the truth from beyond the grave, Aunt Miriam can.

~Rebecca Olker

Chapter
8

Happy,
Horrible Holidays

Nothing says holidays like a cheese log.

~Ellen DeGeneres

66

Merry Christmas, I Broke into Your House

Perhaps the best Yuletide decoration is being wreathed in smiles.
~Author Unknown

Maybe it was the army of bleeding Jesus candles greeting us in our foyer. Or the suspicious pieces of tinsel squished inside our doormat. Or, perhaps, the new wreath lovingly placed on our front door, gently flecked with spray-on snow and plastic "dew."

It had finally happened. Our home had been visited by Santa Claus! And, apparently, Santa was drunk.

Let me back up. Just two days prior, my husband and I had hosted our very first family Christmas party. We were a young couple, and we'd been living in this house together for just over a year. In the past, we had gamely divided up our Christmases between two families in different cities, one pair living north of us, the other living south. No more. This year, my parents would come up for Christmas Eve, and his parents would get to see us on Christmas Day, at their home. We thought ourselves brilliant tacticians. My parents graciously accepted the invitation.

The day before the Christmas Eve party, Ross and I set about decorating our humble little Christmas tree. Up went the ornaments passed down to us from family: a pewter silver bell with our wedding date engraved, some ceramic candy canes, the store-bought colored globes. Around went the twinkly lights, white with a few burnt-out bulbs. Ross is a teacher, so we proudly hung the misshapen pipe-cleaner-and-paper creations his students had made for him. It was our first tree. We admired it with pride, a funny symbol of our still-new domesticity.

My parents arrived the next evening, presents and potluck dishes in hand. In short order, my uncles, a few cousins, and even more presents tumbled inside. We had just put on a Christmas CD and poured a few glasses of champagne when our final visitor arrived.

"HEELLLOOO!!!" came the bellow from the foyer. "Hello, excuse me! I'M HERE!"

Aunt Frances.

"Is anybody home? I brought ROLLS, people. Where do ya want 'em?"

"Frances. It's so good to see you!" I ran into the foyer, greeting my eternally wild-haired aunt. Frances is my mother's older sister and always knows how to make an entrance.

"Hi, sweetie. Your auntie is HERE! I've got BAGS of presents." (Literally. She was carrying trash bags.)

"That's so kind of you, Frances. Here, let me take these."

I led Aunt Frances into the living room, and Ross looked at me with an expression that said, "There's a pair of acid-washed jeans waiting for me in those trash bags, isn't there?"

You should know that Aunt Frances is kind of crazy. This is one of the reasons that I adore her. She tends to be what some might call an "extreme personality," with a heart that has room for both the Holy Spirit and vodka on the rocks. In fact, this combination has led to the occasional prophecy from Frances, where she sits me down and tells me what the Lord has on his mind. The last time we spoke, the Lord told me (through Frances) I would not be raped (yay?), but even so I didn't have to wear so much tacky eyeliner (boo).

Another one of Frances' quirks is her abnormally large heart. This leads me back to the acid-washed jeans thing. You see, Frances has never been a rich woman, but she absolutely loves to indulge her family members with presents. The solution? Blowout thrift-store shopping sprees.

"You wouldn't BELIEVE the deals I got at Goodwill!" said Frances, proudly holding up the plastic bags and giving them a little shake. "Your Auntie Frances got you A FANNY PACK, and a whole box of MUGS! I think they have goldfish on them."

"Shh, we want to be surprised!" I interrupted her with a smile. "Can't wait to open them."

I handed the bags off to Ross. He carefully wedged the mass under the Christmas tree, and we led everyone into the kitchen to serve themselves dinner.

The rest of the night was a blur of clinking champagne glasses and spirited rounds of *Balderdash*. When everyone was good and ready, we opened presents. But out of the corner of my eye, I kept catching Frances stealing glances at our Christmas tree. She looked vaguely troubled.

"Tolly," she whispered raspily in-between presents, "where is the Christ child?"

"Eh, I don't think we have a Christ child," I said.

"I see."

"But we did have a star, so we decided to put the star on."

"Wait. Angels, honey. Where are the angels?"

"Hmm?"

"Well, sweet girl, it's not exactly Christmas without Jesus and angels on the tree, now is it?"

I earnestly agreed. Next year, I told her. Next year, Frances, that tree would be downright dripping with Jesus and angels.

As it turned out, we didn't have to wait that long.

The day after the party, Ross and I had a quick turnaround Christmas trip to see his family. We laughed and ate, unwrapped gifts and played with our in-laws' toddler son. In less than twenty-four hours, we were back on the road, knowing we had more guests coming to visit and a messy house to clean. We pulled up in the driveway and got out of our car. Our eyes immediately fell to the wreath.

"Um... who's been here?" I asked Ross, cautiously pushing open the unlocked door.

The tinsel. The bleeding Jesus candles. We walked farther.

Then, we saw it.

Our Christmas tree had been wholly redecorated.

Gone were the dainty candy canes, scattered around the tree's base like last night's party accessories. In their place hung large, red felt stockings, the kind one would normally hang on a fireplace mantle. They were accented with glitter and had different people's names on them: "Merry Christmas, Aaron!" "Happy Holidays, Ruth!"

Huge plastic balls with scenes from the nativity printed on them now graced our tree's branches as well, along with gilded, cut-out ornaments proclaiming "JESUS CRISTO" at various branch intervals. There was a set of star-shaped frames carefully hung on the highest branches, filled with faded photographs of smiling children... stranger children. Children we had never seen before. Our strand of white twinkly lights now served as a dual-purpose Virgin Mary hanger, with about thirty-eight thimble-sized Virgins dangling off. Tiny plastic rays shot out from behind their heads.

And on the very top, bending the highest branch under the weight of its holy mass, perched a giant ceramic angel. Playing a bugle.

You know the show *What Not to Wear*? This was like the Christmas tree version. Only I was staring at the After, not the Before.

This was the most bizarre thing that ever happened to me. I got a little weirded out. Who breaks into someone's home on Christmas Day, never mind the fact that they broke in to give you stuff? I had a hunch who it was.

"Is this a Goodwill receipt?" Ross said, picking up a piece of white paper from the floor. It was dated from the day before. Frances.

My husband laughed, holding the receipt between his fingers. "C'mon, Tolly, it's funny. And sweet."

He was right. My aunt wanted to spoil us, wanted to give us a better tree. She didn't have much, but she spent what she could to give us something that was, in her eyes, lavish. Sure, it was a little...

odd. But this was probably a tree Frances would have liked to have for herself. Rays-shooting-out-of-head Virgin Marys and all.

It's funny to admit this, but looking back, breaking and entering into my home has been one of the kindest things a family member has ever done for me.

~Tolly Moseley

A
Hand-Me-Down
Prom Dress

It's always the badly dressed people who are the most interesting.
~Jean Paul Gaultier

Trick-or-treating was always an extended family affair. If some of the bad-blood relatives weren't part of the voluntary tech crew—application of makeup, costume design, etc.—they volunteered ideas and contributions of old, retired clothing that carried the promise of a Halloween outfit. If they didn't fall naturally into the first two categories, they would be visited by the happy Halloweeners—all six of the Kish kids—during this eve of revelry and mayhem.

Mama Dida, Granny Sol, and my Auntie Mart were conferencing about the costumes and making heady decisions about what could be worn and who should don these fine, creative pieces of cheap, crafty apparel. I might add a note here that with our lower economic circumstances, there was never any thought about a store purchase. No, the most that was allocated for a frivolous Halloween costume would be for a simple black mask.

Mama Dida, Granny, and Auntie Mart all had limited sewing skill, and nothing elaborate was ever planned in advance. The long day sashaying into the seductive night of Halloween was deemed fully adequate for makeshift costume design, including props.

This three-woman design panel, however, took their assignments seriously. They scrutinized their six midget models and made quick costume decisions. If there was a western-styled hat that fit one of the five boys, there would be a cowboy outfit designed on the spot. And if there was a stray feather floating about, one of the other boys would end up being a scantily clad Indian. Due to the budgetary restrictions, you could always count on at least one of kids being dressed as a hobo, complete with a traveling sack of clothes hung on the end of a broomstick handle.

Although the costumes were obviously important, all of us kids took great care in designing the all-too-important, inverted grocery bag that would carry the treats. We used crayons and did our very best to Crayola a design that fully complemented our assigned costume. I favored Carnation Pink, Cerulean and Indigo, and felt Crayola founders Edwin Binney and C. Harold Smith would have been quite impressed with my executed design.

One particular year, Auntie Mart brought along a never-before-used, crinoline prom dress to toss into the mix of assorted, cast-off clothing choices.

"Somebody can wear this. We'll cut it down to fit one of these pint-sized rabble-rousers," Auntie Mart shouted out as she entered the house holding up a formal dress in one hand and a Salem—the ciggie with air softening in every puff—in the other.

Immediately, my eyes sparked to double their normal size, and I thought: fairy princess, queen, or ballerina. Auntie Mart thought my older sister—by a full year and a few days—could surely wear a cut-down version of this mass of material pinkness, but alas she was too skinny to carry the weight of the multiple layers. It fell to me to save the day and make very good use of such Halloween generosity. I had the stronger, larger frame on which to hang such finery, so I hopefully waited.

"We've got a baseball player, a sailor, a cowboy, and a hobo," said Granny Sol.

"If no one wants to wear the prom dress, I'll wear it myself," said Auntie Mart, still miffed that her date did a "no show" on the night of her senior prom, never providing her with an excuse for that failed appearance.

"Well, it's too much of a dress for skinny Mary Lou here, so…" said Mama Dida.

My tiny boy fingers were daintily crossed behind my back, hoping against hope that I would get to wear this very pink, virgin prom dress. I was already thinking of accessories: shoes, stockings, and a very light shawl.

"Cut it down and let Jimmy wear it," said Granny Sol. "Hand me those pinking shears."

"No, let me do it while I think of 'he-who-did-not-show,'" demanded Auntie Mart. "I will think of him while I cut, especially one manly part of him."

"It will do you good. Here, take the shears and go at it," encouraged Granny Sol.

"That's not a costume for a boy," Mama Dida suggested.

"It's Halloween. Anything goes!" said Auntie Mart. "Besides, with his long lashes, we won't even have to use any mascara."

It was decided—two out of three in favor of the assignment—and so I was quickly fitted up with pink crinoline. Exacting measurements were taken, and the material was carefully cut and pinned and sewn. I was delighted but, to keep face with my brothers, I had to fake a protest.

"Oh, Ma, that's so girly," I said loudly. "But if there's nothing else…"

"There's nothing else, and the material's already cut," Auntie Mart interjected, quickly ending any opportunity for further arbitration on the subject. Yippee!

Granny Sol applied the lipstick and rouge. She instructed me to wet, and then smack my lips together—just like real women did—after the first application of lipstick. I kept smacking my lips like an old man who had misplaced his dentures; I couldn't get enough. I thought, however, that Granny Sol put way too much rouge on my cheeks, as she did with herself, on every occasion. One of the three women—I can't remember who—designed, at the very last minute, a magic wand, and I started granting wishes to all those who asked nicely.

My sister's costume—a hula dancer—did not, even remotely, compare with mine, and I could tell she was envious and semi-angry with herself for being so skinny. I, on the other magic-wanded hand, looked so convincingly pretty. As we visited the houses in the neighborhood shouting "trick or treat," no one guessed that I was a boy. They were flabbergasted to say the least when I announced that I was little Jimmy Kish. I was quickly rewarded with extra treats, obviously for daring-do and authenticity.

This youthful experience laid the foundation for so many Halloween cross-dressing experiences to follow, and I owe Mama Dida, Granny Sol, and Auntie Mart big time for allowing me to feel so comfortable—as well as dainty—in my first crinoline frock.

It's remarkable that I have no memory of my father's reaction to this experience, although he was the night's chauffeur who kindly drove us to the various relatives' homes in and about town. Perhaps he was silent for good reason, knowing that his argument had no voice against three formidable females in the family, whose combined rank outweighed his, especially on a night of trick-or-treating and adolescent cross-dressing.

~Cuauhtémoc Q. Kish

68

Is Everybody Smiling?

Family quarrels are bitter things. They don't go by any rules.
They're not like aches or wounds; they're more like splits in the skin
that won't heal because there's not enough material.
~F. Scott Fitzgerald

In my family, no gathering is complete without a camera. It's genetic, inherited from my father. Dad would have liked pictures taken at his funeral, too, but none of his five children were speaking to each other at the time. Requesting a sibling to "smile for the camera" would have been considered speaking first. It's a well-known rule that if you speak first, you lose. We're a family of winners.

It is amazing that in this clan of chronic chroniclers, we had been missing the picture that became so important to my mother that it forced all of us to spend our first Christmas together in six years.

The hole in the family album was pointed out to me one December morning when my mother and I passed the piano in my living room at the same time. Mom cast a longing look at a picture of my late father taken at his wedding to my stepmother. He was surrounded by his five loving children.

"What's wrong, Mom?" I asked as I watched her pick up the picture.

"Oh, honey, I'd love to have a picture of myself with all of you kids like this one. That's all." Sniff, sniff.

"Sure, that would be good," I said as I removed the picture from her grasp and put it back on the piano top. "Don't you have the one from when you and Larry were married? I can have mine copied for you." I handed her that picture.

"This was taken nineteen years ago."

"But we all looked good. Everyone was smiling." My hair had looked spectacular.

Does the expression "if looks could kill" mean anything to you? "I was thinking of next Christmas, dear," she said as her jaw set and her mouth tightened into a straight line.

"Oh," was the only thing I could say that wouldn't be the subject of a prayerful letter to Sister-Mary-What's-Her-Name at the monastery. Plus, this was December twenty-sixth, and she might forget by next year. Let one of her other children question the sanity of this. Not me. I knew I was not the only one who had no interest in celebrating anything together, but I was still trying to redeem myself for my behavior during my teenage years, when the letters to Sister Mary began.

My family hadn't always been like this. My three sisters, my brother and I, dubbed the "Taylor Tots" by my dad when we were younger and forced to dress alike, had been very close. We spent a lot of time together, especially after Mom gave up on the matching outfits. Sundays meant Lake Harriet. The children swam, the men read the newspapers, and the women gathered in lawn chairs at the water's edge, adding a fresh coat of burn to the previous Sunday's tan. Ours was a family that couldn't imagine celebrating anything without each other. I have the pictures to prove it.

Times change and so do families. We all got busy. The three younger siblings married and began having children at the same time the two older divorced and remarried. Still, no one would have thought to stop celebrating Christmas together. We gathered at Dad's condo: Mom and her husband, Dad and his wife, the five children and their spouses, fourteen grandchildren, a grandchild's spouse, two grandchildren's intendeds and a great-grandchild. That's a lot of flashbulbs.

Then Dad passed away. Grief turned to anger. Even the pictures stopped. Christmas wasn't a consideration with no one speaking to everyone. Oh, this one spoke to that one but not to this other; if you spoke to her, you'd better not mention him. It required a scorecard, and we were allowed no errors. Why? The usual after-a-parent-dies stuff: misunderstandings, hurt feelings, words said that shouldn't have been.

That's how we got to the day after Christmas and my mother's incredible wish. Praying that she'd forget was useless because Sister Mary and You-Know-Who were on her side. In fact, Mom's memory improved now that she had a mission. When she brought up the subject in March, I told her about my brainstorm.

"This is perfect, Mom. We set up appointments at a studio, and each of us can go in for a separate picture. We never have to speak to each other. They can take a picture of you, put it in the middle and have our pictures circled around yours."

"Oh, you're so full of good ideas, aren't you?" I said goodbye to redemption.

The year passed faster than any I remembered, and the picture was a certainty as far as my mother was concerned. Unfortunately, I was the only one who knew about it, and the responsibility of being the oldest and doing the right thing was a burden. My youngest sister called from Florida; she and her family were coming for Christmas. I became suspicious.

By the end of summer, the picture was taking over my life. Why was this so important to her? Whenever we spoke, there was a sniffling sound and some mention of the picture. Why did she want to force us to pose for a family picture when we weren't feeling familial? Who was going to host this celebration? Not me. I wanted to be able to make a quick exit when the yelling started.

Saved! My otolaryngologist, Dr. Super Hero, recommended I have sinus surgery. He assured me there would be swelling and heavy-duty bruising. He mentioned black and blue. I scheduled the operation for the week before Christmas and then rushed to the phone to share the sad news with my mother. And garner some sympathy.

"You'll be all right in time for THE PICTURE, won't you? Your sister's going to have Christmas." Yikes! Which one? It didn't matter; Mom had been working on this behind my back. I canceled the surgery.

Christmas arrived. I was fat. My hair was too short, and I was overdressed. Why hadn't I gotten cucumbers for the vegetable tray? I should have made dill dip, not spinach. I was sweating. The flu. I prayed it was fatal.

"You look great, honey, even better than the vegetable tray, which is a work of art," sang my husband, Mr. Wonderful. Couldn't he see I was dying?

Flu or no flu, I found myself standing at my sister's door, wondering if I should knock or walk in like "the old days." Four children answered the question for me as they came barreling out the door, carrying sleds.

My husband joined the brothers-in-law in front of the television. The teenaged nephews had assumed their now-rightful places among the men in the family. Who was trouncing who on the football field was all that mattered to them.

I put the vegetables on the dining room table and made my way slowly toward the kitchen, stopping in the bathroom first to check my oh-so-short hair. What had I been thinking? I was bald.

There they were — mashing potatoes, stirring gravy, talking. Talking? I took a step. They turned toward me.

"Cute hair!"

"Get her some champagne."

"Someone take a picture of that cute haircut."

I finally got it: my family doesn't say "I'm sorry," or "I love you." We say it in other ways like "Cute hair." Could "Take a picture" mean "I don't want to forget you"?

A year and a half later, four daughters and one son walk down the church aisle to place a gold-framed copy of the picture next to their mother and to say goodbye. We realize that Mom hadn't needed the picture for herself. She wanted it for us, for this day — for the mantle, a table or the top of a piano. Mom knew if she could get us all together that Christmas everything would be as it had been — a family not perfect, but connected in spite of its imperfections. We turn to take our places in the front row — together, the way our mother wanted us.

~Andrea Langworthy

Thanksgiving
with Mary Jane

Small cheer and great welcome makes a merry feast.
~William Shakespeare

When you're a teenager, there are a million places you'd rather be than at a family gathering. However, when I was fifteen, Thanksgiving at home with my relatives was the best turkey day I've ever celebrated.

A week earlier, the postman had delivered a package from our hippie uncle in Oregon, an artisan potter. Gathered in the kitchen, my two sisters and I watched my mother open the Christmas gift from her younger brother. Inside was a hand-crafted mini broom, a leather strap nailed to its handle for hanging at the hearth. Perfect for our 1916 bungalow's fireplace.

While we read the card wishing us a happy holiday in my aunt's blowsy writing, my mother unwrapped another present: a large freezer bag of homegrown cannabis. Our eyes widened. A resinous, earthy green scent overwhelmed the yellow-tiled kitchen.

My mother froze, holding the illegal parcel from her off-the-grid brother and his part-Blackfoot wife. My grandparents had bought the younger couple a house just so they wouldn't live in a tent on a Santa Cruz mountain, and they stocked my wild cousins with cotton panties so they wouldn't run around without underwear. Compared to that branch of the family tree, our household was conventional. Mom pursed her lips.

My Bohemian New York father swooped in from the living room.

"I'm going to put it in the stuffing," he crowed, snatching the bag from Mom.

"Oh, Charles," my mother sighed as he sprinted up the stairs with the Christmas contraband. A capricious architect, my Lithuanian father liked to bait her about the in-laws.

My traditional Italian grandparents did not embrace my father. They were in the habit of warming to respectful young men in crisp white button-down shirts when my father showed up on their middle-class doorstep in 1959. He was an art-school Beatnik in a ripped T-shirt. Still closely shorn from his stint in the Army, where he'd met my mother on a French base, in no other way was he regulation. He snubbed social convention, burying his nose in political paperbacks during my grandparents' cocktail parties with their keeping-up-with-the-Joneses neighbors. Their proper daughter, an elementary school teacher, could surely do better.

Our nuclear family usually observed holidays at their San José ranch house on a staid cul-de-sac filled with cookie-cutter residences. My dad would be gritting his teeth the entire time. But this year my conservative Chicago grandparents had accepted our invite. They didn't enjoy visiting "fruits and nuts" Berkeley, our feisty university town famous for sparking the Free Speech Movement and agitating against the government's foreign wars. My grandfather complained there were never any spots on the hilly, busy streets to park his boat-like Oldsmobile. Accustomed to La-Z-Boys and sturdy American pieces in walnut from Mervyns, my grandmother found our wicker French café chairs uncomfortable and the Joe DiMaggio giant mitt baffling. "Who wants to sit in a baseball glove?" she protested about the cult classic some Italian designer thought up. We may have lived an hour apart in the San Francisco Bay Area, but we really lived in different worlds.

Another reason my parents didn't host often: Mom wasn't a cook. In fact, my kitchen-averse mother was so grateful when my father offered to deal with the big bird that she christened him the turkey expert and let him do whatever he wanted. So the turkey was Dad's rightful domain, and this year my grandparents would be eating it. They were also bringing a recently widowed neighbor, Mary Jane. I can't say I forgot about the surprise stash, but we all dismissed the stuffing threat. Crazy talk was my father's specialty.

On the morning of November 24, 1979, Dad got up at dawn, prepared his poultry, and went back to bed. By noon, my grandparents had arrived with the sweet-natured widow. The eight of us squeezed into our places at the round butcher-block dining table, café chairs grinding against each other. The turkey was nicely done, not dry. Polite conversation flowed due to the gentle outsider, Mary Jane, who asked a lot of questions.

Suddenly, I spied a big brown bud on the edge of my grandfather's plate, speckled with bread and celery. I glanced at my sisters to see if they had noticed. Pushing food around their plate with secret smiles, they obviously had.

"Your stuffing is very spicy, Charles," effused the widow. "Is that sage?"

We kids stifled giggles.

I couldn't look at my mother. Dad was poker-faced.

"Oh, I'm tipsy! It must be the champagne," tittered Grandma, leaning in to shoulder-nudge her neighbor like a schoolgirl.

After my finicky grandfather cleaned his plate, he went to recline on the Italian baseball mitt. Soon, he was sprawled across the giant glove like Fay Wray in King Kong's hand, snoring. The seventy-something dandy in a mint-green Qiana shirt and white leisure shoes looked comfortable—and finally at home in our place.

We devoured the pumpkin pie and Grandma's anise cookies, but didn't budge from our rosy circle. For the first time, I saw my family as individuals rather than role players. In the lanky figure of Grandpa in repose, I recognized the easy character captured in a 1928 photo of him squatting in front of a baseball dugout. Witnessing chummy Grandma, I understood her life-of-the-party image from a Wisconsin lake in the 1940s, an arm slung around her ten younger siblings. Inside my strait-laced mom, I sensed a woman appreciating her daredevil husband's off-kilter view of the world. And I realized my rebel father wasn't really antisocial if he brought us all together. My sisters suddenly seemed like fellow sojourners navigating teenhood, as well as my natural allies in this normal-slash-bizarre family. They weren't so bad.

When the three seniors said goodbye, our hugs were heartfelt. My father asked Grandpa which route home he'd take, a mellow and unnecessary exchange between the two men.

"Your family is lovely," Mary Jane exclaimed, kissing each of us. "Today was the best since my husband died!"

As the five Ashmans gathered in the kitchen to do the dishes and review the day's events—with uproarious laughter and genuine shock—I found myself thinking of the untamed Oregon folk who couldn't be with us. Their holiday gift ensured they were here in spirit. In that moment, I grasped the meaning of family.

In retrospect, I realize how unorthodox this recipe for a happy family gathering was. But I'll never forget the spirit of 1979's seasoning and what I learned about my relatives that day.

~Anastasia M. Ashman

A Third Scent

You're only as sick as your secrets.
~Author Unknown

"**I**t's so good to see you, girl," Aunt Carol sings out, as she draws me closer to her body. She hugs me hard and holds on for a long time, longer than normal. She kisses my cheek and presses her face against the side of mine. The smell of perfume and Listerine wafts by my nose. But there is something else, a third scent. Vodka? Rum? I can't tell which one. But I can tell that Carol is drinking again.

"I have missed you. What's been going on?" she asks.

I tell her that not much is new. I have been working, taking classes toward certification, and writing as often as possible.

"Well, how is Craig? Does he like his new job? Has he made it down to Winston-Salem yet? Are you going to visit him? Oh, my gosh! How is Tyson? Did he do okay with his surgery? Has he healed up nicely?"

I'm not sure where to start, which question to answer first. It doesn't really matter, though. She won't remember my response. She'll ask me the same questions in five minutes, half an hour, and again the next time I see her. And, unfortunately, that is becoming less and less frequent.

Carol is an alcoholic, a functioning alcoholic, to be exact. Her house is orderly, her clothes coordinated and pressed, and her make-up flawless. She goes to church, visits her friends, cooks for her husband...

and drinks. She begins her day with a screwdriver, nurses several cocktails in the morning hours, and closes the day with a nightcap.

In my early twenties, I thought Carol was merely a social drinker. I liked sipping Bloody Marys on her porch while we talked about my college classes and current boyfriend. If she was refilling her glass more than I was, I didn't notice. She never appeared drunk. She never seemed out of control.

She had what you would call "with-it-ness." She was together, presentable and intelligent-sounding. And with a blood alcohol content high enough to kill the average person, she continued to accomplish more in six hours than most people do in an entire week.

But one day, dinner was not on the table when her husband, Rob, came home. And Carol was passed out on the couch. Rob immediately called my parents.

"Something is wrong. I think Carol needs some help," he said. "I think she is mixing alcohol with her medicine."

"Do you want us to come over?" my parents asked.

"Yeah."

My parents drove to Carol and Rob's house. They tried to talk to her about treatment, explaining that they wanted her to be well again. They told her that she was killing herself and that they didn't want her to die.

"I don't care," Carol said. "Who do you think you are, anyway? Do you know who you're messing with?"

She became belligerent.

My mom threatened to call the police if Carol wouldn't agree to get help.

"Call them!" she screamed. "What are you waiting for?"

My mom dialed 911, and in a few minutes, a very kind, soft-spoken, patient officer showed up.

"I didn't think you'd really call them," Carol said.

But she seemed to like the police officer. He took an interest in her, talked to her about her feelings, and convinced her to get help.

Carol went to a treatment center. We were ecstatic and relieved.

She checked herself out two days later.

It was awkward at first when Carol returned. She distanced herself from the family. She said she just needed some space. She meant that she needed us to leave her alone. So we did.

Eventually, Carol called to say she was sorry and that she hadn't intended to hurt us. She also said she was better, sober. She said she hadn't had a drink in thirty days. We believed her.

It has been more than a year since Carol attended her two-day treatment facility. We knew that two days wasn't long enough, but it wasn't our decision to make. And for the large part of the year, she appeared to be doing quite well.

"Merry Christmas, sweetie," Carol said, as we walked up the steps this past December.

We had gathered for our annual holiday dinner, a tradition we have had as long as I can remember. We ate ham, chicken, casseroles, and homemade rolls. We exchanged gifts and discussed changes in the weather. The women washed and dried dishes, and the men went for a walk.

And until this year, we used to wrap up our evening with a cocktail or a glass of wine. But we can't do that anymore. We have to be supportive of Carol. We have to show her that we are here to help her through this.

That night, I walked into my aunt's bedroom to get my coat. Through the window, I saw Carol open her car door. She pulled something out from under the car seat. She opened it, tilted her head back and gulped it down. She didn't see me. She came inside and went to the restroom.

We said our goodbyes a little while later. I hugged my aunts, uncles, and cousins. I wished them all a Happy New Year.

"Merry Christmas, sweetie," Carol said. She put her arms around me and hugged me tightly. "Call me this week when you're out of school." And while she wrapped her arms around my shoulders and planted a kiss on my cheek, I could smell her perfume, her Listerine, and something else.

~Cora Rogers

71

The Christmas Cat-astrophe

Christmas is not as much about opening our presents as opening our hearts.
~Janice Maeditere

"She's not coming, is she?" I knew by the look on my mom's face as she hung up the phone that my grandma wasn't coming for Christmas. Ever since we destroyed her decorations last Christmas, things just hadn't been the same.

It all started last year on Thanksgiving Day. We had just finished stuffing ourselves full of turkey. The twins were wrestling over the large end of the wishbone when my Aunt Melinda walked in carrying one of Grandma's old hats.

"Everyone needs to draw a name. That's who you'll buy a present for this Christmas."

"What?" Uncle Dan hollered.

"Listen," Aunt Melinda explained. "Our family has grown so large that it's hard to buy something for everyone. We thought this might help relieve some of the burden."

"Burden!" Aunt Mary Beth snarled. "I realize that I have more children than the rest of you," she went on while motioning to the twins who were still duking it out on the floor and her three daughters who were slowly lowering their cell phones to listen in on this conversation, "but I never realized that we had become a burden."

"Now, now," Grandma stepped in. "Never have any of my darlings been anything of a burden. It's just that… well… I'm not getting any younger, and you all are always so busy. Your sister just thought it might be easier on all of us if we didn't have to buy quite so much this year."

"Well, I've never heard of such a ridiculous idea," Uncle Dan bellowed. "No offense, Mama, but I thought Christmas was supposed to be a time of giving… to all, not just one person."

"So… who gets to buy Mama's present?" my mom asked.

"Well, whoever draws her name," Aunt Melinda answered.

"Humph!" Uncle Dan snorted as he pushed back from the table, knocking over half-empty glasses of water and sweet tea. Grandma's favorite cat, Snookums, had been sleeping under the table and shrieked as someone stepped on her tail. She scurried into the kitchen. My cousins and I snickered as Grandma flew after the cat, yelling, "My sweet little dumpling! I'm so sorry."

"Dan, watch what you're doing!" Aunt Mary Beth yelled, snatching up the fallen glasses and dabbing at the spills with her napkin.

"Dan, I just gave Mama that tablecloth for her birthday. Now it's ruined. Why do you have to be so difficult?" Aunt Melinda yelled.

"You know what?" Uncle Dan replied. "I'm done with this. Happy Thanksgiving everyone." He turned and walked toward the door.

"Dan, you haven't drawn a name yet."

"Oh, whatever, Melinda. Just pick one for me. I don't care."

"Fine," Aunt Melinda huffed.

"Love you, Mama!" Uncle Dan called as he stormed out the front door.

Christmas Eve arrived, and we all came to Grandma's house with our "one" present. Everyone, that is, except for Uncle Dan. He showed up with a truckload of gifts. He brought something for everyone and even a few extra, which was great since Aunt Mary Beth's girls brought their boyfriends.

Aunt Melinda was fit to be tied when she saw Uncle Dan come in with an armful of presents. She started snatching boxes and throwing them under the tree.

"Hey, watch it, Melinda!" Uncle Dan hollered. "Some of those are breakable."

"Oh, excuse me, Danny Boy. I didn't mean to ruin all your fun."

"Oh, build a bridge and get over it, Smelly Melly."

"We were having a nice time until you got here. Why do you always have to stir something up?"

"Me?" Uncle Dan yelled. "I'm not the old Scrooge who decided to be stingy with the gifts."

"Come on, you two," my mom interrupted. "It's Christmas Eve. Can't you at least try to get along? Look at the example you're setting for the kids."

"I guess you're right, sis. I'm sorry," Uncle Dan answered.

"I'm sorry, too… Danny Boy," Aunt Melinda chided while Uncle Dan glared back.

The rest of the night, Aunt Melinda sat in the corner pouting while everyone "oohed" and "ahhed" over Uncle Dan's gifts.

My dad and my uncles spent most of the night setting up the new surround sound that Uncle Dan bought for Grandma. Mom and Aunt Mary Beth sat in the kitchen discussing what to do about the neighbor who Grandma suspected was stealing her Sunday papers. Aunt Mary Beth's daughters flirted with their boyfriends. We did our best to avoid collisions with the remote-controlled helicopters the twins flew all over the house. I pretended to listen as Grandma showed me our family album for the one-hundredth time.

Dad turned on the surround sound but didn't realize the volume was on high. The blast from every corner of the room caused Grandma to wail and fling the family album into the air. It landed on Snookums, who'd been resting at Grandma's feet. The poor cat let out a howl like I've never heard before and leaped smack dab into the Christmas tree. As the tree toppled over, the red and gold angel that stood peacefully atop Grandma's tree for as long as I could remember took flight and landed right in the middle of the fireplace. It went up in flames as we all watched in horror.

The adults started fussing and blaming each other while trying to clean up broken ornaments and salvage family pictures. We just tried to stay out of the way. Finally, Grandma told us to leave. We hadn't had a family gathering since then.

So here we were a year later, and it didn't look like Grandma was coming to Christmas.

"Well, is she coming or not?" I asked again impatiently.

"Grandma... had a heart attack," my mom answered, her voice beginning to quiver. "She collapsed in the grocery store, and the paramedics are rushing her to the hospital. Go get your coat while I call Uncle Dan."

When we got to the hospital, most of the family was already there. Everyone was hugging and crying and trying to figure out what had happened. Uncle Dan rushed through the door just as the doctor came in.

"Is she going to be alright?" Aunt Melinda asked.

"Yes," the doctor answered. "We're running some tests on her heart to determine the extent of the damage. She hit her head pretty hard when she fell and has suffered a mild concussion. She's resting now, but a few of you at a time can go in to see her."

Uncle Dan and Aunt Melinda stepped forward at the same time. The rest of us held our breath. And then, do you know what happened? They looked at each other and said, "You go first."

Grandma ended up spending Christmas in the hospital, but believe it or not, we all got along. We brought presents to Grandma's room, and Uncle Dan snuck Snookums in when the nurses weren't looking. Don't get me wrong, the tension was still there just under the surface, but we all realized something important that year. Although we may have our differences, we are still family, and we need each other. We may have to work a little bit harder at getting along, but if it makes Grandma happy, it's worth it.

~Christy Westbrook

Reprinted by Off the Mark and Mark Parisi
©1996

Easter Js Over

You can learn many things from children.
How much patience you have, for instance.
~Franklin P. Jones

Easter was quickly approaching. My extended family was planning to arrive at our home after church services for a potluck luncheon. The food would be plentiful and delicious. The kids would have a wonderful time searching for eggs. After the egg hunt, the adults would have an even better time exploring the dessert table. And I was looking forward to the upcoming Sunday as much as a root canal.

I was anxious about it because this would be our first holiday without the portable television, or as my son Garrett calls it, "the little TV." The little TV was a thirteen-inch combination television and DVD player. It only came out of the garage for special occasions, like anytime we had visitors.

Garrett was born with Smith-Magenis Syndrome, and he does not appreciate the change in routine that a family gathering brings. When people are meandering through the kitchen, Garrett is not able to line up his plastic army men in a single file down the center of the floor. He is not permitted to go to the family room and turn the vacuum cleaner on, and off, and on again. But, worst of all, Garrett cannot hear our television in the living room. So, we allowed him to take the portable TV into his room where he could watch his *Barney* DVDs and hide from the overstimulating crowd.

"Garrett will be ten this year, and I think it is time he start joining in the family dinners," I told my husband after the TV died during the Christmas party. I was so brave when Easter was still four months away.

I began preparing Garrett for Easter Sunday as we colored eggs and decorated the house. I showed him where the family would be eating, and we discussed the menu. If he asked about the little TV, I would remind him that it was broken. I explained to him that he could watch his DVDs after the party was over and people went home.

When the day finally arrived, Garrett was in good spirits. I thought we had finally reached another milestone, and he would be a part of our Easter celebration. And then we sat down to eat.

"Can I watch *Barney*?" Garrett stood behind my chair as I tasted my first bite of ham.

"Not yet, Garrett," I answered. "It's time for lunch."

"Can I watch *Barney*?" he asked again.

"No," I replied. "Do you want a sandwich?"

"Can I watch *Barney*?" he asked while wringing his hands. I could tell he was starting to realize the gravity of the situation.

"Garrett," I whispered softly. He had to lean in to hear me. I put my arm around him, hoping to keep him calm. "Remember how I told you all our friends were coming over today? It is a special day! We will turn on the television after everyone has left."

Garrett stood back up, cupped his hands around his mouth and shouted, "Okay, everyone. Time to go home now. Easter is OVER!"

~Tina Marie McGrevy

73

Mom's Empty Glass

What we see depends mainly on what we look for.
~John Lubbock

I was raised by two loving parents. My dad, a fat, jolly Irishman, always made jokes and had us in stitches with his stories and tales. Mom, a little Italian, had more of a "glass half-empty" outlook on life. While they were both wonderful in their own unique way, it was Mom's visits that would often leave me feeling I had once again "failed."

If I repainted the walls, Mom would let me know that the color was "way too dark" or "not dark enough." If I got my hair cut, it was either "way too short" or just a "little too long." When it came to buying her gifts, I would follow directions to a T, but for whatever reason it was either "too tight" or "not the exact shade of blue" or "just a tad scratchy around the waist." I just couldn't win.

That half-empty glass was never more apparent than at the holiday dinner table. I would work for weeks in preparation for the "perfect" holiday setting. Making my menu, shopping, baking, cleaning, setting the table… everything had to be magical. After all, it was a holiday, and whether Easter, Thanksgiving or Christmas, I was making memories for my children to cherish for the rest of their lives.

Being in a house full of men, I had the "pleasure" of doing everything myself. (Can you hear the martyr in my voice?) My four sons, my husband and my brother would sit and watch sports on the television and eat all the appetizers I had prepared so lovingly. Mom would sit in the big corner recliner and take her afternoon nap. I would be held prisoner in my kitchen all alone, adding the final touches to an already "perfect" meal.

Everyone would make their way to the table, taking their usual spot. Al and I each sat at the ends of the table, the boys scattered at our sides, and Mom was directly next to me so I could help her cut her meat — and also so I was in direct earshot of anything she had to say. I would carefully present each dish and place it on the table. The wonderful smells filled the room. Martha Stewart would be so impressed. I would assist Mom in making her plate as her failing eyesight and weak fingers did not allow her to lift the heavy dishes. We would say grace and then silence lingered as everyone waited for Nana (Mom) to open her mouth with some statement of eternal wisdom. At eighty years old, surely she had something to share.

"These beans are not cooked enough for me."

"I like my vegetables soft so they are easy to chew."

"Why did you get these rolls? I like the ones you made last year."

I would smile and continue with my meal. My children would look at me with a huge thumbs-up, knowing that my heart was breaking behind my grin. It became a holiday tradition, odd as that might sound. I had worked so hard and, still, it was not good enough... at least not for her. As everyone complimented me on the meal, Mom sat and cleaned her plate to the bare china.

"Would you like a little more, Mom?"

"No," she would say, "the meat was a little too dry for my taste." I already knew the answer, but I had to ask.

When it came to my Christmas cookies, I was reminded every year that my spritz cookies were not as good as Sue's (Mom's old neighbor) or that my pumpkin pie had just a little too much nutmeg. (One year, I left out the nutmeg on purpose, but yes, there was still "too much"!)

Hearing what was wrong became a part of our holidays. We often took bets on how long it would take before I was told where I had screwed up this time. I really don't think Mom meant to be hurtful. It was just her way. She loved me, this I know, and she loved being at our house. She loved being a part of things. And, most of all, she loved being around her grandsons. If she only knew how her words hurt. Yes, I often told her, but she just said I was just being "too sensitive," so I kept my feelings to myself. By the time we had to take her back to the nursing home, I was drained, physically and mentally, but I wouldn't have had it any other way. I wanted to spend as much time as I could with her. I knew her time with us was winding down.

We lost Mom a few years ago. I held her tiny, weak body in my arms as she faded away. She was on a journey to meet up with the husband she loved and lost so many years before. I cried as I kissed her goodbye, wondering how I would survive without her in my life. As difficult as she could be, she was my mother, and I had no idea how I would manage with her gone.

There is an empty place at our dining room table. I still do all the same prep work, often killing myself as I strive for perfection. We still sit in our assigned seats, and I still present my dishes in the same manner, but there is an eerie silence at the table. We are talking and laughing and telling stories, but "something" is missing. A strange peace is around us. The knot in my stomach is gone. I am not worried about anything. I savor each morsel that I place on my tongue. "Delicious," I think to myself.

It's a little too quiet, though. Something is "just not right," and as I scoop all the leftovers into storage containers, I find myself thinking, "Are these beans cooked right?" "Was the meat too dry?" "Does this pie need more nutmeg?"

I guess I'll never know.

~Trish Bonsall

All in the Family

Chapter 9

Reunited

Every parting is a form of death,
as every reunion is a type of heaven.

~Tryon Edwards

Never Too Late for Family

Other things may change us, but we start and end with the family.
~Anthony Brandt

I sat with my husband and three children in a hotel in St. Petersburg, Florida, where we visit my husband's relatives each winter. But this year was different. This time, I would be seeing my family. Any moment, my sister would arrive from her home ninety miles away. As I waited in the lobby, my cell phone rang every few minutes. "I'm almost there!" she'd say. Finally, a black SUV pulled up.

Alexa jumped out and into my arms. I had been waiting for that hug for thirty-eight years.

Alexa and I had not seen each other since she moved away from Massachusetts when I was eight years old and she was one. That also was the last time I saw our father.

And now, all these lost decades later, we were hugging and crying outside a Florida hotel.

My parents divorced when I was three and my brother Ethan was one. For the next five years, I cherished my father's occasional visits and phone calls, even though he often let me down. I met his new wife and loved playing with their baby daughter, Alexa. But when I was eight, my father moved his new family to Pennsylvania and eventually to Florida.

I felt loved and cared for by my mother and her parents, who we moved in with. But a deep sadness was with me always. My father had left us. He did not know me as I grew up, and I did not know him. I felt different from other kids, but I would not let it show. I inherited my mother's determination and realism, which helped me. And I was glad she was always open with me about her efforts—relentless, but unsuccessful—to get child support; about my paternal grandparents, who lived nearby but had almost nothing to do with us; and, in my teens, telling me that my father had a wife and two sons before us.

When I was growing up, we occasionally heard from my father's sister. That is how we knew he was no longer married to Alexa's mother. He had married a fourth wife and had three children with her. We never heard from him. That didn't stop me from wishing that I could know my father, but I could not bring myself to call or write. It never felt like the right time to reach out. "It's not supposed to be me looking for him," I thought. "He is supposed to be taking care of me."

I was an adult with children of my own when Ethan went to a wake for our father's uncle, hoping our father would be there. He was not, but Ethan had taken a step toward re-establishing contact with our father's family. A few days later, at my aunt's request, I visited her for the first time in twenty-seven years. For the next eight years, I sent her a holiday card each year, and she responded with an update on my father.

Still, I could not bring myself to contact my father, even when she told me that he was sick. I had three children of my own by then, and I knew the power of love between a parent and child. How could he throw it away? It didn't make sense. I never stopped wondering why he left me and my brother.

When my father died, I could not cry. I wanted to mourn, but no emotions came. That bothered me, and I sought guidance from my rabbi.

"Your mother and your grandparents were your parents. They raised you," she said. "He was your father only biologically." And she suggested his behavior was that of an unhealthy person.

This opened up a different way of thinking for me. Maybe I had mourned him long ago with all those childhood tears. Still, I felt shock that he was truly gone. I had always held the thought deep down inside, and especially since becoming a parent, that any day my father would call me. With his death, I felt that it was over. I felt closure… or so I thought.

What I did not know then was that my oldest half-brother, Dan, had sought out our father and established a relationship with him in the years before his death. After our father died, Dan got in touch with me. We lived just a few towns apart and arranged to meet in a seafood restaurant not far from our homes. After forty years, I was finally making a connection to my father.

I wanted to hear every detail, to piece together a picture of our father as a person. "What was he like?" I asked. "How did he act?"

Dan told me that he was friendly and charismatic and easy to be around. "And he loves chocolate ice cream," he added. My heart jumped. I am a fiend for chocolate. It was a connection, however small.

What I had not expected was the connection I felt to Dan. It was so easy to talk to each other. We shared the same circumstances — we had both been left by our father as children. In other ways, we were so much alike. I had a new half-brother.

A few months later, I was styling a bride's hair. She was so excited that her half-sister was travelling a great distance to attend her wedding. Suddenly, I ached. I had a half-sister, too. But I didn't know her.

I asked my aunt about Alexa. Her mother had recently died. I got Alexa's number and dialed.

From that day on, Alexa and I talked every two weeks. I reached out, and she reached right back. Alexa opened up doors for me into the life of my father. He was a good father to her, even after her parents divorced. He was involved in her life, supportive, and attentive. I was glad he could be so nice. All my life, I'd wondered, "Does he have a heart?" But I also learned that he was a womanizer who liked to drink and gamble.

Of all my half-siblings, Alexa was the one I'd longed for. I had a late-1960s photograph of me standing behind her, holding her hands as she toddled forward toward the camera. Alexa kept a photo of me, too, cradling her in my arms.

Suddenly, here we were, grown women hugging outside a Florida hotel. After six months of phone calls, we had decided to meet. With our husbands and children, we spent two wonderful days together. The new cousins got to know each other, laughing over the similarities in their moms—in our upbeat personalities and more.

In Florida, my aunt showed me photographs of my father throughout his life. She also had a framed picture of me that my grandmother always kept and another in a locket of my grandfather's. I had never known they even thought of me. Looking at those pictures, I didn't feel so forgotten. But I still wondered, "Why didn't they reach out to me all these years? How could they have just ignored us?"

The biggest question of all lingered for me: "Was my father sorry?" Dan never asked him directly, but he sensed his regret. That gives me a little peace. I know he would have liked me. And I would have loved him—even though I think he was a coward.

With my half-siblings, there is no such baggage. We are innocent people in the irresponsible, kooky, maybe even wicked life of our father. He never took responsibility.

With my father's death, I have found a new family. When he was alive, no one was willing to challenge him or ask him questions. He kept such secrets. But his death opened things up. At first, there was just me and my brother. Now I have all these people in my life who love me. They have formed a circle for me—Dan and his brother, then Alexa and her family, and maybe others I will eventually meet. And I trust them one hundred percent, in a way that I never could have trusted my father. They give me so much more than he ever could.

I can't dwell on the past or be sad about it anymore. I have so much more now that is new and blooming. During my Florida visit, I kept staring at Alexa, thinking, "She's half me." Each day since, I marvel, "I have a sister!" These are words I have not said or thought since I was eight years old. How lucky I am to be able to say them now at age forty-six. And it is also easy to say: "I love my sister."

~Robynn Ashwood

Emma's Castle

There are no rules of architecture for a castle in the clouds.
~G.K. Chesterton

y son held the phone with shaking hands. "The office is calling through to their classrooms now."

A moment later, he looked up. I will never forget his face.

"They're gone. She took them straight from the classroom. Without their coats."

That's how we found out his three children, our grandchildren, had been kidnapped.

For fifteen years, the entire family had tiptoed around Lisa. We had been told that childhood abuse was responsible for all her rages, melodramas, bizarre behavior, chameleon personality, and apparent inability to feel empathy for anyone but herself.

Now Lisa had suddenly ended her marriage and ripped the children from their everyday lives with a text message sent while Jim was in the final stages of a job interview.

That first night was the longest of my life, longer even than the one that had ended just before dawn years before when my father had come home from the hospital and announced that my big brother Jamie had "gone to heaven."

Now I waited at my son's big, empty house, praying Lisa would relent. My shell-shocked son slept fitfully on the couch, waking often in a jumble of tears. I sat in little Emma's favorite chair, watching the minutes roll round on the clock.

Just after midnight, I heard a car door slam. I strained my ears to catch children's voices, a faint clatter of feet. A kaleidoscope of emotions flashed through my mind, the strongest being relief.

I waited, willing myself to hear Caitlyn, Andrew and Emma tramping upstairs, chattering as they always did at top decibel. In a few moments, Jim would wake to be bombarded with three voices competing to pour out whatever terrible or interesting adventure the day had held from their point of view.

But the voices and footsteps died away. The house settled back into absolute silence. To this day, I don't really know what I heard or if it was real.

For the rest of the night, I sat unable to doze until my husband Don arrived to take over at dawn.

When it became clear Lisa wasn't returning, our daughter Lucy and her husband rushed down from Ottawa. We took turns staying with Jim or shadowing him at the construction site where he worked alone. Still trying to adjust to the sudden, complete loss of his family, his shock was disabling at times.

Between us, we helped him make phone calls, talk to police and lawyers, and (terrified she had taken them across the border) alert Lisa's relatives in Utah.

When two burly policemen turned up at Jim's door one day to serve him with a detailed restraining order, we finally found out what happened. Lisa had fled to a woman's shelter, full of lurid tales of spousal abuse. We were allowed no contact.

I will never forget the pain of being suddenly and totally separated—perhaps forever—from grandchildren who had been part of my daily life since their births. I missed Caitlyn's phone calls. Chatty as a sparrow, she had rushed to phone me every day, the moment she got home from school. Andrew, the middle child, loved nothing better than to "hang out" in my "girl-free" zone while I plied him with cookies, carrot sticks and attention.

And then there was Emma, age five. The last time I saw Emma

was on my birthday, right before the abduction. Emma proudly took me by the hand and led me to her favorite chair (the one she always fought over with her two older siblings). Beaming with pride, she offered me a present she had obviously wrapped herself, her little face shining as I opened it.

"See, Grandma? You've got your very own Pez and a supply of Pez candies. Wasn't that very clever of me?" I assured her it was, and I meant it.

And then, face glowing with love, she earnestly invited me to her impending birthday party at Chuck E. Cheese, anticipated for weeks. "You're the only grown-up I've invited," she whispered.

But Emma's birthday passed with no word and no contact.

I couldn't imagine what she was feeling, what she had been told. She wouldn't understand "restraining orders." She wouldn't understand why her world had changed forever. Would she think her daddy, Grandma, Poppa, Aunty "Lulu" and Uncle Tony didn't love her anymore? Would Lisa make sure she had her Chuck E. Cheese party?

As for me, in the long weeks that followed, I faithfully ate one of Emma's Pez candies every day. I tried not to think of how I would feel when the precious supply ran out. I wondered if I would ever again look out my glass kitchen door to see my three rascals tumbling out of their daddy's car and rushing up my path, eager for another "adventure."

In the months that followed, the lawyers wrangled their way through court. Jim dealt with everything bravely. We learned, too late, more than we ever wanted to know about Borderline Personality Disorder, which explained Lisa down to the last dot, sudden abduction and all.

The children were all we were concerned about now. Without Jim to act as a buffer, what were they going through? I couldn't help listening every night to the collection of precious messages saved on my answering machine. Listening to those bright little voices hurt as much as it helped, but it was all the contact I had left. Then, one black day, an overly helpful telephone company representative decided to upgrade my services. I discovered the treasured messages, dating back almost to Caitlyn's babyhood, erased. I phoned my husband at work. I couldn't stop crying.

Don came home with a Sonotube, a heavy industrial cardboard cylinder for use in pouring footings for house foundations. "Let's make Emma a castle...."

I chose a doll and spent an entire week carefully re-rooting its head with the longest, most golden hair that any children's fairy tale had ever seen. I gave "Rapunzel" the ultimate pink princess dress, dotted with roses and sparkling trim. My husband spray-painted the Sonotube with "rock" finish and cut an elaborate Gothic window into it.

We both got totally caught up in the project, our thoughts now focused on reunion. We added a windowsill made from painted foam popcorn, dozens of individual craft-stick "shingles," miniature weathervanes, furniture, and a floor for Rapunzel's chamber. Emma's castle kept us going.

We showed our project to Jim. We made him promise he would tell her about it the instant he saw her again. He looked at the pastel-shingled roof and Rapunzel's impossibly long hair, and he smiled for the first time in weeks.

One never-to-be-forgotten Friday, Don and I returned from grocery shopping to find the light blinking on our answering machine. I pressed the button, and Emma's little voice wavered out.

"Grandma, once you're home, could you please come over and bring me my castle?"

We were in the car before the machine even shut off.

~Rosemary Merritt

eMaybe Next Time

In true love the smallest distance is too great,
and the greatest distance can be bridged.
~Hans Nouwens

My phone rang, making me jump. I saw "Home" on the caller ID and flipped my phone open.

"Mariela?" my mom said. She always says my name as a question, as if anyone else was going to answer my cell phone. "Jesse is here. I'm coming to pick you up," she continued. I froze. I could hear something between excitement and sadness in her voice.

I quickly gathered my things from my friend's floor to wait by the door. As my mom pulled up, my stomach was in knots. I didn't know what to expect. I didn't even know if I would recognize him. We rode home in silence, keeping our thoughts to ourselves.

The last I'd heard about Jesse was that he'd been in jail due to illegal drug use two years ago. My parents always tried to protect me from the things that affected them the most. My brother wasn't a topic that came up very much in conversation. I knew my parents adopted Jesse when he was nine. Before that, he'd lived with his abusive, mentally ill mother from whom he was taken away when he was four. Jesse ran away from our house when he was fifteen, the year I was born. He packed knives in a backpack and began a new life on the streets. He met a woman named Lisa who had a daughter, Monica. She helped him get back on track, but after seven years together, drugs entered his life once again, and everything started to fall apart.

When we pulled up to the house, I hurried to the door. I hadn't seen my brother for at least a year. I paused, gripping the door handle. I heard a muffled laugh from inside. It sounded familiar, yet distant at the same time. I got up the courage to open the door handle. As I stepped inside, a man, about six feet tall, stood in front of me, facing the opposite wall. He was talking to my dad, telling a story involving wild hand gestures. He wore a dirty white T-shirt and baggy shorts. His face was freshly shaven, but his hands were coarse and dirty as if he'd just come from work. Instinct immediately told me to run up and hug him. He was my brother, but in so many ways, he was a stranger just stopping by for a visit.

The things in my arms fell to the floor, and he turned around at the sudden noise. His eyes were the same striking blue they had always been. He looked at me only for a second before scooping me up in his arms and squeezing me until every bit of air had been forced out.

"Sis!" he exclaimed. He'd called me that ever since I can remember. He looked me up and down, taking in everything he'd left behind.

"I've missed you," I said. He smiled warmly and set me down on my own two feet again. He continued with his story about living in the woods in Boulder Creek. He caught his own food and lived off the land. My parents always asked if there was a way we could reach him, and the answer was always no. The only way to see him was when he randomly decided to show up at our house. What made him decide that? We didn't know.

The whole time he told his stories, excitedly waving his arms and describing every detail of his life in the woods, I didn't talk. I never ask questions when he visits. A part of me wanted to tell him how much I'd missed him. I wanted to tell him what had happened while he was gone and ask him if he was happy. But a bigger part of me was afraid that if I opened my mouth, what came out wouldn't be what I wanted to say. I was scared that, instead, I'd tell him how much he hurt me. I was scared I'd tell him I was angry. I was angry that he had to live on the streets, even if it was by choice. I was angry that he left. I was afraid I'd ask him, "Why?" Why didn't he want to be part of our family? Why couldn't he have stayed at home and been my brother?

There are times when I see or feel something, and I know he's missing from my life. My family sits at the dinner table every night, and I stare at the empty seat across from me, wondering about the person who's supposed to be sitting there. Wondering where he is and if he's alright. Wondering if it was my fault he left in the first place. I hate not knowing him and not being able to talk to him. I hate not knowing if he's okay or if he's even alive. I hate wondering if he ever thinks about me. I hate dreaming that someday he'll come home again.

Each time he visits, I get closer and closer to talking to him, but something stops me every time. Maybe I'm waiting for the right moment when I know all the right things to say. A moment when my parents step out of the room, and I've collected all my thoughts, so nothing comes out wrong. At this point, I feel like everything is too jumbled, and if I say all the things I'm thinking, I could do the one thing I am sure I don't want to do. I don't want to hurt him. If I hurt my brother, just like everyone else has in the past, I may never get the chance to see him again.

Jesse reached out a hand and tickled me out of my thoughts. I squealed, suddenly being brought back to reality.

"I should get home," he said reluctantly. I saw everyone's smile fade. We walked him outside. The starry night sky was filled with goodbyes hanging heavy over our heads. I hated goodbyes more than anything. My parents each gave him a long hug, taking in everything about him, so that they would never forget. My mom repeated the words she said to him every time we had to say goodbye. "Don't be a stranger," she said.

And, like every time, he replied, "I won't." But by now I've learned that it could be years before I see him again.

He saved my hug for last. He picked me up off the ground again with his strong arms, squeezing me tight. I squeezed him back. He pulled away to look at me, telling me, "Stay in school, kid. Don't do drugs. Don't smoke, and never take your mom and dad for granted." They were the same words that had been regurgitated to me so many times before, but somehow from him, they meant so much more. I silently promised I would.

"I love you," I whispered into his ear.

"I love you too, sis," he whispered back. "Never forget that." I watched the headlights of his car fade into the distance, leaving behind only those words that I couldn't forget if I tried.

~Mariela Tsakiris, age 14

A Daughter Moves Back Home

To a father growing old nothing is dearer than a daughter.
~Euripides

"**D**ad, I am coming back." These five words changed my world.

My daughter, Amy, had left home seven years before to live in San Francisco shortly after her brother Matthew's suicide. Over the years, we had talked on the phone, written letters, and spent time together during her infrequent trips back East. Whenever she came home, however, there was always a tension between us. Because of my work, I had been under a great deal of pressure when she was growing up, and I would occasionally "pop my cork." Amy was a little afraid of me.

It was late October when Amy arrived after driving across the United States. Almost immediately, we got into a conflict over some minor problem. I became worried that I might not be able to handle living with her. I had accepted an early retirement incentive and would be home a great deal. Amy would also be there working as a freelance writer for a publishing company in California.

When I retired from my job as a social studies teacher in an urban school system, I decided to write a book about my experiences. I had finished a number of drafts before Amy arrived, but I knew the manuscript needed a great deal of editing. Amy agreed to help me, and we set up a weekly meeting in which we went over her suggested changes.

It was rough for me in the beginning because it was hard to accept that my "masterpiece" was far from perfect and that it needed extensive structural changes. Amy was gentle and supportive as we worked together. Week after week, she skillfully helped me to improve my work. I was unsure of my writing skills in the beginning, but she was a wonderful teacher and mentor.

We met every Tuesday morning at eleven o'clock in the kitchen. "Uh-oh, I see a lot of purple," I would say as I looked at my inverted manuscript from the other side of the table. (Amy used a pen with purple ink to make her edits.)

"Dad, you can't just tell people what happened. You have to show them. Put more of you in your work," she said. "Most readers want to know more about the people in a situation than the event itself. Don't hold back. You need to use more dialogue. Your work is improving, but I am raising the bar."

My spine tingled whenever she would say, "You nailed this section." I also noticed, as time went by, that we started to talk about many things besides the manuscript.

She shared the pain of coping with her brother's death and her battles with alcohol and depression. Through my writing, she began to understand why I was under so much strain when she was little. I also talked about my struggles with Matthew's death. I cried a number of times at these meetings. Many of our sessions ended with a hug.

As we got closer to the end of the editing process, Amy said to me one morning, "Your book has saved my life. I was beginning to wonder if anything was worthwhile. Using my skills to help you with your manuscript has been my anchor over the last six months." Talk about crying.

It was awhile before words came. "Amy, you have enriched my life," I answered. "You have inspired me with a great love of writing, and an even greater love of a wonderful human being and fantastic editor, who just happens to be my daughter."

Two years before, fear had invaded me as I was deciding whether to take the early retirement incentive. Financially, I knew it would be a stretch. I took a long weekend in the mountains to make my decision. As I walked along a beautiful trail with large, powerful-looking trees, I thought of Robert Frost's words in "The Road Not Taken": *I shall be telling this with a sigh somewhere ages and ages hence: two roads diverged in a wood, and I—I took the one less traveled by, and that has made all the difference.*

Over the first hill, I met my daughter.

~Edward A. Joseph

Finding Marie

There can be no situation in life in which
the conversation of my dear sister will not administer some comfort to me.
~Mary Montagu

"I love you, bud." These words come at the end of every e-mail my biological father sends me. If it wasn't for one eleven-year-old girl, I probably never would have believed him.

My mom was out of town one weekend, so I was stuck home alone with my stepdad and four wild brothers. Fortunately, MySpace came to the rescue as always. After I had logged on and replied to all my friends' messages, I noticed that I had a new friend request from an unfamiliar woman named Allison. I was about to hit the decline button when I noticed a note beside the picture of her and two young girls. It took me a second to understand what the woman was trying to tell me in such a short note, but then it was only a moment before tears started to roll down my face. The message read, "Hi, Dallas. My name's Allison, Marie's stepmom. She really wants to talk to you. You're her big sister!" That was all she wrote.

I felt like those words were screaming at me over and over again. I didn't know what to do or what to say or even how to process it all at once. Another name raced into my head from that old, dusty folder that has been hidden deep in my heart for over a decade. Richard. My father. The man I hadn't spoken to since I was five. It all still didn't make sense, even though I read the message over and over again.

At last, I came to the conclusion that it was real, and it was really happening to me. It was a moment I had been dreading all my life.

Knowing that I'm a role model for Marie and that I mean so much to this stranger who lives 1,539 miles away in Arkansas is the strangest feeling for a fifteen-year-old. It makes me want to try harder. I want to be there when she cries because a silly little boy hurts her or when she laughs at a Saturday morning cartoon. I feel responsible for her, almost like a mother does for her own child, even though she's only four years younger than me.

Marie has changed my life forever. My thoughts and feelings about life shifted almost instantaneously. As soon as she said hello, I was hers forever. Every day, I wake up and remember that not only am I a sister to five brothers, but I'm an older sister to a girl who deserves better, but still chooses to love me and all my flaws. She's my total opposite—short and blonde with gorgeous blue eyes—but in the end we're always in perfect sync.

Because of Marie, I also met the one true thing we truly have in common: the man who is responsible for our shared DNA. All my friends say I look like Wayne. As soon as I saw a picture of him, I immediately knew where I got my red hair. I'd been mad at him for so long that my anger had become second nature to me. My mom talked to him on the phone a couple of times, and she would ask me if I wanted to speak to him. I would say the first thing that came to my mind: no. Of course, I felt guilty for it later, but I couldn't give him the satisfaction of knowing he could disappear for years and come back thinking that it was all going to be okay.

Finally, I gave in. After listening to him apologize for twenty minutes, I asked him the question I'd been waiting to ask my entire life: Why? Why did he leave? Why did he hide? Why didn't he call? And, most important, why did he choose to come back now when I was nearly grown and didn't need a father figure anymore? His answer hit me like a wrecking ball. He was just as clueless as I was. He said there was no answer, no excuses or anything of the sort. He was young and reckless and had no clue about the life he was missing out on. I wasn't angry or upset. I was relieved in a way that's impossible to explain. And that was that.

I haven't forgiven him, and probably never fully will. There's a love between us, but it's a very different kind of love. Any man can be a father, but it takes more to be a dad. I just thank Richard for letting me and Marie have the relationship we have to this day. I've only known her for about a year, but she has affected me in more than a million ways. I think she has made me a better person, more responsible and aware of the effects of my actions on the people around me. If it wasn't for MySpace, I wouldn't know Marie. And not knowing Marie is like not knowing me.

~Dallas Kuzinich, age 15

The Hug

Forgiveness is a funny thing. It warms the heart and cools the sting.
~William Arthur Ward

The first letter arrived a few weeks before Christmas. My heart stopped when I saw the return address. I was pleased but apprehensive. I dropped the rest of the mail on the counter and sat down at the kitchen table.

I had written to ask him for my family's medical history. The reply was long, as it had the information I had requested and then some. It explained a little of my past, but still kept me at arm's length. I reread it a few times, and then wept and set it aside.

Life goes on, and many things sit and collect dust in the back of one's mind. A year later, an unexpected Christmas card with a family photo arrived from his wife. She said he was busy working out of town but that he would write soon. I studied the picture. Immediately, I knew where my looks came from. I really didn't bear much resemblance to my mother's side of the family, but here was a man staring back at me who looked familiar in so many ways. He had a grown son and daughter—a family of his own who looked so happy together. They wanted to get to know me and asked if I could send a picture of my family. I wasn't sure. Did I have the courage to go forward?

A mere week later, my aunt reminded me, "When one door closes, another opens." I had not thought of it in that way. My mom had just passed away. My aunt encouraged me to write back.

The reply came in February. As I read his letter, my eyes misted over. He would be in Manitoba in March. Could he and his wife stop by to see us? After almost thirty years of absence he wanted to meet me.

Excitement, happiness, fear, and sadness washed over me all at once. My toddler wanted to know why I was crying. I told a white lie. "It's okay. They're happy tears." To be truthful, I had no idea what those tears represented.

I was only two years old when they divorced. As hard as I had tried over the years, I had no memory of him. Divorce laws were not necessarily fair in the 1960s. My mother did not allow any contact—no cards or letters, no phone calls, no pictures, no visits. He did not want to make a bad situation worse, so he reluctantly agreed to stay away. Being two provinces away did not help. When my mother remarried, I still retained my father's last name so I always knew of his existence.

When you are young, you accept your life as it is. It was not until I had children of my own that I really began to question my parents' decisions. How could they have thought this best? It was likely complicated, but no one ever offered an in-depth explanation.

Now, here I was a parent myself, but feeling very much like a child all over again. I had a month to pull myself together, a month of waiting and wondering. It wasn't as though I wouldn't be busy. I had a two-year-old son and a newborn daughter. The end of March would be here before I knew it.

Then panic set in. Would I be ready? How would I look? How would I feel? He was coming to Manitoba in March… what if it stormed? Our yard always looks so bleak and unkempt that time of year. Would he get lost trying to find our place in the country? Would I have the house clean enough? Would he think I was a good parent? What if he didn't like me? Would they stay for lunch? What would I cook for two people I didn't know? Was this really a good idea? I was reeling and overreacting. I needed to breathe… three deep breaths in and out. It wasn't working so I tried again, slowly this time. Don't worry, I told myself. It will be fine. I needed to calm down, but couldn't help feeling terrified.

The days and weeks slipped by, and March 23rd arrived. The weather cooperated. The roads were fine. Our son and baby daughter had slept well and looked sweet and innocent. I, on the other hand, looked tired and nervous.

We watched and waited. A car pulled into the yard. They got out, opened the doors to the back seat and pulled out gift bags. They had brought presents. I had nothing for them. Lunch alone would have to do. They saw us in the window, smiled and walked to the door. I welcomed them into our home. He put down the bags he was carrying and came up the three stairs toward me. Then, the unexpected.

He reached out and hugged me. It was a big bear hug filled with emotion. It spoke volumes. I have never been hugged like that before or since. The hug said, "I'm sorry." It conveyed, "I've missed you. I'm so happy to see you." It expressed, "I love you." It made up for every missed birthday and Christmas. It explained, "I wish I had been there for all your firsts, for every accomplishment, and for every time you needed a shoulder to cry on."

I didn't want to let go, and it seemed he didn't either. The hug replaced my worries with comfort. Words were not needed after all, but introductions were, and so the hug ended. It was time to relax and visit. We had a lot of catching up to do.

~Sandi Knight

There Is a Tree

If you feel called to share a message,
it's because there are people in the world who are waiting to hear it.
~Michael Port

On the plane headed to Detroit for my grandparents' sixtieth wedding anniversary, I gazed out the small cabin window. My mind wandered as I reviewed the past year.

I had moved to Phuket, Thailand, where I had become a scuba dive master and taught children at a local school. I didn't have a good answer as to why I left home. I just needed to escape from my life as it was.

After living in Thailand for seven months, I got a call from my brother.

"I just got back from Iraq again. A lot has changed in my life, and I have so much to tell you!"

"Well, when can you come out here to visit me?"

"I don't get out of the Marine Corps until next March. When are you coming home?"

That was all I needed to hear. I decided right then and there to return home to see my brother and family as soon as I could wrap things up in Phuket.

First, my mom flew out to see what life had been like for me in Thailand. We spent seven weeks exploring Southeast Asia and parts of Europe before returning home. We then drove through the southwestern United States and along the West Coast to visit my brother and two sisters.

It struck me that I had traveled to ten countries and, now on my way to Michigan, ten states within the course of a year.

I pulled out my travel journal, weathered by months of tropical sea air and endless carry-on chafing. And I began to write....

Months later, my family gathered in Arizona for our first Christmas together in three years. My brother was home from Iraq, and I was back from years of international adventure. My mom wanted it to be the best Christmas ever.

We had all decided to have a "Come as You Will Be" party to celebrate our dreams as a family and our commitment to getting along and growing together. When it was my turn to talk about my dreams, I revealed my intention to be a writer. I even had my first work with me, a short parable I had recently written. Although I wanted to read it to them, an overwhelming sense of vulnerability emerged, and I changed the subject. Then, suddenly, I was interrupted with, "Let's hear it!"

Somewhat surprised that everyone seemed genuinely interested, I read what I had written on the plane two months before.

There Is a Tree

There is a tree whose roots sink deeply into the very core of the earth. Its branches soar up through the sky and out into the universe. Its trunk is so wide, no one really knows where one side begins or the other one ends. On that tree, there are so many leaves that, from far away, they seem to blend together as one.

But, up close, each leaf looks completely separate. Because of this, most leaves overlook the fact that their stems are attached to small branches, which give way to all the other branches and ultimately connect to every other leaf on the tree. Most leaves forget this connection and feel separate and alone.

When it rains, the leaves think they must accumulate more drops on them than the others, or they might die of thirst. So they compete with each other for the limited raindrops, forgetting that they all share the same roots, which absorb the water when it moistens the earth.

When the sun comes out, the leaves are again worried, this time because they may not get enough light. When they see other leaves getting more sunlight than themselves, they feel resentful and envious, forgetting that when the sun shines on any one of them, the warmth and energy strengthens them all.

Some leaves don't remember that they are part of a tree until they fall to the ground. But from the ground looking up, they can plainly see that all the leaves are growing from the same tree. Once they remember, they transform into nourishing soil and continue on as a different part of the tree.

Some leaves, on the other hand, remember before they fall from the tree. When it rains, these leaves relax and trust, knowing that the water will moisten the soil below, and the roots of the great tree will absorb it, providing plenty of water for each leaf.

When the sun comes out, the leaves bask in its warmth. When they see other leaves getting more sunlight, they are delighted, knowing that they all benefit from each other's success.

But the most amazing thing is that when one leaf remembers, sometimes other leaves notice. And then, slowly, they begin to remember, too. And before you know it, on a tree whose roots sink deeply into the core of the earth with branches that reach all the way out into the universe, there are leaves that, even up close, don't seem so separate.

I looked around. Everyone was quiet.

Today, if you were to say to me, "Thailand?! What made you want to move there?" I would have an answer. Only after all the people I met, after all the places I saw, after all the experiences I had, and only after being with my family, as if for the first time, can I say in earnest, "I just needed to find my way home."

~Kimberly Anne Reedy

Sisters by Choice

The hardest thing to learn in life
is which bridge to cross
and which to burn.
~David Russell

In my fifties, I often masked my heartache by relying on the popular statement, "Girlfriends are sisters by choice." Unfortunately, my real-life sister, Peggy, and I were estranged.

Peggy got to rule the roost for two years prior to my arrival. We endured the usual "Get your foot off my side" arguments, but growing up, Peg was someone I looked up to and often leaned on.

As adults, we went through periods of emotional separation. We always lived at least two hundred miles apart, and our hot-and-cold pattern persisted regardless of how often we saw each other. Better times found us sharing holiday dinners together, along with our husbands and our children.

In our early forties, we lost both parents to cancer within a two-year period. Their deaths left us with challenges some people don't face when parents die. Mother and Dad were married fifty-four years, and we cherished our good memories of them. But our earliest memories also included their arguments and frequent criticism of one another. Even so, we knew that, to have stayed together over half a century, they must have filled each other's needs on some level. Did Dad's controlling personality complete Mama's child-like, dependent nature? Or did Dad's upbringing as a preacher's kid forbid divorce in his mind?

Regardless of the glue that held them together, their harsh exchanges lasted until the first one died. In spite of the raw emotions Peg and I carried away from decades of their interaction, we loved our folks and buried them beside one another with the knowledge they were, at last, at peace. We settled the estate and worked together, cried, laughed, and loved each other through those years.

I thought our closeness would last forever, but fifty years of dysfunction finally led us to part ways. I wondered if the ties that bound us simply died with Mama and Daddy. For eight years, I closed my mind as much as possible to the memory of a sister. I gave up hope we'd reunite, and I stored pictures and gifts. My girlfriends became sisters by choice, and these friendships brought the supportive sisterhood I missed.

While living in Florida in 2007, I had a chance meeting with a woman named Carolyn who had attended my Dallas high school. She graduated three years ahead of me, and she knew my sister. Carolyn and I soon had dinner and discovered we had much in common. As the year passed, our friendship grew. She thought the disintegration of my relationship with Peggy was sad, and since Carolyn's only sibling was deceased, she hoped Peg and I would reunite.

By now, my daily prayer list often included a good relationship with Peg—something I believed only God could orchestrate. Throughout 2008, thoughts of Peggy and the bond we once shared strengthened my desire to know her.

Carolyn invited me to attend her October high school reunion in Dallas, and I thought I might see folks who knew my sister. But I wasn't prepared for the number of people who asked about Peggy, causing me to invent answers concerning a life I knew little about. I left feeling melancholy but more assured than ever that God would reunite us in his own time.

Another former classmate from our high school was compiling a book that would contain pictures and former students' written memories. A friend asked me to submit my memories, and I initially hesitated. Going back to my childhood would require me to examine feelings I'd long since left behind. But, as someone who likes to write, I faced the challenge.

One of my written memories of Peggy stated she was always around to welcome me to new schools she already attended. I followed that sentence with two special words, "Thanks, Peggy!" Would she ever see the book, read my words, or recall the many good memories we shared? Through friends, I knew that Peggy sometimes attended the annual high school alumni gatherings, where the book would be introduced in 2009. On November 5, 2008, I placed the outcome in God's hands and felt peaceful as I e-mailed my submission to the book's author.

My birthday was November 8th, and by that day, cards from friends and family had all arrived. No birthday cards appeared to be in November 8th's mail stack until I got to the bottom. An innocuous white envelope was suddenly in my hand, but the handwriting was unmistakable. I quickly opened the card that contained the following printed words:

My Sister —
There have been times when I felt we were really close
And times when we each sort of went our own way
But I want you to know there's never been a time
I didn't love you, and I hope you know I always will.

She wrote at the bottom, "Happy birthday. Love, Peggy."

Tears filled my eyes as God's goodness overcame me. The postmark on Peggy's card was November 5th — the date I had e-mailed my memory submission for the high school book. My sister and I had reached out to one another on the very same day. Even so, I wasn't sure about the best way to respond. I looked for a similarly heartwarming card and found none. Should I call Peggy instead? What if, in my nervousness, I said the wrong thing?

Carolyn and I had lunch at an Asian restaurant on November 10th, and I shared my good news with her. After we ate, Carolyn said,

"Pick out a fortune cookie. I think it's going to contain a message relating to your sister."

I laughingly replied, "You're funny. Every fortune cookie I've ever opened contained absurd ramblings."

Carolyn watched while I broke open the cookie, and our eyes grew large as I read the message aloud: "Sister... Everywhere you choose to go, friendly faces will greet you."

I'll never forget the power of the words inside that fortune cookie. I called Peggy that afternoon, and God's wonderful orchestration of our reunion led to a long, loving conversation. We've been together many times during the past eight months despite the miles between us. I would choose Peggy as my sister and my friend over and over again, and we can honestly say we are glad to be sisters by choice.

~Betty Bogart

All in the Family

Chapter 10

Brothers and Sisters

*To the outside world we all grow old. But not to brothers and sisters.
We know each other as we always were. We know each other's hearts.
We share private family jokes. We remember family feuds and secrets,
family griefs and joys. We live outside the touch of time.*

~Clara Ortega

My Homeless Brother

Wherever a man turns he can find someone who needs him.
~Albert Schweitzer

No one ever dreamed my brother would end up homeless on the streets when he won a National Merit award in high school. Bruce had a near-genius IQ level. We were all a little stunned to find out how intelligent he was. He had gotten lost in the crowd of a large family. My older brother was the high achiever. I was the only girl. My youngest brother was into sports. Bruce had always been in the middle, somewhat of a loner with a tender heart. Yet he had a talent to fix anything and created the most ingenious inventions to help our family business. It was when his own young business began to fail in his early twenties that we began seeing outlandish behavior. It was like something in his brilliant mind snapped.

Paranoia caused him to believe international agents were out to kill him. He could not go past certain unseen boundaries, and he was somehow entangled in every world news event. With irrational thinking, he turned real information into crazy fantasies. It became too challenging to be around our family, so he began to come and go. I felt compelled to try to help him. Many hours of research caused me to diagnose him as paranoid schizophrenic (although I have no qualifications as a doctor). Determined to make my family get him help, I called family meetings, educating them on what I had learned and how we could help. No one wanted to admit there was anything wrong. Sadly, even if we all agreed, Bruce was an adult and could not be forced into treatment.

Bruce left home, traveling across the country any way he could. Sometimes, there were collect calls when he was terrified for his life. At times, he would scream on the phone, saying someone was attacking him. We had no way of knowing if it was real or not. It was very real in his mind! Other times, we would get calls when he seemed very peaceful, even praying with us. We never know if he's alive until he calls again. At times, he sends boxes or newspapers home with clues, messages or for safekeeping from whoever is "after him." We've learned to stay calm and provide steady access to reality when he makes contact.

Bruce has been mentally ill for twenty-five years and homeless for eighteen. Many cold, snowy nights I wonder if he has some kind of shelter. At meals, I often worry about whether Bruce has something to eat. When one of us gets a frightened phone call, we anxiously wonder how anyone could live with such deep fear all the time. After years of worrying about him and praying for him, the thought has come to me that God has taken care of him so far. Bruce is surviving. I should trust God to look after him, wherever he is.

I have learned from my brother that I can't fix everything. There are no easy answers for mental illness or for homelessness. My husband and I go spend time on the streets with the homeless about once a month. We can't resolve their issues, but we can offer them the love of Jesus right where they are. I can look in their eyes, knowing they are someone's brother or son. I can look past their appearance or odd behavior and treat them with kindness and pray with them. I can respectfully visit with them, as a real person, instead of ignoring them like they aren't even there. We minister to them, but we always feel we have been ministered to by them as well. I'm always surprised at the faith someone can have in the midst of dire circumstances. God is with them, even on the streets. I've also discovered there are friendships and a code of ethics in the homeless community. It helps to know my brother must have friends.

It is easy to judge someone standing on a busy corner with a sign begging for money. Now I realize not everyone is able to hold a job or have the security of a home. Each individual has a whole life story that I don't know. It's not always appropriate to get out of my car to talk to them, or I may not feel right giving them money, but I try to keep a supply of zip-lock baggies ready to hand out. The bags have toiletries, a snack, a small devotion book and a letter telling them that I am praying for them like I do for my brother. As I hand it through the car window, I always ask their name so I can pray for them. When I reach out to someone homeless near me, I trust that God is leading someone to reach out to my brother in another state.

I don't know what will transpire in Bruce's life. He may never stabilize, but I know God is with him. I trust that he will be made whole in heaven! My family has learned much compassion for the homeless and mentally ill. I will continue to walk among the homeless and mentally ill with the love of Christ, and minister to them as if they were actually my brother Bruce.

~Eva Juliuson

They're Listening

From now on, I'll connect the dots my own way.
~Bill Watterson, Calvin & Hobbes

She had changed her legal name at least three times, and I had not seen her in more than forty years, but when the note arrived without a return address, I knew exactly who it was from. In tiny, scrawled, almost illegible handwriting, the invitation said, "Living in OC. Visit me if you'd like, but send me a photograph so I can recognize you. Enclosing one of me. Meet me at the library by the periodicals."

I sent back my photograph and the date of my arrival.

The two-hour drive to Ocean City was pleasant and filled with expectations of a friendly reunion. I had packed an overnight bag and told my family I would return in the morning.

Arriving at the periodical section, I searched the room for a face to match the photo. Perhaps she decided not to come. Perhaps she got her days mixed up. Perhaps I was too early. And then I spotted her. She was at least thirty years older than the woman in the photo, but some of the features were the same. A plaid woolen scarf was tied under her chin, and she was wearing a long coat that would have fit a much larger woman.

She remained seated until I spoke. Then she put her finger to her lips to shush me and made a gesture that we should leave.

"I brought my bike. Follow me."

What I saw next will be forever embedded in my memory. She

placed a knitted cap with an aluminum foil pompom over the plaid scarf and carefully tucked every stray hair into it. And then she rode her bike down the center line of every street on the way to her apartment, with me following closely behind in the car.

"I'm back, so all of you can stop staring and go into your houses now!" she shouted into the air as we walked up to her building. There was no one in sight, but she continued, "Get away from the windows and mind your own business!"

Before entering her apartment, she took me to the basement to show me where all the "beams" were coming from. The rooms were musty and dark and scared me more than any possible "beams" she imagined. She stowed her bicycle behind an old oil heater, but kept her protector hat on until we got inside her living room.

At that point, I got a real glimpse into the life she was leading. There was no phone and no TV. Dark lined drapes covered the windows, and an assortment of castoff furniture littered the room. Old books with stories by Kierkegaard and Kafka covered her dining room table. Filthy dishes, glasses, and pans covered the kitchen counters. Empty plastic water bottles were strewn everywhere. She was afraid the city water was poisoned, while I feared the bacteria encrusted on those dishes.

She ushered me into her bedroom and lifted the covers to point out the aluminum folding table under her bed. "This reflects the beams." In the spare bedroom, she lifted the covers to show me the table and whispered, "You'll be safe." Evidently, she was expecting me to stay.

"Let's get dinner out," I suggested. "I'll drive."

With a questioning look, she put on her protector hat and handed me one, too.

"No, thanks. It's really too hot for me."

Before she would sit in the car, she had to inspect the glove compartment, radio and seats. Satisfied that no one could hear us, she made herself comfortable on the leather cushions. I was driving across the small bridge when she placed her hand on my thigh.

"Your mother said I was trying to drown you, but I wasn't." I remained as calm as possible, steadying the wheel, eyes straight ahead.

My mind flashed back to one of my few memories of her, lying on the blanket at the lake, spending lazy summer days flirting with the lifeguards. She was stunning in her black bathing suit with a black lace insert. She laughed and joked, with her full red lips and white teeth glistening in the sun. I was an awkward pre-teen; she was a beauty queen.

"I've always wanted a chum. We can be great friends," she promised.

We arrived at the Crab Trap, and I asked the receptionist for a small table in the back. Margaret ordered the same entrée and drink as I did, but she would not eat it. She watched as I tasted the food and then signaled for the waitress to come to our table.

"This is too rich for us. We'd both like salads instead." The waitress looked at me, with the food still in my mouth, and questioned, "Is that right?"

"Bring two salads and leave these. Thanks."

Two salads were served, and Margaret watched again as I ate mine. She signaled the waitress again.

"We just want coffee."

"But you didn't eat anything."

"What! Is there a law that a person has to eat in here? Can't a person just have coffee?" Margaret challenged in a raised voice.

The waitress looked at me, and I promised, "I'll pay for the food. Please bring the coffee."

After I paid the bill, Margaret started toward the ladies' room when she saw an obese woman eating something very creamy.

"Look at you! No wonder you're fat! You shouldn't be eating this!" I tugged at her and apologized, without mentioning my sister's diagnosis.

I was washing my hands when I heard what sounded like a scuffle in Margaret's stall. Then I smelled sulfur from a lit match. "Is everything okay in there?"

She washed her hands, exited the room, and whispered, "You have to cover your DNA."

Arriving at her apartment, we decided to take an evening stroll on the north end of the boardwalk. It was not near the vendors and the air would be refreshing. This time she insisted I wear my protector hat, and I acquiesced. Arm in arm, we made quite a pair. She told long stories and revealed more details about her life than I felt comfortable knowing. She made several references to important men she had known, always saying she could not reveal their names because they were married and in prominent positions. "Someone might get hurt," she repeated, and I began to believe she was the someone. The conversation came to an abrupt halt every time we passed a streetlight, because the communicators were listening.

At her front walkway, she issued a different version of the warning I heard earlier. "You can get away from the windows now. We're home for the night. You can stop waiting for us!"

My mind was on overload, so I retreated to the guest bedroom. I closed the door, turned off the light, and lay on the bed. But I did not get changed. Something in my gut told me to be prepared for anything. I recalled the day's events, chuckled to myself about the look on the waitress's face, and realized that it's very freeing to be with someone who's a little off. Sometimes you can pretend you're the caretaker; sometimes you can pretend you're just as eccentric.

It was two in the morning when my door creaked open. Margaret did not enter, but I saw her silhouette pacing back and forth, back and forth. She was like a caged lion. At first, I thought she was afraid of something outside. Then I realized I was the something outside who had invaded her sanctuary.

"Don't worry, I won't hurt you. Don't worry, I don't have a weapon." She uttered these words over and over. Her voice was husky and strange. It was her final claim that really startled me. "Don't worry, I don't have a knife." Now she was naming the weapon.

I slid out of the bed quietly, reached down for my overnight bag, and waited until I heard her walk into her room. I quickly headed for the front door when she confronted me.

"What are you doing?"

"Margaret, I can't sleep here. I miss my family, and I really need to get back to them."

She must have been just as relieved as I was because she did not try to stop me.

"I'll write to you, and we will see each other again. You will know the letter is from me because I will write the words 'Rice Krispies' for the return address. My family and I use those words to say we are safe. I had a good day. Thank you."

And then I was out the door and on my way home. It was too late to call and have my husband worry about my return trip at that hour, so I slipped into bed next to him around 4:00 A.M.

"Why did you change your mind?" he mumbled.

"I needed to be here with you." And then I said a thankful prayer for the life I am blessed with.

~June Waters

Sanity and Soda

A sibling may be the keeper of one's identity,
the only person with the keys to one's unfettered, more fundamental self.
~Marian Sandmaier

Some people think that my brother John is crazy just because he spent some time in a mental hospital. I cannot agree with such logic. That's like saying that I am a hamburger because I spent some time at McDonald's. When it comes to decision making and planning ahead, John is one of the most rational people I know, and I am blessed to have him in my life.

John is ten years my senior and was diagnosed schizophrenic when I was only twelve. He is very smart and came within months of graduating college. He has memorized a list of vocabulary words and uses them correctly. He gets up every day and tries to make himself a better person and contribute in some way to the world.

When I am at a useless office meeting where they are discussing minute details such as changing the name of a department that has done the same task for twenty years or out for dinner in a wildly painted Mexican restaurant, I often ask myself, "What would John think of this? What would he see?" It sharpens my perspective.

John shows me that there is no one right way to look at the world. He teaches me that the world is not always nice or kind, but it can be more interesting with a sprinkle of fairy dust and imagination. He takes many things personally and feels that balloons on real estate signs and flags at the car dealership are put there just for his pleasure.

Sometimes, we talk about crazy feelings or crazy things. We have a sibling bond of shared secrets, and we still cherish that. At times, I find it's very enlightening to hear his perspective on craziness. John will share stories of times that he threw apples at nurses when he was first diagnosed and say that he is sorry that he acted in that way.

One day, John told me, "The craziest thing I ever did was when Rick and Jim and I went swimming in Surf City after that hurricane on Long Beach Island. Now, THAT was crazy!"

I laugh because he is right. Sometimes there is such a fine line between everyday behavior and that which is considered crazy.

John is free to admit his faults and weaknesses. He is completely addicted to soda, and while my mother treats this like he was addicted to gambling or drugs, the truth is that he does his best. I refuse to chastise him for his "drinking problem," and he excuses it by saying, "Sometimes I just need to look forward to a little soda, you know?"

John still admires the heroes of childhood: Dumbo and Charlie Brown and Rudolph. He watches the DVDs and empathizes with the misfits of his youth. He knows he does not fit in. While at times it makes him sad, it does not make him ashamed. It makes it so much easier for me to admit the times that I don't fit in when I see how John bravely accepts this about himself.

John also teaches me to be easier on myself. He lives quite independently in a supportive residence near my mother's house. Once in awhile, he calls me up and says, "Sometimes, it is really hard to just do what I have to do every day." He is absolutely correct. John hates Valentine's Day and usually has himself "a good cry." On those days, John takes special care of himself and listens to his favorite band, U2, so he doesn't feel so alone.

There are days when I need to look at myself with the same acceptance and kindness that John does. Life is hard, and sometimes it is okay to turn off the ringer on your phone, drink lots of soda, and watch cartoons. Sometimes, it's not just okay, it's necessary.

~Susan LaMaire

Sharing Everything

If your sister is in a tearing hurry to go out and cannot catch your eye,
she's wearing your best sweater.
~Pam Brown

My family is a source of amusement at all times. Even at funerals, something will happen to prompt a giggle. I guess we learned it from my grandmother, whom we affectionately called "Ma Ma Baker." She taught us that laughter is the best medicine. We learned that if you cannot laugh at yourself, you'd better just hide your head like an ostrich. Life goes on.

Our family consisted of all girls. Not that my mom and dad did not keep trying. You would have thought that after three, they would have given up on the boy. I think they knew, though, that the best was yet to come. That was me. I'm number four. Then they messed up and had my baby sister. Accidents happen. Really, they do. My mother wrote my dad's mom a card and said, "Guess what? We're having another baby! April Fool!" The "April Fool" was my mom. She found out she was pregnant. Girl number five was it. No more trying for "Jr."

Poor Dad. He said he should have bought stock in all of the girl products. He would have received a great dividend just on us. Daddy came home all excited one day. He said, "I found the perfect house for us!" Then he burst out laughing and said the convent had come up for sale. We could each have our own bathroom and bedroom. No more fighting for primping! That would be heaven (no pun intended) for all his girls, his wife, and his mother-in-law. And my dad would never again have to hear, "Are you finished in there yet?"

The biggest problem with girls is sharing. Sharing without asking. Now, some people would call this stealing. I did call it that. My sisters didn't. They called it borrowing. Until I did it. Then it was stealing. Go figure. My mom could not keep a handle on her items either. She tried to hide them. She did pretty well for the most part until we got older. Then the make-up was a free-for-all for everyone. The laundry would be mixed up, people would take things without asking, and Mom… she would lose control. When she lost control, she was also the best target for laughter.

Trying to get ready for church on Sunday mornings was like a mad dash with everyone trying to get ready at the same time. They all made fun of me because I was eighteen, and everything—and I mean EVERYTHING—had to look right. I even had Bibles in different colors to go with my outfits. No, really, I did. One particular Sunday, I invited a boyfriend to go to church with me. He came to my house to pick me up. I soon figured out that maybe this was not a good idea. Sunday morning at my house? What was I thinking? Okay, I wasn't. I was too worried about matching Bibles. I went back to my bedroom to retrieve the burgundy one instead of the red. As I came out of the bedroom, I heard this commotion going on. It was my mom in her bedroom. Some comments about clothes. Something about stuff. Something about not being able to find anything. Then the door flew open, and out came a raving Momma. "Do these look like mine? Huh? Do these look like mine?!" The raving lunatic in her slip and too-small pantyhose must have scared the bejesus out of my boyfriend, but he never let on… nor did he skip a beat. Greg just looked at her and said, "Nope. I really don't think so!" My red-faced mother slinked back to the bedroom.

Greg probably went home, washed his eyes out, and had nightmares. He never told. Come to think of it, he and I never dated much after that! Mom will never, ever live it down.

~Libby Hires

Our Last Goodbye

In time of test, family is best.
~Burmese Proverb

Sisters are funny creatures. People say you grow closer as you get older, but that wasn't the case with my sister and me. We were extremely close right up until she was seventeen and I was nineteen. That's when Kara became pregnant.

"I'm giving the baby up for adoption," she announced one brisk January morning.

"Adoption? Why?" I stared at her huge, round belly, dumbfounded.

"We can't afford to feed a baby. We can barely afford to feed ourselves."

"We'll find a way," I said, clinging to the hope she'd change her mind. I had looked forward to this baby for the past seven months.

"Stacy, with Mom and Dad gone, you can't support me and a baby."

"Yes, I can." I wasn't sure I could, but I'd give it my best shot. "There are a lot of programs out there to help pregnant women. We could apply for every available assistance there is."

"I'm sorry, Stacy. Marcus and I have made up our minds. We're giving the baby up for adoption."

For the next month, I tried in vain to convince Kara that I could raise this baby if she wanted. Kara wouldn't hear of it. Tension grew between us, and within the next year we went our separate ways.

Kara moved in with Marcus. I met my husband, and we moved two hundred miles away to Rhode Island to start a family of our own.

I lost touch with Kara over the years. In fact, it wasn't until twenty years later that I heard a peep about her. We didn't have any family after Mom and Dad passed away from cancer. We only had each other until we disagreed about giving the baby up for adoption.

I received a call from a friend of a friend with whom I went to high school. She was working for the local hospice and thought I should know that my sister was dying. She had lung and brain cancer. Just like our mom and dad.

My husband held me as I cried that day. Why had I let so much time pass without talking to Kara? She only had weeks, if that, to live. I packed a bag and drove through blinding tears for three hours into the early morning until I reached the hospital.

I didn't go in right away. I sat in my car trying to clear my face of the red blotches. I wanted Kara to see I was strong. I didn't want her to see the fear I felt. I wasn't sure she'd want to see me.

You see, the person who called did so without Kara's knowledge. She was breaking confidentiality by calling me, but she thought I needed to know and that Kara needed her sister.

Finally, I worked up the nerve to enter the building. I asked the woman at the information desk where I could find my sister. She gave me the room and advised that she was very sick and on pain medications, so she might not recognize me. I was taken aback. I never dreamed Kara wouldn't recognize me. New fears crept into my mind. What if she didn't? What if it was too late to make amends? I trudged forward, determined to heal old wounds before my sister slipped to the great beyond. I didn't want her dying thinking I didn't love her, because I did.

When I entered her room, I was surprised to find Marcus sleeping in the chair. Kara lay in the bed looking frail. Her once full head of blond hair was now sparse. She looked weak and feeble. This wasn't the vibrant sister I knew twenty years ago.

Slowly, I walked over to the bed and slipped into a chair. I stared at my sister for a good half-hour before I gave into my fears and took her frail hand in mine. She stirred and groaned.

"Kara?" I whispered.

"What are you doing here?" Marcus spat.

"I've come to be with my sister. She needs me right now. You should have called."

"She hasn't needed you for twenty years. You don't get to come in here and play all nice when she's dying."

"Marcus, please," Kara said in a weak voice. "I want her to stay."

We both looked at my sister, who looked so pale. There was pleading in her blue eyes.

"Fine. I'll run home for the girls. I'll be back. Is there anything you want me to bring you?" He gazed upon his wife with such love and admiration. It broke my heart to think they would be separated after all these years together. It also shocked me to hear they had girls. I didn't know they had more children.

"No. Thank you." She kissed the palm of his hand. "I love you, Marcus. Tell the girls Mommy misses them."

He nodded and hurried off.

"How long have you been sick?" I asked her.

"Almost a year." She coughed as she tried to sit up.

I helped her as best I could.

"Kara, I'm so sorry. I wish I could take back the past twenty years, erase them, and start over. I can't believe I let so much time pass without speaking to the only family I have left."

"Me, too. I'm sorry I disappointed you."

The pain cut deep. "You didn't disappoint me, Kara. I was young and naïve. I thought I knew what was best for you, but clearly I didn't."

"We have two beautiful daughters now. They're six and nine. My only regret is I won't be around to watch them grow."

Reality was like a slap in the face. Poor Kara wouldn't get the joy of seeing her girls grow up, get married, and have babies of their own. How could I have been so selfish in thinking I knew what was best for my sister and her baby? Why had I wasted so much time?

"Marcus still loves you as much as he did when you were fourteen."

She smiled. "He's wonderful. He's trying to be strong for me and the girls, but it's killing him not to be able to make this go away."

I shook my head. "I can't believe this is real."

"It is, Stacy. I'd like you to promise me something."

"Anything," I said, and I meant it. I would do anything for my sister.

"Be an aunt to my girls. They're going to need someone strong in their life while Marcus grieves."

"Of course. I'd be honored."

"Thanks, sis."

Kara died three weeks later, and I've kept my promise to her. Every weekend, I meet Marcus and bring the girls to Rhode Island to play with my children. There are times when it's tough on all of us, but we've kept our promise to Kara. And when I watch her girls, it reminds me of us when we were that age. I'm determined not to let any riffs come between them, no matter what.

~Tina O'Reilly

That Did It!

The highlight of my childhood was making my brother laugh so hard that food came out his nose.
~Garrison Keillor

y little brother, Gabriel, had a fear that never made sense to me, but was fun to mess around with from time to time. All I had to do was say, "That did it!" and he would take off running and screaming for our father. He would run up and grab Dad's leg, like little kids do. But as Gabriel got older, the weight of him would take Dad's leg out every now and again. I started thinking of it like bowling!

One time at a cookout, I could see Dad talking with some friends and holding a plate of food in his hand. I realized that Gabriel might just be able to take him down to the ground in front of an actual audience. This was gonna be great! I looked over at Gabriel and yelled, "That did it!" and he took off, full tilt, right into the back of Dad's leg. Dad never saw it coming, but he didn't fall down, much to my disappointment. I can't remember if Gabriel got him to drop his plate, but I bet at the very least a hot dog was sacrificed to the Grass Gods.

For the first few years of this, Dad would yell at Gabriel, and I would get away with it. I always wondered if Dad believed that Gabriel had this compulsion to run into him at full speed for no reason. How do you get a kid help for that?

"Doctor, I think there's something wrong with my son. He keeps running full speed into my leg for no reason. I don't know why, but he won't stop. Do you think he's going insane?"

Then, when Gabriel got old enough to articulate why he was running, I was blamed for it every time, whether it was my "That did it!" that did it or not. So, in a way, I guess it all balanced itself out.

As for scaring Gabriel all the time, I couldn't help myself. It was funny to see him take off, just a streak of blond hair and feet. I guess it also felt great to have that power over another person, even if he was only five.

You see, in my everyday life, I was afraid of everyone, and I got teased and picked on by bullies half my size. So I got a chance to feel intimidating. But I also knew deep down that my teasing of Gabriel had no real lasting effect after he ran away screaming. Dad would yell, and then Gabriel would always come right back and continue what he was doing, mostly because my threat never led to any consequence. I never hit him, or threw him in a room and locked it, or tickled him until he peed himself. Gabriel wasn't afraid of me any other second of the day, and he had no need to be. But if I said, "That did it!" it sent him running like he was late for a free ice-cream giveaway two towns over.

Maybe he was fearful of me because I was ten years older than him. Or it could have been that I was his only brother, and things like that are ingrained in DNA. Also, at fifteen years old, I had been bigger than our father for about two years, making me the biggest person he knew. Scary to a little guy!

Sometimes, my intimidation served a useful purpose. For example, if I wanted to sneak a kiss with my girlfriend, a "That did it!" would free us of an audience in an instant.

My favorite "That did it!" moment happened early one Saturday morning. I had spent the weekend over at Dad's apartment and was watching cartoons in the living room. Gabriel came walking in carefully carrying a bowl of Froot Loops. Every step he took sloshed Froot Loops up to the sides of the bowl, but not going over. Gabriel was happy with himself and proud of the job he was doing, and I'll never forget the look on his face.

Then I thought to myself, "You know, if I said 'That did it!' right here, right now, I bet he'd throw his bowl of cereal into the air and take off running. Sure, I'd get yelled at and have to clean it up, but it'd be worth it."

I know. I'm a bad, bad brother. I don't know why siblings do these things to each other, but we do.

Then, I thought to myself, "If I do this, I can't yell it. It is far too early for yelling, and I think I heard Dad walking around. But would a 'That did it!' work without the yelling?"

"Hey, Gabe…"

"Yeah?" he replied, still concentrating on his task at hand.

"That did it."

Gabriel froze. He looked at me and then back at the bowl. He was still a good five feet from the coffee table, and he tried to move quickly while his little eyes shifted back and forth from brother to bowl. Finally, he reached the table and sat the bowl down, not spilling a drop.

Darn, he made it. Oh, well, I tried.

That's when Gabriel took off!

All you could hear were the sounds of bare feet slapping on hardwood floors and his high-pitched screams echoing in the hallway. "Well, so much for being too early for yelling!" I thought to myself.

That's when I heard a crash and things falling, and my father yelled out a very loud obscenity.

I had no idea what happened, but I was afraid to move from the couch in the living room.

"Ben, I ought to beat the heck out of you!" my father yelled out.

I tried not to laugh as I nervously asked, "What happened?"

"You made him run into me while I was going to the bathroom, and he made me pee all over the walls!"

I slowly walked down the hallway to the bathroom where I found Gabriel on the floor against the open door, frozen in fear. The cup and toothbrushes were knocked into the sink, and my father, all five feet, eight inches of him, was beet red and angry, clad only in a pair of gray sweat pants cut off into shorts.

Apparently, my father was using the bathroom with the door open when Gabriel ran right into the back of his leg, causing him to urinate a line starting from the wall above the back of the toilet and extending over to the right and onto the tiled walls of the bathtub.

I remarked, "Hey, at least you eventually made it into a drain."

By now, Dad was fighting back laughter, but he grabbed me by my shirt and said, "Now, you'll have to clean it up."

Ten minutes later, Gabriel was eating his cereal in the living room, watching cartoons with a smile, as Dad stood in the doorway of the bathroom, supervising my cleaning. Every time I laughed, I was met with a smiling Dad kicking me in the behind.

As I was applying Comet to the bathroom tiles, I thought to myself, "And you thought you would only be cleaning up some Froot Loops. Man, you didn't see this one coming!"

You know what? It was still worth it.

~Ben Kennedy

Our Little Man

Ruin and recovery are both from within.
~Epictetus

My brother Brian's story starts out like that of too many other bored teenagers—a kid with nothing to do but drink beer and party.

I think I realized that my brother had a problem one night when we were having a party at our house while our parents were out of town. Everyone was drinking and dancing, having a good time. I don't drink for my own personal reasons, but the majority of his and my friends did.

At the time, Brian was dating a girl named Melissa who also drank, and I was hanging out with them in our kitchen. As we spoke, I quickly figured out that Melissa and Brian were already pretty drunk. I said something that must have upset him (it is my job as the little sister), and he blew up. My usually sweet and warmhearted brother yelled at me at the top of his lungs. And then he slapped me. I am by no means saying that my brother is an abusive guy. I believe to this day that the alcohol just set something off inside him.

I cried at the time and didn't talk to him for a while. His girl-friend finally made him apologize. He called me his "baby sister," and all was forgotten. At least, it was for him. I don't think I will ever forget the anger in his eyes that night.

•••

"So, I leave June 20th, and I'll be back around July 23rd." Brian and I stood in the back room of the restaurant where we both worked, talking about an event that we all expected but somehow didn't exactly see coming. My nineteen-year-old brother was going to rehab for his alcohol problems. He had finally gone too far one night with his drinking and earned himself his ninth MIP (Minor in Possession). He would be gone thirty days and miss my sixteenth birthday.

"But..." I started.

"Sara, I can't do anything about the date. I know I'll miss your birthday, but I'll call you guys." And then he just left. In his defense, his shift was ending as mine was starting, but his walking away still felt more symbolic than a simple matter of scheduling.

I had always looked up to my brother. In our large family, we had always been the odd ones out, so we always stuck by each other. Being so close in age, we'd grown to have some of the same friends and really appreciated each other's company. But though we'd always been pretty close, there was always the ever-present sense that we are completely different people. Of course, now that we're older and have both matured exponentially, we share an even greater bond.

But I'm getting ahead of myself. Back to rehab.

None of us really thought this rehabilitation center would help my brother in any way. After all, he was a teenager who loved to drink. He didn't possess many goals, awards, or motivations. He would probably just go, be back in a month, and return to his usual ways. At least, that was the pessimistic thought I had until my visit.

It was a Saturday. It was about a four-hour drive during which I had plenty of time to think about what might come of this trip. I considered many outcomes. Sometimes, in my head, my brother was a living zombie in that place, craving alcohol by day, sneaking sips of liquor by night. Other times, he was God's perfect angel, the most positive person in the center, waking up extra early to write poetry about his recovery.

My mom must have seen the anguish in my eyes as we pulled up to the rehabilitation center. She said simply, "You'll be impressed."

She and my dad had visited my brother previously, when I was tied up at work, and said that he was doing well. We still had different expectations. I just wanted Brian to be sane, and they wanted him to be "clean." As we got out of the car, we saw him standing there, smoking a cigarette and laughing with an older man who was also smoking.

"Hey, guys!" he exclaimed, carefully putting his butt in a cigarette disposal. He waved to his friend and strode over to us with assurance. There were no dark black circles under his eyes, nor a halo around his head. He was just Brian. He was my brother, whom I loved more than anyone else, but for the first time, in my eyes, I saw a man. I hadn't quite realized it yet as I sat through his normal day of classes, recreation time, and lunch, but he had changed. He wasn't a teenager who liked to drink anymore; he was a man who had learned that he was a better person.

I wouldn't say my favorite part of our story is about Brian being in rehab, although it might seem that way. I would say that my favorite part has yet to come. It's the next few years. My brother has been out of rehab for five months now and hasn't had a drop of alcohol. That means so much to me, but it also means a lot for him. It means no more partying with the guys who grew to be his drinking partners and, ultimately, his best friends. No more drinking until he can't see straight and no more of the old Brian that the kids of our town had known. He went into rehab a boy and came out a man. Five months later, he's regained some of his old friends and thrown himself into his work. He works full-time at a different restaurant now and is taking classes at our local community college part-time. He's also saving up money to get himself an apartment.

My parents still worry from time to time about whether my brother is staying sober and behaving, but not me. Now I know that if he's out at two o'clock in the morning, he's at his twenty-four-hour gym, not drinking.

I'm not sure exactly how to end the story of my brother because it hasn't quite ended for us. Every day and every night is another chapter in Brian's story of recovery, and I can't begin to predict what will happen next. I guess my ending is... happiness. I know that sounds corny. All of us — my mom, my dad, me, and my brother — are happy for different reasons, but we all share the unique story of how our "little man" became an adult.

~Sara Wessling, age 16

We Buried My Sister Alive

It was nice growing up with someone like you—someone to lean on, someone to count on... someone to tell on!

~Author Unknown

was about five years old at the time. We lived in a big white house with blue trim. It had a wooden front porch with wooden steps. I remember it was June, and the sun's hot rays were beaming down on us. My mother told us kids to go outside and play while she cleaned the house. We were all bored with nothing to do. We didn't know it then, but this was a day we would never forget.

While the rest of us kids were in the front yard playing chase, my oldest brother George and my oldest sister Carrie went off by themselves. After a little while, William and Sharon went to the big oak tree that stood in the front yard. They called us to come over to them. We started talking, and then all of a sudden Sharon collapsed to the ground. We were all in shock because we didn't know what was happening!

As we all stood around her, William leaned down to check to see if she was breathing. He looked up at us and announced that she was dead. We all started to cry. Then William said that we needed to dig a hole and find just the right spot to bury her. We finally decided on the front side of the house, close to the fence where some trees and purple and yellow wildflowers were growing. It took us hours to dig a hole that was big enough to fit her body. After we finished, we looked around for something to put her body in. We finally found an old brown potato sack that smelled like rotten potatoes on the back porch. Her body was limp and heavy as all of us kids lifted her into the sack. Then we laid her in the hole that we had dug. We started covering her up with the soft brown dirt from the hole. We could smell the freshly picked flowers as we laid them on her grave.

We started crying again and were saying a prayer for her when all of a sudden we saw a hand coming out of the dirt like it was trying to climb something! Then we saw a second hand coming out of the ground! We were all scared and started to scream. Sharon came up out of the ground with dirt all over her. She held both arms straight out in front of her, and her eyes looked like they were going to pop out of her head. It seemed like something was wrong with her legs because she was sort of dragging them and moving really slow. She started coming toward us, yelling, "Brains, brains, brains!" We were all running, crying, and screaming.

My older brothers and sisters ran for the big oak tree that stood in front of the house. They could reach the branches better than I could and climbed the tree so that Sharon couldn't reach them. I started screaming for them to help me up, but they refused. Sharon was coming closer to me, so I ran to the house. As I was running, Sharon was on my heels. She seemed to be moving a little faster than she had before. I reached the house and tried the door handle, but it would not open. I started banging on the door, screaming and yelling for my mom. Just as Sharon was about to grab me, my mom opened the door.

Mom tried to calm me down and tell her what was wrong. She looked at Sharon, who had stopped laughing and wouldn't say anything. My mom yelled for the other kids to come in the house, where she sat me down on her lap until I had settled down. The other kids started telling our mom what had happened. William had been in on the prank, but when Sharon came out of the ground, it had scared him so badly that he was the first one up the tree. Our mom told us to go find a switch, so we all went outside and picked one out and carried it back to our mom. She told us to line up for our spankings, which we did.

When my stepdad came home from work, we heard our mom telling him what had happened that day. We could hear them laughing all the way into our bedrooms. After that incident, my mom would tell us, "Go outside and play, but do not bury anyone!"

~Melissa Pannell

Normally Dysfunctional

Our brothers and sisters are there with us
from the dawn of our personal stories to the inevitable dusk.
~Susan Scarf Merrell

"At least you're not my real mother!"

My daughter's words interrupted my tirade. I was fixing dinner, worrying about work, and wondering why my husband was late getting home. Six-year-old Marcy had brought me some small problem. It was one thing too many for my frazzled brain, and I yelled at her across the kitchen island.

But her tear-filled eyes and quiet voice stopped me. "What on earth do you mean?" I asked.

"I know I'm adopted."

I stared. Was she in that phase already? For years as a child, I had wanted to be adopted, painfully embarrassed by my not-so-cool mother and father. Surely my real parents were out there, I thought, ready to sweep me away to a world where I would be pretty and popular. If only I could find them. But my desire for different parents hadn't surfaced until I was a preteen. At six, I hadn't worried about where I fit into the world.

And my yearning to be adopted hadn't lasted long. Once I could calculate that I was born nine months and ten days after my parents were married, and knew the significance of that timing, my dreams were dashed. I couldn't be adopted. No one in their right mind would adopt a kid that soon after marriage, particularly not a good Catholic couple, who were far more likely to have been surprised by their quick fertility than to have sought to raise someone else's child.

But that evening Marcy was serious. She thought she was adopted. I needed to set her straight.

"Marcy," I said, "I was there when you were born. Trust me, you weren't adopted. I'd know. Besides, you know people always say we look alike." Back then, she did look like me.

Marcy looked dubious. But she didn't say anything more. I never heard her mention her adopted status again, and I forgot about this incident for years.

Marcy and her older brother Jamie grew into young adults. We had our ups and downs. Some undisclosed speeding tickets, some underage drinking. But they both got good grades and worked hard most of the time. Jamie did well in forensics, and Marcy in athletics. Both could hold their own in dinner-table discussions. By the time they graduated from high school, they were good company.

After they left for college, my husband and I didn't see much of them because they went to school far away. But we enjoyed them when they returned home on breaks, which came less and less frequently.

One holiday when they were both home, the kids and I were chatting. The conversation turned to how they had gotten along as children. I suspected there had been more sibling rivalry between them than they had disclosed when they were younger. They confirmed my suspicions.

"You know, Mom," Marcy said, "Jamie convinced me I was adopted when I was a kid."

"What?" I exclaimed.

"Yep. He said you and Dad didn't want me to know until I was older, so I wasn't supposed to say anything to you."

"You believed him?" I asked, incredulous.

"For two or three years."

I sat in shocked horror. My baby had thought she was adopted?

And then I remembered the incident when she was six.

"How could you have done that?" I asked Jamie. "Why were you so cruel?"

He just shrugged and smiled sheepishly.

We talked some more about the awful things that family members do to each other. They mentioned friends, some of whom had serious problems with substance abuse or eating disorders, whose parents had gone through nasty divorces, or who were unable to cope with the stresses of school and peer pressure.

"I've always been grateful our family was just normally dysfunctional," Marcy said. "We may have done mean things sometimes, but we generally liked each other."

Normally dysfunctional. I raised my kids in a normally dysfunctional family. I still think that's the best compliment I've ever received as a mother.

~Theresa Hupp

Bridezilla

A wedding is just like a funeral
except that you get to smell your own flowers.
~Grace Hansen

My sister is engaged. If you don't understand how horrifying that sentence is, you've never met my sister. I swear, the minute the ring found its new home on her finger she turned from nice sister to evil Bridezilla.

I'm not making this up. And yes, after she reads this I will probably be murdered by some sort of wedding accessory, like a cake knife engraved with the lucky couple's initials. That's okay. Makes it easier for the CSI team to close in on her. Look, the woman is crazy. Her wedding isn't for a year, but already she's evil. Pure, unadulterated, Bridezilla evil.

It started with the dresses. Seriously, the dang ring wasn't on her finger two seconds and she was already at the bridal shop picking the outfits for the Big Day. For her this means that she goes to a shop and tries on every single dress there, takes a cell phone picture of it and then e-mails it to everyone on her contact list. Every time my cell phone tells me I have a new photo, I want to crawl inside a closet and scream.

Once she finishes trying on the dresses in one shop, she moves on to another. It's a wonder she finds time to work or spend time with the groom-to-be. Fortunately, she called the other night with the earthshaking news that she finally narrowed her search to three dresses. One was simple and nice; the second was a bit fancier and, frankly, needed more bosom than my sister can provide on her own; and the third, well, the third was what is referred to in the wedding biz as "traditional with a full skirt." In English, that means "poofy as heck in case you're bloated on your Big Day."

Unfortunately, the picking of the bridal gown means she's moved on to selecting the dreaded bridesmaids' dresses. Without elaborating on her choice, let's just say that bosom isn't a big deal in our family. So the dress requires some, er, padding. And if that weren't humiliating enough, the dress is in a color called "truffle." Yeah, I didn't know what color that was in the real world either. Turns out truffle in bridal-speak is actually brown. We're going to look like Puffy Marshmallow Girl and the Four Doo-Doos.

And let's not even get into the ugly shoes she wants dyed to match our doo-doo dresses.

Of course, it doesn't end with the clothing choices. Over the past week, I've received seventeen phone calls pertaining to music. For Pete's sake, who cares? Give out free champagne and everyone will do the Macarena to James Blunt. But the music questions don't end there. There's the whole question of which DJ? Live band? iPod plugged into a speaker? Drunken best man and a karaoke machine? The choices are endless.

But even the phone calls don't compare to the 152 e-mails with links to possible wedding locations. Have I mentioned my sister lives in Florida, a state I've been to a grand total of one time? The only places I know are Gator World, the Everglades and some wild animal park. All those places sound good to me, but I think even the gators at Gator World would run and hide from this Bridezilla.

And then there are the daily e-mails with attachments of centerpiece photos. After a while, all the flowers look the same. But when I said that to Bridezilla, she shrieked at me. Apparently, one had a red rose instead of a white rose in the center. How silly of me to have missed that fine detail.

So far, I've only had one e-mail regarding the food, which is fine. Everyone knows the wedding food will stink anyway, so who cares what we are having? Just bring on that free champagne and the antacids, and everything will be just ducky.

Of course, I can say none of this to my sister. My sister believes that she is not only Queen for the Big Day; she is, indeed, Queen of the Entire Year Leading Up to the Big Day. She also believes that no conversation with her is complete without at least 400 mentions of the wedding and/or the tremendous amount of pressure she is under to make it perfect.

I think I'm just going to forward her an e-mail with a Vegas wedding chapel link in it. Maybe Bridezilla will get the hint. Or maybe I should get used to looking like doo-doo.

~Laurie Sontag

Chapter
11

Parents and Kids

Love is the chain whereby to bind a child to its parents.

~Abraham Lincoln

Always an Adventure

*Children are a great comfort in your old age—
and they help you reach it faster, too.*
~Lionel Kauffman

Just when I thought it was safe to resume a normal life, one of my kids phones with the joyous news: "I'm going back to school for a PhD."

While this sounds like a perfectly reasonable idea—something that should elicit a round of applause—my immediate reaction is a feeling of utter terror and doom. The only question that goes through my mind as she's waxing eloquent over her plans is: Who's going to pay for it? I control myself, however, and immediately reply:

"A PhD... how wonderful!"

I turn to my husband, who is snoring away beside me, and poke him in the ribs. "Wake up, darling," I demand. "Guess who is on the phone and wants to get a PhD? Your daughter!"

"A PhD? At one o'clock in the morning?" comes the tired response.

"Your father is overjoyed," I tell her. "Here, he wants to talk to you."

I hand him the phone. In a groggy voice, he asks, "What's this about a PhD?"

Silence.

"Uh-huh."

Silence.

"Uh-huh."

Silence.

"We'll discuss it in the morning."

"What did she say?" I ask.

"She said she wants to get a PhD."

"A PhD in what?"

"I forgot to ask her," he says. "I was too busy worrying how much it was going to cost us."

"It's probably a PhD in psychology. She likes to analyze everybody. PhDs make a lot of money."

"She'd better make a lot of money because by the time we're through paying her tuition at another fancy grad school, we'll be broke and out on the street eating baked beans and sleeping in a cardboard box."

"Beans have lots of protein," I say.

The following night, our son-the-lawyer calls to say he's thinking of giving up the law, and although he's making a bundle, it's not turning out to be the challenge he had hoped it would be.

"I've decided to move to a farm in Vermont," he informs us, "to commune with nature and get my hands in the soil."

"He has a Thoreau complex," I say. "He wants to live off the land."

My husband grabs the phone. "We didn't send you to law school to get your hands dirty."

"I'm a lawyer, Dad," he reminds him. "How much dirtier can I get?"

"How can you live on a farm?" I ask. "You have a Manhattan apartment. You carry a briefcase. You own a Rolex watch."

"I'd rather drive a tractor," he says. "I'd rather spend my time in a pig sty than a West Side apartment."

"Your apartment is a pig sty," I remind him.

When the third child phones, she is polite enough to ask, "Did I wake you guys up?"

"Wake us up? Of course not. Dad and I are always up at 2:00 A.M. watching reruns of *The Dating Game*."

"Good, because I'm so excited I can hardly stand it. I just had to tell someone."

"What is it, sweetheart?" I rub my eyes from a deep sleep.

"I just met HIM."

"Who is HIM?"

"Mr. Possibility, that's who. He has all the right attributes except for one teeny flaw."

I nudge my husband. "Wake up this instant. Guess who finally met a guy with a teeny flaw."

"Your father wants to know about his flaw."

"He's unemployed. But he has potential. He's an archaeologist. He goes on digs. Next month we're going to Peru to look for old bones."

"They're looking for bones," I scream at my husband.

"What is he... an orthopedist?"

"No, an unemployed archaeologist."

"I was wondering if you and Dad could lend me some money for our plane trip to Lima."

"She wants money to dig," I translate.

"I'll give her money to dig!" he says. "Tell her to call her brother on the farm. Maybe he can lend her a spade."

We thought things were under control until our son-the-investment banker called to tell us he wasn't coming home for the weekend as planned because he was going bungee jumping. This news, like the rest, was presented to us at an ungodly hour of the night. That way our kids figure we'll be too tired to really comprehend what they're saying.

"What is it now?" my husband asks when I pick up the phone.

"It's your son."

"My son the farmer or my son the non-conformist banker?"

"It's David. He can't be with us this weekend because he's going bungee jumping."

"How much is that little diversion going to cost me?"

"What do you mean how much? Your son is in a very precarious position. He's putting his life on the line. Bungee jumping is extremely dangerous."

"How much?" he asks.

"It won't cost you a penny he says."

"Good," my husband says, pulling the covers over his head. "Let him jump!"

~Judith Marks-White

The Perfect Mom for Cooper

Happiness is life served up with a scoop of acceptance, a topping of tolerance
and sprinkles of hope, although chocolate sprinkles also work.
~Robert Brault

*J*slumped in the doctor's office chair. "Your son exhibits the symptoms of Asperger's syndrome," the doctor said. "It's a form of autism." While she danced around the words, careful only to say he had the symptoms, I tried to remember what I had read about this confusing, multi-faceted syndrome. Did kids with Asperger's function at a high level, or were they the children who rocked silently in corners? I searched my memory while she casually knocked my world off its axis. "Cooper is very highly functioning," the doctor told me as she picked hairs off her sleeve. I wanted to scream and shake her, but I sat and said nothing.

Questions raced through my mind. Does she mean that Coop will never be normal? What is normal anyway? Why do I have a child with autism? Why would God give me this child when I was clearly not ready for him?

For months, we had suspected something was wrong with Cooper, so we started him in speech and occupational therapy. Twice a week for seven weeks, I piled all four kids in the hot van for the forty-five-mile trip to the therapist. Tired, frustrated, and overwhelmed, I now faced the ugly truth.

Will Cooper ever want to play with the neighborhood kids? Will Cooper ever have a friend when he can't reach out? How will he communicate when his little world is black and white and the English language is shaded gray?

It wasn't fair. I didn't ask for four children, including a set of twins, but I'd rolled with the punches and kept smiling. I loved them, watched over them, and prayed for them. All I wanted was normal children.

But Cooper had Asperger's syndrome along with developmental delays. There was no cure, no known cause. Over the next few weeks, I struggled to control my emotions. As a mother, I felt disheartened. As a follower of God, I felt angry. Why would God do this to me? To my family. To my child. Could someone please tell me how God was taking care of this mother of four? Was I some cosmic joke to Him?

All of my children would be affected by Cooper's problem. Was the situation fair to them or to Cooper? Stumbling, swearing, and just about cursing God, I found no answers and put away my Bible in disgust.

A few weeks later, the phone rang. "God put it on my heart to call you," my sister Dawn said. She asked how I felt, and I opened the vault. I cried and yelled and cried some more. When I was spent and exhausted, Dawn quieted my heart. "God knows you are angry, and this is not about you."

"What do you mean this isn't about me?" I said. "This has everything to do with me and how Cooper's autism affects my family. I have to change our meals, our schedules, and everything about our daily lives. How in the world is this not about me?"

Dawn answered with God's truth. "This is about God giving Cooper the perfect mom for him," she said with love. "God knows you will stand up for Coop and fight for him. You'll care for him, and Cooper will become the best Cooper possible because of you." She paused and added, "You are the perfect mom for Cooper."

Dawn was right. At that moment, I felt God's undeserved grace wash over me, filling me with strength. I couldn't focus on me; I had to focus on Cooper. I would be his protector, the one who let him explore and expand. I would be his advocate in countless school meetings and doctor appointments. When I didn't have the strength to go on, I would open my Bible and pray. I'm not a perfect mom and never will be, but I could be a pretty good mom for all my kids, especially Coop.

I still struggle with my son's autism. I battle to accept who Cooper is and what he can do without limiting or overprotecting him. I cry when I make Cooper study his spelling words one more time because he spells words according to their sounds rather than the dictionary. I rejoice when he gets 100 percent on the same test he took the previous week. If a new treatment doesn't work, I try something else. I can never cure Cooper, but I help him start the day calmer and handle situations differently. My son is funny and wonderful, and I laugh at all the "Cooperisms" that come from his mouth.

You see, motherhood isn't about me. It's about God giving a mother to four wonderful children, including one who stands out and demands a little more work. I am God's gift to Cooper, the perfect mom for a unique child. And he is God's gift to me.

~Kay Klebba

The Classics

One man's trash is another man's treasure.
~English Proverb

As a mother, I've learned that having grown sons often demands long suffering. Their toys aren't picked up as easily as their Matchbox cars once were. Take Ryan's motorcycle, for instance. Though he hadn't ridden it in years, the bike held a place of honor in the blackberry bushes. "I'm gonna restore it someday, Mom. I can't get rid of it!" My youngest child knew he could usually wrap me around his little finger. As a teen, he'd once accused me of child abuse for buying fat-free ice cream. When he drove off to college in a Toyota pick-up, he abandoned his first love—a 1977 Camaro—next to his brother's red 1967 Firebird and a brown 1979 Datsun with no windows. Next to the cars, a sixteen-foot boat and trailer languished in the sun.

Home for summer break, Ryan was in the backyard tenderly spreading gobs of Bondo over the rust spots on his Camaro. "Listen, Ryan," I said lightly, "since you drive the truck now, why not sell the Camaro?"

"Sell the Camaro?!" Ryan gasped as if I'd asked him to cut off his foot. His expression of sheer terror let me know that I'd have to tread carefully. He continued, "When I get it all fixed up, it will be worth a lot more than I paid for it. It'll be a classic someday!"

"I can hardly wait," I muttered before returning to the house to consider my next tactics.

Number-one son, Shawn, the owner of the Firebird and Datsun, came over to work on a marine engine. I found him under the sundeck, muscles rippling as he hoisted an outboard motor into a barrel of fresh water. I sauntered over: "Say, Shawn, have you considered selling that Firebird? You don't drive it anymore." Shawn wiped grimy hands on his jeans. His blue eyes stared as though I'd said something ridiculous. "Mom, that car has sentimental value. I bought that in the Navy, remember? It took me ages to pay that thing off. Besides, it's almost a classic!"

"Well, what about the Datsun?" I persisted.

"Aw, Mom, nobody will buy that thing the way it is. New windows will cost more than it's worth."

I sighed and went back in the house. I recalled the day that Shawn parked the Datsun at the top of the road with a "For Sale" sign. In the middle of the night, vandals broke out all the windows. The next day, Shawn sadly drove it down the driveway and parked it next to his Firebird.

My husband, Ted, came up from the basement. "Carol, have you seen my torque wrench?"

"I wouldn't know a torque wrench if I stumbled over one. Try the backyard."

"Those guys never put anything away," he mumbled.

"Ted, our backyard looks like a junkyard," I said, seizing the opportunity to complain.

"What's wrong with it?"

"It's all those cars! Shawn's Firebird, the Datsun, that junky boat and trailer nobody uses, and Ryan's Camaro and truck."

"There's nothing wrong with Ryan's truck."

"That's not the point! With our cars, and all their junkers, our place looks like a used car lot in a bad part of town! This is a nice neighborhood, or at least it used to be!"

"I would like to get rid of that Datsun," Ted admitted. "It's a shame about those windows."

As the summer progressed, I grew to hate those cars. I prayed that God would spur my boys to car-selling action, or maybe consume the cars in a freak fireball. Everyone who entered the yard was asked the same question: "Do you know anyone who wants an old Datsun with no windows?" No one jumped at my offer.

One day, I got tough. "Shawn, it's almost wintertime. You'd better do something about that Datsun, and soon!"

"Okay, Mom, I promise I'll do something tomorrow."

When I came home from work the next day, the Datsun was draped with blue tarps. "Aughhhhhhhhhh!"

By spring, the tarps had blown off, and mushrooms were sprouting in the back seat. "Please, Lord," I prayed. "Send someone to take this wreck away."

Meanwhile, Ted was asked to consider running for president of the small mission congregation we attended. He prayed about the matter, but heard nothing. Pastor Tim said he needed an answer by the following Sunday. All week, Ted wrestled with his decision. By Saturday afternoon, he was still undecided. "You'd better let Pastor Tim know your answer pretty soon," I said.

Ted sighed. "I just don't know."

"Hey, why don't we put out a fleece?" I suggested.

Ted frowned. "What kind of a fleece?"

"You know, something so out of the ordinary that if it happens, you'll know for sure that you're supposed to serve as president. Hey, I've got an idea. Let's tell God that if somebody walks down our driveway tonight and buys that old Datsun, then you'll know."

Ted laughed. "I guess we're safe on that one!"

"I'm serious. Let's pray."

About 9:30 that evening, Ted said, "I'd better call the pastor. I hate to let him down, but…"

Just then, the doorbell rang. Our teenage neighbor, Alex, and a friend of his greeted us. "Hi, Mrs. Genengels." He nodded politely. "Mr. Genengels."

"Hi, Alex, what's up?"

"Well, my friend here was wondering if you'd take fifty bucks for that Datsun."

We doubled over.

"What's so funny?" Alex asked.

"Are you sure you want that car?" Ted said.

His friend answered, "Yeah, it's perfect for the demolition derby. I've had my eye on it for awhile."

"You've got yourself a deal," Ted said before excusing himself. "I have to go call someone."

Ted served as congregational president for two years. Eventually, all the "classics" found new homes, and we got our yard back. Through it all, I've discovered that being the mother of grown sons has its own special challenges, but I wouldn't have it any other way.

~Carol Genengels

I Will Always Be Your Son

Everyone is kneaded out of the same dough but not baked in the same oven.
~Yiddish Proverb

Several years ago, when my husband and I married and blended our families, we were suddenly a stepfamily with thirteen children. The year we married, we had five weddings—ours and four of our children's—and we already had more than a dozen grandchildren. The process of blending families can present a myriad of challenges that increase exponentially with the number of people involved, and for us, it was a circus, to say the least.

When we married, my husband was still deeply grieving the death of his first wife, and I faced ten stepchildren who had recently lost their mother. My husband and I knew that we faced some challenges, but we weren't prepared for the tsunami that was to hit our family, threatening its very foundation. It broke our hearts when our youngest son decided to leave our home before he graduated from high school. We are so thankful for loving friends who provided him refuge during those difficult times.

We often found ourselves locked in conflict with our children. We knew that if we pulled together instead of apart, and prayerfully asked for God's help, we could find solutions to our problems.

Have you ever tried to pray when you were angry with someone?

I found that when I prayed, my prayers were mostly about asking God to fix everyone else. But it just didn't work, and I felt devoid of God's spirit. It was very scary and lonely.

Sometimes taking offense and seeking revenge feels like the right thing to do when you're in the thick of things with someone. It was that way for us. Our natural response to hurtful comments and unkind behavior was to defend ourselves with more hurtful comments and unkind behavior. But we quickly learned the destructive power of those "natural" responses when we saw our conflicts becoming deeper and longer-lasting. We needed to find another way to deal with our differences if we hoped to keep our family together.

Being devout Christians, we were drawn to the scriptures to find answers to our conflicts. Over and over again, we were reminded of the necessity to "love thy neighbor as thyself," and to "love thine enemy; pray for them who despitefully use you and persecute you."

Those words pierced my heart. But how many of us, when we are in deep conflict, have the self-control to step back and try to see our enemy as a friend? I realized that that is exactly what I had to do. So, once again, I turned to the Lord for help.

My prayers began to change, and I began asking for help in softening my own heart. As I drew up enough courage to look within myself instead of blaming my stepchildren, I discovered much that didn't belong there. I discovered that the way I was responding to things they were doing was only making matters worse. So I began thinking about practicing acts of kindness toward them instead of plotting revenge.

One day, I knew that my stepson, who was away at college, was having his wisdom teeth pulled. I called a local grocery store in his neighborhood and arranged for them to deliver him some cartons of his favorite ice cream and boxes of Popsicles. I had them enclose a note saying I hoped he would feel better soon and told him I loved him and was thinking about him. It was signed "From Your Wicked Stepmother." That was the last thing he expected from me, but it made an impression on him. More importantly, it changed something in me.

Another time, soon after that, my husband and I showed up on my stepdaughter's doorstep early one Saturday morning with tools to wallpaper her two-year-old triplets' bedroom. She seemed to be having the hardest time of all dealing with the death of her mother, and my heart ached to be able to comfort her in some way.

Things had been especially volatile between us for a long time, and showing up to redecorate her children's room was the last thing she expected from us. I had hoped that our service to her would cause a change in her attitude toward us, but I never expected the profound change that occurred in my own attitude toward her.

As I worked in her home that day, I began to feel what it must be like for her with three little toddlers, while homeschooling her other three children. I realized how overwhelming and exhausting it must be for her to do everything she had to do to care for them. As I began to see her in a new way, all the bad feelings evaporated, and I was filled with love and a deep respect for her.

An amazing thing happened as I changed my way of responding to my stepchildren. Even though I hoped that the acts of kindness I was showing them would soften their hearts, I soon discovered that I was the one who was changing. Their behavior soon lost its sting, and I was able to see past their rejection and look into their hurting hearts instead. Then I set about trying to find ways to heal their hurt. As I did so, I could feel the healing in my own heart.

That is when I learned the greatest lesson about love: Love is a decision before it is a feeling. Once I decided to truly "love" my stepchildren, by overlooking the hurtful things they were doing and by looking into their hearts, I became healed. As we found the courage to do what we already knew to do, the miracle happened, and our broken hearts and broken relationships began to mend.

I received a letter from my stepson shortly before he returned from his mission for our church — the one who couldn't live at home and had to move out because of the unresolved issues between us — the one I had prayed over for five years, and whom I struggled in every way to gain as a friend. He wrote:

I just wanted to take a moment to thank you for all the support you have given me on my mission. I honestly have no bad feelings from what has happened between us. You have been my greatest support on this mission, and a lot of my enthusiasm came from knowing that you were always there, being such an incredible help.

I may have told you this before, maybe not, but one time, shortly after my mother died, I was sitting in a [youth meeting] and the speaker said, "The person who will write you the most faithfully on your mission is your mother." I knew that this was not the case with me because my mother was quite beyond the realm of writing to a missionary. I figured communication on my mission would probably be pretty slack and that I would miss my mother fiercely. In my notes I still have written in saddened black pen, "Not I, said the cat!"

But the speaker was quite correct. You get the award! You have indeed written me the most faithfully throughout my mission. Thank you forever for your support. Although you may not be my mother, I will always be your son.

All thirteen of our children are now married and raising their own families. Our ranks have grown from twelve to forty grandchildren, with more on the way. Though there are still some rough edges that come up from time to time, we are getting better at working through them to the love on the other side.

~Ramona Watson

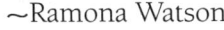

Door Man

Never lend your car to anyone to whom you have given birth.
~Erma Bombeck

All my mom could do was smile; all I could do was stare at the door.

It all started a couple of months earlier as an innocent drive to the local bowling alley with some friends in our family minivan. I had had my license for about six months, so my parents were comfortable letting me drive our family's minivan with three friends and my boyfriend to go bowling.

After bowling, while waiting in the bowling alley parking lot for our friend, my boyfriend and I started to argue. The ensuing fight turned into a teenage melodrama fit for TV. *Beverly Hills 90210* was a comedy in comparison. I yelled at him to get out of the van and to find his own ride home. He refused to get out and continued to fight with me.

I have a bad temper, but I have since learned to control how I deal with my anger. But that night, full of teenage hormones, rage and a lead foot, I threw the van in reverse and slammed on the gas. My thought was that I could scare my boyfriend into exiting the vehicle in fear for his life. As an added guarantee to his flight from the passenger seat, I started to swerve.

I must say, I had seen that light post in the middle of the parking lot many times. I even drove around it that very night upon arrival at the bowling alley. But in my teenage tantrum, I was not paying attention to that trusty old light post behind the van as I sped backward, swerving as I went.

I think it was the post that actually stopped the van, not my delayed reaction to hit the brake when I heard the horrible crunch of metal. I jumped out of the van and ran to the passenger side of the van. That is where my life as I knew it had ended. How could one little light post do so much damage? That was the first thought that whipped through my mind. The next thought was that my parents were going to kill me.

As I looked at the damage and started to cry and scream, "I'm dead, I'm dead," my friends came running out of the bowling alley, and my boyfriend crawled out of the window of the passenger door. Starting at the passenger front door handle all the way back to the taillight, the once shiny paint was now deeply scratched, and the metal underneath was crunched and dented inward. The sliding door was completely caved in, and neither it nor the front passenger door could be opened.

I ran into the bowling alley and called my parents. I bawled on the phone that I had backed the van into a light post. Their first question was, "Are you okay? Can you drive home?" I answered yes. They remained calm and said to come home right away so they could survey the damage for themselves.

I cried all the way home. When I came into the house, they were waiting in the living room. I sat down and proceeded to tell them what had happened. However, I neglected to tell them that instead of just backing into the post, as they thought, I had in fact almost sheered off the entire right side of the van. My dad was a little upset but said that accidents happen, and he and my mother ventured out to the van to assess the damage.

As they walked up to the back of the van, they were bewildered by my crying hysterics on the phone and profuse apologies in our living room. They could only see a little scratch on the taillight. For some reason, though, my father followed that little scratch to its origins on the right side of the van.

From my vantage point in the house a hundred feet away, I could see my father's face go from confusion, to shock, to a festive shade of Christmas red as he walked to the right side of what used to be his immaculately cared-for vehicle. My mother just stood beside him in shock. Then my dad turned around and headed for house at a pace that my mother struggled to keep up with.

After the lengthy scolding and threats, I was to pay for some of the damage and grounded from using the van for anything but errands for my parents for two months.

One glorious sunny day in July, two months after my "accident," my family and I pulled up to our hotel after a long seven-hour drive to my fastball tournament venue. My dad got out and came around the passenger side to unload the luggage and equipment, and I got out of my teammate's parents' car to help my dad unload. As I stood waiting, he opened the recently fixed, freshly painted sliding van door, which suddenly fell to the ground as he pulled back on the handle. My father was still holding the handle as the door hit the ground with a crunch that sounded eerily like what a van sounds like when it hits a light post.

As my dad looked up at me, memories of the recent damage that he had just repaired came flooding back at the same speed as the blood rushing to his face. All I could do was stare at the door and think, "How ironic."

My mother, who had watched this whole thing unfold, sat back and smiled, struggling to keep from laughing lest she send my dad over the edge. She, who had witnessed the carnage my father had inflicted on many a vehicle they owned, knew that this was just another way that my father and I were very much alike.

~Tara Schellenberg

Flower Cower

Family is just accident.... They don't mean to get on your nerves.
They don't even mean to be your family; they just are.
~Marsha Norman

My sister and mother fight like they will live forever. This is because they are the same person, split only by cells and decades. They work together at my mom's flower shop, Enchanted Florist. It's a 10x10 room, painted blaring neon pink and green, with old stems and leaves covering the floor. Receipts and bills are stuck to the walls with push pins, and the cash register was bought used from the Salvation Army. Customers are surprised to see my mother chomping down on a sandwich in the middle of their wedding consultations. My sister is often barefoot. The air is clouded with flower spray paint, and the plumbing rarely works. Any workplace is subject to hormonal cat fights or the occasional co-worker spat. But when a mother and daughter are the only two employees, things can get downright terrifying.

These tear-streaked, screaming estrogen fests usually have no impact on my own life, unless I have previously announced a visit. On these special occasions, I get a horror-film phone call from Haley. She cries and spits out violent threats of matricide while simultaneously telling me to go find out if she's been fired. If there's one thing my sister is good at, it's being unemployed. Before she started working at the shop, she was fired by an astonishing repertoire of bosses. Our mom is the only one to keep her on long enough to earn healthcare benefits, if she provided any.

When I arrive at the shop, I find my mom hacking the stems off roses. She immediately rolls her eyes and wields the shearing knife madly, motioning for me to come in. Her left hand is covered in metallic gold, and her right, a dark shade of magenta. Her face is contorted with anger and sparkling from the flecks of embedded glitter. To a passerby, she'd look as if she's just murdered an eighties hair band.

"YOUR sister is working on my last nerve!"

She always emphasizes "YOUR sister," as if I was the one to bring her into my mom's life. Like I had come home from school one day with this little hobo child and begged for her to be taken in. The fault lies with me.

"Mom, Haley wants to know if she's fired...."

"I haven't decided yet."

"Okay... that's not exactly HR..."

"Don't you start with your wordy, smart-aleck words! YOUR sister is ungrateful, and I just can't handle her anymore. I'm done!"

She's angry at me because she knows I'm secretly satisfied. I once explained that this employee/boss relationship would be detrimental, but both parties decided I was being crazy and irrational. My silent "I told you so" is on constant repeat, but I will never say this aloud to either of them. They are equally horrifying.

"Mom, just call her. She's really sad and..."

"The phone works BOTH ways, you know!"

"Okay, yeah, but I think you're both just so... so similar that it's hard for her to..."

"HOW are we similar? She's crazy! She has NO consideration for other people."

"But you're both crazy. Crazy in a good way..."

"That's RIDICULOUS. I'm the sanest person in this world!"

"Mom, just saying THAT is crazy..."

This is where her eyes become wide, almost inhuman, giving her that "renegade Muppet" look. I know that all rage will now be deflected to me. I quickly turn around and put my hands up in the air, attempting an apology and shielding my eyes from thrown thorns. I walk out the door before the lecture starts with "You think you're better than everybody else!"

Immediately afterward, she will call up my sister. Their prior, career-changing argument will be null and void. Mom will manipulate my actions until you'd think I had just committed a hate crime, and Haley will completely agree.

"Well, YOUR sister just told me I was crazy."

"OH, I KNOW! You should have heard her on the phone..."

I stay tucked away on the other side of town for about a week. Afterward, I reemerge, and my family is once again a happy and gainfully employed unit. I walk into the shop to find them singing Frank Sinatra songs and laughing about some poor woman's unfortunate eyebrows. The room smells of lilacs and fried chicken, both of which are strewn about the countertop.

A part of me is jealous that I can't be more involved. I'm only the unfortunate mediator to our little lives. My own career choice has been a corporate jungle gym. I wear suits and get up hours beforehand to do my makeup and hair. While Haley and Mom are busy creating cherished arrangements, I prepare Powerpoints that are disregarded fifteen minutes after presented. If I get fired, there are no second chances. I would pack up my non-sentimental work belongings, and security would escort me out.

I will never work with my mother or share intimacies with my sister on a daily basis. Our phone conversations consist of "seeing how you're doing," instead of poking fun at ugly brides with disastrous color schemes. However, just knowing the shop exists gives me a sense of accomplishment. I know that my superiority complex keeps me on the outskirts, but it's also what keeps me coming back. I need to know that all is well in their world before I can sit back comfortably in my own.

~Courtney Rae Wick

A Nice Italian Boy

Any intelligent woman who reads the marriage contract,
and then goes into it, deserves all the consequences.
~Isadora Duncan

My Italian mother ignored the fact that I was a half-breed. I looked Italian so, as far as she was concerned, I was Italian. My German father's genes didn't exist. I was her immaculate conception, another of the many miracles in her life. If the electric bill was lower, it was a miracle. If it stopped raining when she went outside, it was a miracle.

In accordance with the unwritten rules of the culture, a good Italian girl married a nice Italian boy — out of respect for the family. Some marriages were prearranged at birth, but the prospective bride and groom never knew. Their parents worked like secret agents to make sure that the couple fell in love.

When the chosen girl walked into a room, the boy's father nudged him, raised his eyebrows and smiled. Siblings were encouraged to tease their brother and were spared from bodily harm when possible. The mothers of the destined couple arranged for them to attend the same social events, sit within sight of each other in church, and take the same bus.

Some families did not embrace the custom of arranged marriages, but ventured into matchmaking after watching their son or daughter blow out sixteen candles. My mother had a potential Italian husband in mind for me before the smoke cleared.

Angie—a girl I only knew to say "hi" to in passing at school—invited me to a "pajama party," now known as an "overnight." I was elated. I should have been suspicious.

My mother bought a new pair of pajamas for me to wear "to make a good first impression." I wasn't sure who I was supposed to impress since all the girls at the party were in my P.E. class, and we had seen each other in our underwear.

When the boy-talk started, Angie passed around a photo of her boyfriend Frankie. The general consensus amidst squeals and sighs was "He's cute!" She casually mentioned that he had an older brother.

I'm still not sure how it happened, but Angie and Frankie and Frankie's older brother, Tony, and I went on a double date. It was a smooth set-up. More double dates followed, and soon Angie and I were calling each other regularly to plan the next Saturday night date.

In a matter of weeks, I had a best friend, a boyfriend, and a happy mother who hummed incessantly, smiled when she looked at me, and pinched my cheeks a lot.

I enjoyed dating Tony, but I wasn't in love with him. Unlike many of my peers, I was not interested in getting married and having children. I wanted to have fun. Tony was two years older than me and had a different agenda.

We had been double dating for a few months by the time the holiday season arrived. My mother was the personification of holiday spirit and arranged a get-together of her Sicilian clan and a few friends. "I want everything to be perfect," she said, and I cringed, knowing what that meant.

We spent two days cleaning and polishing everything in the house, and one entire day cooking. My mother was either smiling like Mona Lisa or singing duets with Dean Martin recordings.

I had a twinge of suspicion when she suggested I invite Angie and Frankie and Tony. "So you will have someone your own age here, too," she said. On previous social occasions when I complained, "There won't be anyone my age there," she was unsympathetic. Her standard response was, "So, act younger or older, and you'll fit in."

Then came the dreaded shopping trip for "something nice to wear for the holiday," which really meant, "I will choose a dress, and you will wear it." We walked into the dress shop, and I went straight to the rack of dresses with Peter Pan collars and gathered skirts and waited. She called to me from another rack.

"What do you think of this one?" I shuffled toward the rack assuming the only thing less figure-flattering she could have found was a nun's habit.

I blinked and stared at the scoop-necked, red velveteen dress with the wide belt and straight skirt. I tried it on and waited for her to change her mind. She made small circles with her hand and said, "Turn, turn," and then, "Stand up straight." I completed the circle and looked up to see her smiling and coming toward me with open arms.

"Oh, my little girl is all grown up," she said and wiped a tear from the corner of her eye.

It was one of those surreal moments. Of course, I wanted her to recognize that I was no longer a child, but the sudden leap to "all grown up" left me feeling like I had missed something, like eating an Oreo cookie that had no cream in the middle.

When I came down the stairs in my new dress on the night of the party, my father looked at me and then quickly at my mother and said, "How much?" She waved him off, but he followed her into the kitchen repeating his question until she answered. He lapsed into German. I heard a few familiar words like *dummkopf* as he pounded his fist on the table.

We worked as a team when the guests arrived. My mother greeted people at the door like the Queen of Christmas, and my father stood by like her trusted servant. He took their coats and handed them to me. I piled them on my parents' bed, and the dog curled up on top of them. I figured she deserved the honor since she had endured being bathed, brushed and polished in the pre-party cleaning marathon.

Angela and Frankie came in a few minutes before Tony arrived with his parents. My mother greeted them like old friends, but I had never seen them at our house or heard her mention Isabella and Geronimo. I would have remembered hearing the names of the Queen of Spain and an Indian chief.

While my mother embraced them and kissed their cheeks, I looked at my father, who shrugged and shook his head. But since it wasn't unusual for my mother to cram as many Italians as she could into our house for a Christmas party—her version of the fraternity phone booth stunt—I didn't give it a second thought.

People separated into age-related groups. Older Italians sat around the dining room table, the small kids went downstairs to the recreation room, and the young adults and teenagers played records and danced in the living room.

Tony brought a collection of records with him and took control of the music. Every time he put a stack of records on the phonograph, he looked at his watch. I thought he was concerned about getting his parents home safely before the predicted snowstorm.

I missed the other signs, too. He reeked of Vitalis, he kept his sportcoat and tie on all evening, and he kept grinning like a Cheshire cat.

After the last stack of records had played through, he put a single record on the turntable, looked at his brother Frankie, and nodded. Frankie nudged Angela, who placed her hand over her heart, closed her eyes and sighed when Elvis crooned, "Love me tender, love me long, never let me go."

Tony pulled me close and held me in an upright full body press as we danced. I wanted to protest, but breathing took priority. He twirled me around a few times at the end of the song, and I leaned against the wall and gasped. It was the first and only time he left me breathless.

Everyone stopped talking. That just does not happen when that many Italians are together unless they all die at once. I looked at my smiling mother standing in the dining room archway, her hands clasped under her chin. That instinctive fear of a deer caught in the headlights ran through me.

Tony knelt in front of me, pulled a ring out of his shirt pocket, and in a distinctly romantic recitation in Italian asked me to marry him. No one breathed except me. I was still breathing deeply to inflate my lungs.

This was a life-or-death moment. I knew if I said no, my mother would kill me — later, when there were no witnesses. If I said yes, I would be dragged down the aisle like a sacrificed virgin the day after I graduated from high school.

I had an "aha moment." Italian families coveted a high school diploma. I was a junior. Time was on my side. Time to back out of the deal and leave town before my mother called her uncle Vinnie and added my name to his "contract list."

I looked at Tony and said yes. Shouts erupted. His parents hugged me. My mother hugged him. My father watched with a grim expression, shaking his head like he had just witnessed an execution.

I ran into the bathroom and threw up. My mother brushed it off as "bride-to-be nerves." To this day, my stomach lurches at the scent of Vitalis.

The double dates continued. Tony worked long hours on his parents' farm, and I went to school. I only wore the engagement ring on our dates and justified that to my mother by the classes I took: clay sculpture, chemistry, biology lab, and being on the girls' basketball team. She was satisfied with my reasoning that it could easily slip off my finger or be damaged.

Just before Lent, I ended the engagement. Tony said he understood, and I was relieved he took it so well until I learned he enlisted in the Army the next day.

Consequently, there were mixed reactions to my decision. Tony's mother put a curse on me, his father yelled my name every time he beheaded a chicken, Angela never invited me to another pajama party, and my mother didn't speak to me until Easter Sunday. She gave me up for Lent.

My father gave me a Volkswagen.

~L.A. Kennedy

A Full House

Open your heart—open it wide; someone is standing outside.
~Mary Engelbreit, Believe: A Christmas Treasury

Like most families, mine is, well, a bit unusual. True, I have a father and a mother, who have been married for more than fifty years. But I have had more than forty siblings.

When I was child, I had two sisters and a brother who were many years older than me—fifteen, thirteen, and eleven years older, to be exact. So, in grade school, I was an only child of sorts, who had older siblings drop by once in a while.

Soon after my twelfth birthday, my parents decided to fill our great big house with more children in a rather unconventional way: as foster parents. Through the years, my mom and dad showed love to many children of all ages, whom they treated as part of the family. As for me, I gained numerous brothers and sisters—both older and younger.

There was Hope, who joined our family as a sixteen-year-old and ended up staying for two years. A few years after she left our house, she asked my father to walk her down the aisle at her wedding, a testimony to the special relationship she developed with my parents. Sandy, an eight-year-old with emotional problems, attached herself to me and sometimes would refuse to go to court-ordered counseling sessions unless I accompanied her.

There were newborn babies, like Mark and Stephen, whose smiles and coos are some of my happiest memories of those days. Then there were the twins, a brother and sister who were five months old when they arrived. They, like many foster children before them, ended up staying with us for more than two years and then becoming eligible for adoption. By this time, my parents had already raised four children and were grandparents, but they ended up adopting Jenny and James.

Much has been said about the importance—and necessity—of foster parenting, but being a sibling to foster brothers and sisters brought its own rewards. I reveled in being a big sister to countless children. However, it wasn't always laughter and lightness. I had to share "my" things and "my" parents with other children, many of whom had no concept of family life.

Yes, there were times when I hated having strange kids in my house, playing with my toys and interrupting my schedule. But my parents taught me that these relatively small sacrifices made a big difference in the lives of these neglected and abused kids. I had a real chance to make a difference, to show sisterly love and affection to children whose own families had not shown much love. With my parents' encouragement, I could play a small role in helping to ease their pain and to show them that someone cared about them.

I also knew the love that my parents showered on these children in no way took away from their love and care for me. I never felt neglected or overlooked, no matter how packed the house became or how often I had to sacrifice my wants to their needs.

My parents raised foster children for three decades. Amazingly, many of those foster children who passed through our house—whether for a few months or a few years—kept in contact with my parents after they left. Some send annual Christmas cards, some call my parents regularly, and a few occasionally even visit—all a testimony to the love and impact my parents had on their lives.

Today, as I raise four young children of my own, I look forward to a time when my husband and I might reach out to other children in need of a temporary haven. I hope one day that I can pass along some of the things learned by watching my parents foster children and teach them about love and life.

~Sarah Hamaker

Cheers

Forgiveness does not change the past,
but it does enlarge the future.
~Paul Boese

eer. I don't really understand the fascination people have with it. Personally, I think it is one of the most disgusting things that a human being can drink. I can't stand it. Fermented hops and barley? Um, isn't that what horses drink to wash down the oats and wheat? Anyway, there's something about beer that encourages people to get comfortable, talk, and have fun. I don't know if it's the alcohol content or just the camaraderie that comes from sitting around and sharing a bottled brew, but after a recent experience, I've developed an understanding and appreciation of beer and its "power."

My dad and I don't exactly have the most intimate relationship. I guess it's the stereotypical Asian father/son deal. Sometimes, I hate being around him because I feel a lot of pressure. When we talk, he usually just expresses his disappointment and frustration. I don't really approach him because I don't want to hear it, and he doesn't approach me because he doesn't want to say it.

One night, at the dinner table, the topic of my future came up. As usual, my dad went off. It was pretty much like all the times in the past, so I just sat there and took it. After that, I tried to avoid my dad for the rest of the night, so I went down to the basement. A couple of hours later, I heard footsteps coming down the stairs and figured it was going to be round two: more yelling, more disappointment, and more frustration. It turned out to be completely different. My dad came downstairs with two plastic bags, sat down next to me, and opened them up. One was filled with food, and the other beer.

My dad used to drink beer when he was younger, but when he got older he never drank, no matter the occasion or the company. He was also pretty strict about me not getting into it either. I didn't mind because I had never struggled with it in the first place. So, when my dad came down to the basement and offered me a beer, you can imagine the utter shock and disbelief!

He told me to drink and eat, and then he dropped another shocking surprise. He proceeded to apologize for always being hard on me and for having all these expectations. At this point, I had to take a step back and figure out if this was for real or just a dream. It's a weird feeling for a son to get an apology from his dad. I appreciated it, but I felt so guilty. I'd failed my dad in so many different ways, but it was he who was apologizing to me. So, after hearing that, I took a big, deep breath, an even bigger sip, and apologized to him too. And for maybe the first time ever, we had a "moment." It was one of those weird moments when two men share something big. Things got extremely quiet and awkward, but we soon got over it and moved on, the way that men in these kinds of situations often do.

It's funny how beer played a part in bringing us together. I wouldn't have imagined in a million years that I would be sitting there drinking beer with my dad. But I'm glad it happened. I'm still not a fan of beer, and I can't imagine ever learning to enjoy it, but if my dad offers me another beer and wants to talk, I'll gladly drink to that anytime.

Thanks, Dad. Cheers.

~Dennis Ko

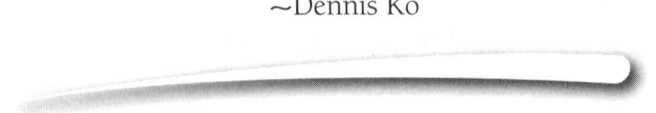

Like Mother, Like...

Fantasy is a necessary ingredient in living.
~Theodore Geisel

My daughter drops a glass of milk on the freshly mopped floor. I stare at her, the words and screams forming at the back of my tongue. She simply says, "She did it," while pointing to her hand. Then she looks angrily at her hand and asks, "Can't you see? Why did you drop the milk?" We're talking about her left hand. She calls it Sujana, which incidentally is the name of my sister-in-law, who isn't one bit pleased about it.

The right hand is called different names according to the occasion. My daughter sometimes grasps her own neck with her right hand and says, "Help, someone help! Don't do it, Mervin! No, Mervin!" I free her from Mervin's grasp and ask him to get out. Mervin sometimes scribbles on the wall, and then he's called Arvi. I look a pretty sight, scolding her hands. When she does something good, I ask her, "Did Mervin clean this up?" She says, "Who's Mervin? I did it myself." It's all very amusing, but she's only three years old, so I worry.

I complained to my sister about this apparent personality problem, hinting at a visit to the child psychologist, but she guffawed. "Personality problem? Now if that's true, and judging by the same yardstick, you're a complete maniac." I knew what she was talking about, so I didn't ask for explanations. As a child, I used to talk to the plants in our garden. Early every morning, I would go to each flower and greet it personally. They were great conversationalists, especially the white lilies. But I didn't particularly care for the black and yellow worms that tried to join in the chat. Incidentally, will someone tell me why those ugly things are so attracted to white lilies? Is it universal or is it me?

We also had Edward roses (at least that's what my mother called them). They were pale pink, and when you took a whiff, you knew you had experienced a slice of heaven. There were also purple verbena and a yellow flower that didn't have a name or fragrance, but looked lovely all the same. Once, mother grew a whole set of bluebells, and boy, could they listen! They shook their heads and agreed with everything I said. It made me feel important. My parents and siblings took great pleasure in watching my exercise. They never teased me about it or interrupted my playacting. I don't remember when I stopped this habit, but it must have eloped with my innocence, I guess.

"So," I ask my sister, "you mean she'll be okay? She'll grow out of it like I did?"

"Oh, yes," she says, "although I secretly hope she continues to do it. It's so funny."

I throw her a how-would-you-like-a-jab-in-the-stomach look, but she is still smiling. "And who said you grew out of it? Yesterday, I saw you talking to the washing machine."

For heaven's sake, I was just asking it whether it had seen my blue stockings….

~Sapna Manoj

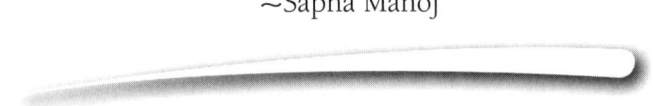

All in the Family

Meet Our Contributors
Meet Our Authors

Meet Our Contributors

Tonya L. Alton is an author of Canadian fiction. She has written her first book, *Under the Sitka Tree*, which is being considered for publication. Tonya is a spokesperson for mental health issues and gives presentations to high schools. Her inspiration is her kind-hearted daughter. Please e-mail Tonya at power2b@shaw.ca.

Sharon L. Andersen received her master's and doctoral degrees in Nursing Education from Teachers College, Columbia University. As owner of Crone's Nest Educational Consultants, she writes programs and does research using photo stories. Sharon enjoys eating out despite past traumas associated with sugar bowls. She thanks her family for their love and inspiration.

Anastasia M. Ashman is an award-winning producer of cultural entertainment. Co-creator of *Tales from the Expat Harem*, a travel collection recommended by *The Today Show*, she's scripting a film about bridging her radical West Coast family and traditional Near East in-laws at a palatial Istanbul wedding. Her microblog is www.twitter.com/thandelike.

Robynn Ashwood resides in Needham, Massachusetts, with her three children, husband, and dog. Besides exercising and practicing yoga, Robynn is a makeup artist and is very involved in her kids' various activities.

Betty Bogart worked at Southwest Airlines for twenty-one years, often ghostwriting for Herb Kelleher and other company officers. She has received awards for her poetry and nonfiction. Her writing has appeared in *The Palm Beach Post, Living the Law of Attraction*, and *Chicken Soup for the Soul* books. E-mail her at texasgirlb@gmail.com.

Trish Bonsall and her husband of twenty-seven years are the proud parents of four sons. She works as a sales manager for a local home builder. In her free time, she enjoys entertaining, reading, and writing. Trish is in the process of getting her first book published. E-mail her at bonz223@hotmail.com.

Marty Bucella is a full-time freelance cartoonist/humorous illustrator whose work has been published more than 100,000 times through magazines, newspapers, books, greeting cards, the Internet, and more. To find out more about Marty's work, visit his website at www.martybucella.com.

John P. Buentello is the co-author of *Reproduction Rights* and *Binary Tales*. His latest short story, *A Certain Recollection*, was published in the Mystery Writers of America's anthology, *The Blue Religion*. He is currently at work on a new novel, a collection of short stories, and a children's picture book. Contact him at jakkhakk@yahoo.com.

C. Hope Clark is editor of FundsforWriters.com, a ten-year-old, award-winning website for other writers. She pens nonfiction articles by day and a mystery series by night. Now that the kids are grown, she and her husband live on the banks of Lake Murray, South Carolina. E-mail her at hope@fundsforwriters.com.

J.M. Cornwell lives in Colorado in the shadow of Pikes Peak in the heart of the Rocky Mountains where she writes essays, stories, and novels. She avoids clock watching, but manages to be always on time. Visit her Cabin Dreams at http://fixnwrtr.blogspot.com.

Anne Crawley has been teaching English to seventh-graders for thirty-four years and still enjoys it every day. She lives in rural Pennsylvania with her husband and two daughters, plus two cats and three dogs. She loves to read, write, swim, and spend time with her family, especially her mother who lives nearby.

R.D. writes both fiction and nonfiction. She is currently working to receive a Bachelor of Arts degree.

Avis P. Drucker retired to Cape Cod with husband Al as "Washashores" in 2001 and discovered the joys of writing. She has been published in several magazines, anthologies, and *Chicken Soup for the Soul* books. She enjoys travel and family time, especially with her two daughters, Leslie and Vicki.

Amanda Eaker grew up listening to family adventures which, along with reading, travelling, and daydreaming, have been her favorite hobbies. She spent the past seven years working with a liver cancer and diabetes research group in Pittsburgh, and is now returning to school to study Science Education.

Susan Farr-Fahncke is the founder of 2TheHeart.com, where you can find more of her work and sign up for an online writing workshop. She is also the author of *Angel's Legacy* and the co-author, editor, and contributor to more than sixty books, including many *Chicken Soup for the Soul* books. Visit her at 2TheHeart.com.

Betsy S. Franz is a freelance writer and photographer specializing in nature, wildlife, the environment, and humorous and inspirational human interest topics. You may visit her online at www.naturesdetails. net or e-mail Betsy at backyarder1@earthlink.net.

Carol Genengels lives by the ocean with her husband of forty-nine years. Her stories have appeared in several books and magazines. She's been active in women's ministries and the National Alliance on Mental Illness (NAMI). She enjoys traveling, swimming, walking the beach, and hanging out with her grandchildren. Please e-mail her at awtcarolg@aol.com.

Mort Gerberg is a cartoonist and author best known for his magazine cartoons in *The New Yorker* and numerous other publications. He has written, edited or illustrated forty books for adults and children, including *Last Laughs: Cartoons About Aging, Retirement... and the Great Beyond.* Contact him at abcmort@aol.com.

Judy Lee Green is an award-winning writer and speaker whose spirit and roots reach deep into the Appalachian Mountains. Tennessee-bred and cornbread-fed, she has been published hundreds of times and received dozens of awards for her work. Her colorful Southern family is the source of many of her stories. Reach her at JudyLeeGreen@bellsouth.net.

C.H. is an ordained minister who founded a nonprofit for abuse victims and survivors. She lectures and writes on the subject of family violence.

Carolyn A. Hall received her bachelor's degree from Kansas State University. She and her husband live on a river bluff overlooking the Kansas River. She loves writing about her family, cooking, and baking. Combining all three, she wrote *Prairie Meals and Memories: Living the Golden Rural.* Please e-mail her at chall711@gmail.com.

Sarah Hamaker is a freelance writer and editor, and author of *Hired@ Home*, a guide to unlocking women's work-from-home potential. She has a master's degree in Literature and Language from Marymount University. Sarah lives in Virginia with her husband and four children. Visit her online at www.sarahhamaker.com.

Melanie Adams Hardy received her Bachelor of Science in 1984 and her Juris Doctorate in 2007. Melanie enjoys cooking, writing short stories, and volunteer work in her church and local community. She plans to write a book of short stories about her unique Southern family. Please e-mail her at rhardy212@charter.net.

Hallie Hastings lives with her husband and three sons in the Midwest. She writes children's books, parenting articles, and humor.

Jonny Hawkins is a full-time cartoonist from Sherwood, Michigan, where he lives with his wife and three kids. His work has appeared in more than 400 publications, and in his own books and line of cartoon-a-day calendars. He can be reached at jonnyhawkins2nz@yahoo.com.

Lori Hein is the author of *Ribbons of Highway: A Mother-Child Journey Across America*. Her freelance work has appeared in publications like *The Boston Globe* and several *Chicken Soup for the Soul* titles. Visit her at LoriHein.com or her world travel blog, RibbonsofHighway.blogspot.com.

CJ Hines is a former newspaper reporter and editor. She is a member of the Christian Writers Guild and has been published in *The Lookout*, *Lutheran Woman Today*, and *Christ in Our Home*. She enjoys quilting, sewing, reading, travelling, and spending time with her family. E-mail her at cjhines@cfu.net.

Libby Hires presently lives in Southeast Georgia. Libby has fond memories of growing up in the Carolinas with her family and friends. She hopes to write more about these experiences. Libby is also looking to have her children's stories published.

Carol Huff is a freelance writer from Hartwell, Georgia. She enjoys reading, writing, horseback riding, and interior decorating. In addition to her many short stories, she has authored one inspirational novel and two romance novels. Please e-mail her at herbiemakow@gmail.com.

Theresa Hupp is a prize-winning author, as well as an attorney, mediator, and human resources professional. She writes short stories, essays and poetry, has completed one novel and drafted her second.

Theresa has a B.A. from Middlebury College and a J.D. from Stanford Law School. Please contact her at MTHupp@gmail.com.

Edward A. Joseph is a former teacher and administrator in the Yonkers public school system. He now works as a freelance writer. His memoir, *The Loneliness of the Long-Distance Teacher*, is available by calling 1-888-795-4274 (option 3) or at amazon.com. Please e-mail him at edwardajoseph@optonline.net.

Mother, grandmother, Christian writer, and grief recovery specialist (www.grievewithhope.com) **Eva Juliuson** sends out a regular short e-mail prayer to encourage others in a deeper prayer life with the Lord. E-mail her at evajuliuson@hotmail.com.

Ron Kaiser lives and teaches in the Lakes Region of New Hampshire with the most beautiful woman you'll ever see. He also has two dogs named Oliver and Ben, and partial custody of a corpulent Chihuahua named Snowflake (don't ask).

Ben Kennedy is a stand-up comedian, actor, and writer from Baltimore, Maryland. He now resides in Charleston, South Carolina, with his beautiful wife and amazing son. (He is not biased.) He plans to release a collection of humorous essays and stories in the coming year. Please e-mail him at bigben@bigbenkennedy.com.

L.A. Kennedy is a writer and artist, and has experience in social services and public education. She began journaling when she was twelve. Her journal entries are the source for her short stories. Lori is presently compiling her first fictional collection of humorous and reality-based short stories about "mature" women. E-mail her at elkaynca@aol.com.

Michael Kilpatrick received his Bachelor of Arts degree from Michigan State University in 1971 and MBA from Pepperdine University in 1976. Recently retired after twenty-four years with the California Lottery, Michael enjoys travelling with his wife, Cecelia, and daughter, Megan. Michael plans a second career writing humorous and insightful children's books.

Cuauhtémoc Q. Kish is a freelance writer and playwright. He is actively seeking a publisher for his short-story collection called *The Sissy Chronicles*. Feel free to visit his website at http://kishwriter.com.

Kay Klebba is happily married to Scott and the mother of four incredible children. Kay's passion is speaking and writing to women about the hilarity of our blessings. Please visit her blog at http://kayklebba. blogspot.com or e-mail her at kayklebba@gmail.com.

April Knight is an artist and freelance writer. She lives on a ranch and enjoys riding her horses, Gypsy Wind and Valley Rambler. Australia is her favorite vacation destination. She has four children and many strange friends who make life fun. Write to her at moonlightlady1@ hotmail.com.

Mimi Greenwood Knight is a mother of four and freelance writer with more than 300 articles and humorous parenting essays in print. She lives in South Louisiana with her husband, David, and enjoys Bible study, butterfly gardening, baking, and the lost art of letter writing. Visit her blog at blog.nola.com/faith/mimi_greenwood_knight.

Sandi Knight lives with her husband and two children on their family farm in Manitoba, Canada. She has been freelance writing since 2003, receiving encouragement and support from an amazing group of local writers called the Prairie Pens. She enjoys gardening, photography, long walks, watching birds, wildlife, and the ever-changing prairie sky.

Dennis Ko was born on June 5, 1984. He enjoys playing and watching sports. Writing is currently just a hobby, but he hopes to one day make a career out of it. Please visit his blog at www.xanga.com/dko. He can be contacted at dennisko@gmail.com.

Dallas Kuzinich is a fifteen-year-old student in high school. She hopes to go to Berkeley and become a social worker so she can help children in abusive homes. Her hobbies include reading, traveling, and hanging out with her best friends: Brittany, Breanna, and Alicia.

Susan LaMaire lives in Parsippany, New Jersey, with her husband, Brian, three hermit crabs, and many fish. She is currently working on a collection of humorous and true short stories. You may e-mail her at hunkoftin8@yahoo.com.

Andrea Langworthy's columns appear in the *Rosemount Town Pages* and *Minnesota Good Age* newspapers. She's been published in *Chicken Soup for the Soul: Divorce and Recovery*, the *2009 St. Paul Almanac* and various Minnesota publications. She teaches a writing workshop at Minneapolis's Loft Literary Center.

Marianne LaValle-Vincent is a registered nurse with a long history of publications. A native of Syracuse, New York, her poetry and short stories have been published worldwide and include two full-length poetry collections. She still resides in Syracuse with her daughter, Jess, and extended family.

Patti Lawson, an award-winning author and attorney, lives in West Virginia with her canine companion, Sadie. Read about Sadie in *The Dog Diet, A Memoir: What My Dog Taught Me About Shedding Pounds, Licking Stress, and Getting a New Leash on Life* (HCI, 2006). Visit www.thedogdiet.com.

Beth Levine is a veteran freelance writer and humorist whose work has been published in many national publications. Visit her at www.bethlevine.net.

Delores Liesner enjoys sharing the hope, humor and adventure of a personal relationship with God — loved by the Father, lifted by the Son, led by the Spirit. A favorite moment of this hyper-grandma's life was her grandson saying, "Gramma, you rock!" She welcomes contact at lovedliftedandled@wi.rr.com.

Stephen J. Lyons is the author of *Landscape of the Heart*, which is a single father's memoir, and *A View from the Inland Northwest*. He writes poems, essays, articles, and book reviews from his home in central Illinois where he works as a speech writer.

John MacDonald received his master's degree in Special Education from the State University of New York at Albany and currently teaches English as a Second Language in upstate New York. John enjoys writing about his family's bizarre but always amusing behavior. Please e-mail him at jmcdon7@nycap.rr.com.

Pat Maloney is a writer and teacher living in Virginia. She enjoys reading, writing, and spending time with her dogs. You can reach her at corgicapers@ymail.com.

Annie Mannix resides in Southern California with her two sons. She has written for several regional publications. She enjoys music, horses, and books that make you smile. She can be reached at eitman@mindspring.com.

After a decade as a copywriter for agencies in India and Dubai, **Sapna Manoj** settled in Sharjah with her husband and two kids. As a full-time mother and part-time scribe, she has managed to strap together a collection of short stories that awaits publication.

Judith Marks-White is a *Westport News* (CT) award-winning columnist of The Light Touch, which has appeared every Wednesday for the past twenty-five years. She is the author of two novels published by Random House/Ballantine: *Seducing Harry* and *Bachelor Degree*. Judith teaches humor writing and lectures widely.

Timothy Martin is the author of four books and seven screenplays.

His script, *Fast Pitch*, is currently in development. The novel version of *Fast Pitch* is scheduled for publication (Blitz Publishing) in 2009. Tim's work has appeared in several *Chicken Soup for the Soul* books. He can be reached at tmartin@northcoast.com.

Toni L. Martin provided publicity and marketing support for an award-winning novel written by a Florida author. She leads a writers group for the Florida Writers Association and was inspired by their inaugural speaker, a *Chicken Soup for the Soul* author, to try writing nonfiction. Her day job includes writing proposals, documents, and training packages.

Jilliann McEwen has written articles purchased by *Faith and Friends* and *War Cry* magazines, and *Seasoned Cooking* e-zine. She and her husband have two children and two grandchildren. They reside in Oklahoma. You may contact her via e-mail at jffchayil@gmail.com.

Tina McGrevy lives in Springfield, Ohio, with her husband, Charlie, and their boys: Garrett, Patrick, and Brennan. Tina writes about the adventures of raising sons and the unexpected joys of Smith-Magenis Syndrome (SMS). She can be reached at tmcgrevy@yahoo.com and invites you to visit www.prisms.org for more information about SMS.

James McMillan is a Grade 12 student at D.W. Poppy Secondary School in Langley, British Columbia. An avid filmmaker, writer and philanthropist, James is planning to attend the Tisch School of the Arts at New York University after graduation and step into the world of independent film.

Lynn Maddalena Menna lives in Hawthorne, New Jersey, with her husband, Prospero, and cat, Toonsie. Lynn is a former educator with the Paterson Public Schools and listed in *Who's Who Among American Teachers*. Lynn is currently and happily retired. Friends and relatives who still speak to her can contact her at prolynn@aol.com.

Anne Merrigan is a therapist by trade, an Irish soul for life. She applies her ancient rhythms in her work with trauma survivors. She plans to write a book reflecting ways to cope with trauma. Besides writing, Anne loves to paint, garden, and spend time with family and friends.

Rosemary Merritt appears to be living life backwards. After marriage, she enjoyed a busy career in publishing. She then attended Georgian College in Ontario, where she graduated with honors in 2005. Most recently, she has been experiencing a happy childhood along with her grandchildren. You can reach her at firefly@netrover.com.

Ali Monroe is a Virginia-based writer who enjoys reading, writing, and shopping. You can contact her at wyndietwil@yahoo.com.

Cynthia Morningstar received her Bachelor of Music in Piano Performance in 1979. She has worked as a librarian for a number of years, and has directed her church choir and taught piano. Her husband, Mark, is a pastor in Indiana. They have three daughters: Amanda, Beth, and Jill. Contact her at cbmorn@hotmail.com.

Tolly Moseley is a publicist and freelance writer in Austin, Texas. She and her blog, Austin Eavesdropper, have been featured on About. com, G4TV, in *Rare Magazine*, and in *The Daily Texan*. Thanks to her aunt, she now knows how to decorate the perfect Christmas tree. Contact her at tollymoseley@hotmail.com.

Rebecca Olker received her Bachelor of Arts from UC Riverside and her master's degree in Taxation from Golden Gate University. She is an accountant in the heart of Silicon Valley. Rebecca enjoys reading, knitting, and walking her dog. When she is not writing, she is surfing the Internet. Please e-mail her at Rebecca_Olker@comcast.net.

Tina O'Reilly is a freelance writer, mother of three, and wife to an amazing husband. She enjoys writing, traveling, reading, the ocean, and her new granddaughter. Please e-mail her at seaswept68@aol.com.

Melissa Pannell is currently working on a degree in web design. She is a foster parent for two of her grandsons with adoption in the near future. Melissa enjoys surfing the net, reading, writing, traveling, and swimming. E-mail her at MPANNELL6@yahoo.com.

Chantal Panozzo is a writer and advertising copywriter. Her articles and essays have appeared in the *Christian Science Monitor*, *National Geographic Glimpse*, and other publications. She recently received the Rosalie Fleming Memorial Humor Prize. An American expatriate, Chantal travels extensively in Europe and lives in Zurich, Switzerland. Visit www.chantalpanozzo.com.

Mark Parisi's "off the mark" comic, syndicated since 1987, is distributed by United Media. Mark's humor also graces greeting cards, T-shirts, calendars, magazines, newsletters, and books. Check out www.offthemark.com. Lynn is his wife/business partner. Their daughter, Jen, contributes inspiration (as do three cats).

Novelist, blogger, and award-winning travel writer, **Perry P. Perkins** is a stay-at-home dad who lives with his wife, Victoria, and their two-year-old daughter, Grace, in the Pacific Northwest. His novels include *Just Past Oysterville* and *Shoalwater Voices*. Examples of his published work can be found online at www.perryperkinsbooks.com.

Nancy M. Peterson has spent her adult life writing for national and regional newspapers and magazines. She enjoys sharing the joys and pain that life brings us, and the wisdom that family and friends impart. Her four books reflect what she has learned about life in the West. Visit her at www.nancympeterson.com.

Kay Conner Pliszka says the dysfunction in her family has helped her face life head-on with a strong faith and a sense of humor. Her work with at-risk students from dysfunctional families has brought numerous awards and honors. Kay is a humorous and motivational speaker. E-mail her at kmpliszka@comcast.net.

Marijoyce Porcelli has been a freelance writer for several years. She is now working on a "cozy" mystery set in Appalachia, as well as enjoying putting together a fantasy novel. She hopes to eventually create a series out of each original manuscript.

Joe Rector is a freelance writer and retired English teacher who has written several pieces for *Chicken Soup for the Soul* and other publications. View more of his writing at www.thecommonisspectacular.com.

Dwan Reed, a licensed Master of Social Work, spends her time as a real estate agent, preacher's wife, youth mentor, women's prison evangelist, and aspiring writer. Dwan, an experienced public speaker, delivers inspiring presentations to audiences throughout the United States and Africa. She can be contacted at dwanbooks@yahoo.com.

Kimberly Anne Reedy is very passionate about connecting with others through writing, travelling, foreign languages, and shared awareness. She has been a business owner, educator, scuba diver, body-worker, and a volunteer in support of Fertility Awareness Method (FAM). Her family has been her inspiration and the light of her life.

Bruce Robinson is an award-winning, internationally published cartoonist whose work has appeared in numerous periodicals, including *The National Enquirer*, *The Saturday Evening Post*, *Woman's World*, *The Sun*, *First*, *Highlights*, and many others. He is also the author of the cartoon book, *Good Medicine*. Contact him via e-mail at cartoonsbybrucerobinson@hotmail.com.

Danielle Rockwell grew up in Ohio where most of her stories take place. Since moving to England in 1991, Danielle enjoys writing about family, friends, and the memories they shared. She has been published in several books and magazines, including various *Chicken Soup for the Soul* titles.

Cora Rogers lives in Virginia and has worked as an addictions counselor. She is currently employed as a special education teacher and writes as often as possible.

Jo Rogers has a Bachelor of Arts in Communications and a Master of Arts in Theology from Fuller Seminary. She has published articles in a variety of magazines, and she is the editor of a national magazine. Ms. Rogers has two children and nine grandchildren. She resides in Orange, California.

Diana Savage, a professional writer, editor, and speaker, has a master's degree in theological studies. She has worked for nonprofits most of her career and has traveled abroad on numerous humanitarian trips. Since her daughter got married, she hasn't sung at weddings or organized reception food. Her e-mail is info@dianasavage.com.

Tara Schellenberg received her Bachelor of Science in Animal Science from Cornell University in 2000 and Master of Science in Epidemiology from the University of Saskatchewan in 2005. She is an epidemiologist in Saskatchewan. Tara is the mother of three, and enjoys fastball and quilting. Please e-mail her at t.schell@sasktel.net.

Michael T. Smith currently lives in Idaho with his wife, Ginny, and works as a project manager in the telecommunications industry. In his spare time, he writes inspirational stories for his weekly e-zine, *Hearts and Humor*. E-mail Michael at reversingfalls@yahoo.com. To sign up for Michael's weekly stories, visit http://visitor.constantcontact. com/d.jsp?m=1101828445578&p=oi.

Laurie Sontag is the author of the popular blog, Manic Motherhood. She has been a humor columnist for California newspapers since

2001. You can see more of Laurie's work at www.lauriesontag.com or e-mail her at laurie@lauriesontag.com.

Jean Sorensen's cartoons have appeared in *Good Housekeeping, The Washington Post* magazine, *The Lutheran*, and numerous textbooks. Her work has also been featured in greeting cards for Oatmeal Studios. Jean lives in the Washington, D.C., area with her high school sweetheart and three children, who always keep her laughing.

Ken Swarner is the author of *Whose Kids Are These Anyway?* He can be reached via e-mail at kenswarner@aol.com.

Marsha D. Teeling is a fifty-six-year-old grandmother of two: Madison, five, and Logan, three. Marsha has been married for thirty years to a wonderful man from Dublin, Ireland. She works as a case manager for critically ill children. Her twin sister lives nearby, and she enjoys gardening, needlework, reading, and friends.

Nori Thomas received her Bachelor of Arts in Journalism from the University of Central Florida. She worked for several newspapers, and later as an educational advisor at a local college. Nori is president of Volusia County Romance Writers.

Mariela Tsakiris is now seventeen and in eleventh grade. She is passionate about writing, languages, and travel. Mariela is currently studying psychology and volunteering at an after-school program for children. She plans to become bilingual in Spanish and to study abroad in college.

June Waters' life has been anything but ordinary. She survived a household with eight siblings and enjoys writing about the chaos. June travels extensively and spends much of the year in Ireland, writing historical fiction for young adults.

Ramona Watson has been married to Dr. John Watson for eleven years. Together they claim thirteen children and forty-three grand-children. They recently moved from North Carolina to Utah to be closer to family. Read Dr. Watson's contributions in *Chicken Soup for the Soul: The Cancer Book* and *Chicken Soup for the Chiropractic Soul*.

Janie Dempsey Watts' stories have appeared in three *Chicken Soup for the Soul* books, *The Ultimate Gardener*, *The Christian Science Monitor*, and *Georgia Backroads*. Janie writes a column for *Catoosa Life Magazine*. Her mother-in-law now lives nearby and continues to share her Sicilian customs, including her delicious meatballs made from her mother's recipe.

Aggie Welsh is a freelance writer who enjoys reading, writing, and spending time with her husband.

Sara Wessling is a senior in high school. She likes to sing and write in her spare time. She is the secretary of student council, section leader in her varsity choir, and producer of her school's video yearbook. Sara plans to be an elementary school teacher.

Christy Westbrook enjoys writing inspirational stories about everyday life. She loves spending time outdoors with her family and friends. She lives in Lexington, South Carolina, with her husband, Thad, and their two daughters, Abby and Katie. She wishes to thank her wonderful critique group for all of their support.

Courtney Rae Wick majored in poetry at Southern Illinois University. She is currently a General Manager with Verizon Wireless in Central Illinois, where she also resides with her husband, Ian. Courtney loves animals, convertibles, and Thai food. Please e-mail her at CourtneyRaedio@gmail.com.

Meet Our Authors

ack Canfield is the co-creator of the *Chicken Soup for the Soul* series, which *Time* magazine has called "the publishing phenomenon of the decade." Jack is also the co-author of eight other bestselling books.

Jack is the CEO of the Canfield Training Group in Santa Barbara, California, and founder of the Foundation for Self-Esteem in Culver City, California. He has conducted intensive personal and professional development seminars on the principles of success for more than a million people in twenty-three countries. Jack is a dynamic keynote speaker and he has spoken to hundreds of thousands of people at more than 1,000 corporations, universities, professional conferences and conventions, and has been seen by millions more on national television shows such as *The Today Show, Fox and Friends, Inside Edition, Hard Copy,* CNN's *Talk Back Live, 20/20, Eye to Eye,* the NBC *Nightly News* and the *CBS Evening News.*

Jack has received many awards and honors, including three honorary doctorates and a Guinness World Records Certificate for having seven books from the *Chicken Soup for the Soul* series appearing on the *New York Times* bestseller list on May 24, 1998.

You can reach Jack at:

Jack Canfield
P.O. Box 30880 • Santa Barbara, CA 93130
phone: 805-563-2935 • fax: 805-563-2945
www.jackcanfield.com

ark Victor Hansen is the co-founder of Chicken Soup for the Soul, along with Jack Canfield. He is a sought-after keynote speaker, bestselling author, and marketing maven. Mark's powerful messages of possibility, opportunity, and action have created powerful change in thousands of organizations and millions of individuals worldwide.

Mark is a prolific writer with many bestselling books in addition to the *Chicken Soup for the Soul* series. Mark has had a profound influence in the field of human potential through his library of audios, videos, and articles in the areas of big thinking, sales achievement, wealth building, publishing success, and personal and professional development. He is also the founder of the MEGA Seminar Series.

He has appeared on *Oprah*, CNN, and *The Today Show*. He has been quoted in *Time*, *U. S. News & World Report*, *USA Today*, *The New York Times*, and *Entrepreneur* and has given countless radio interviews, assuring our planet's people that "You can easily create the life you deserve."

Mark has received numerous awards that honor his entrepreneurial spirit, philanthropic heart, and business acumen. He is a lifetime member of the Horatio Alger Association of Distinguished Americans.

You can reach Mark at:

Mark Victor Hansen & Associates, Inc.
P.O. Box 7665 • Newport Beach, CA 92658
phone: 949-764-2640 • fax: 949-722-6912
www.markvictorhansen.com

Amy Newmark is the publisher of *Chicken Soup for the Soul*, after a thirty-year career as a writer, speaker, financial analyst, and business executive in the worlds of finance and telecommunications. Amy is a *magna cum laude* graduate of Harvard College, where she majored in Portuguese, minored in French, and traveled extensively. She is also the mother of two children in college and two grown stepchildren who are recent college graduates.

After a long career writing books on telecommunications, voluminous financial reports, business plans, and corporate press releases, Chicken Soup for the Soul is a breath of fresh air for Amy. She has fallen in love with Chicken Soup for the Soul and its life-changing books, and really enjoys putting these books together for Chicken Soup's wonderful readers. She has co-authored more than two dozen *Chicken Soup for the Soul* books.

You can reach Amy and the rest of the Chicken Soup for the Soul team via e-mail through webmaster@chickensoupforthesoul.com.

usan M. Heim is a longstanding author and editor, specializing in parenting, multiples, women's and Christian issues. After the birth of her fraternal twin boys, Austen and Caleb, Susan left her desk job as a Senior Editor for a publishing company and has never looked back. Being a work-at-home mother allows her to follow her two greatest passions: parenting and writing.

Susan's books include *Chicken Soup for the Soul: Devotional Stories for Women*; *Chicken Soup for the Soul: Twins and More*; *Boosting Your Baby's Brain Power*; *It's Twins! Parent-to-Parent Advice from Infancy Through Adolescence*; *Oh, Baby! 7 Ways a Baby Will Change Your Life the First Year*; *Moms of Multiples' Devotions to Go*; and, *Twice the Love: Stories of Inspiration for Families with Twins, Multiples and Singletons*. Susan also hopes to venture into fiction writing in the future.

Her articles and stories have appeared in many books, websites, and magazines, including *TWINS Magazine* and *Angels on Earth*. Susan writes an online column for *Mommies Magazine* called "Loving and Living with Twins and Multiples." She shares her thoughts and experiences about raising children in today's world through her blog, "Susan Heim on Parenting," at http://susanheim.blogspot.com. Susan is also an expert on twins and multiples for AllExperts.com, and a parenting expert for SelfGrowth.com.

Susan is the founder of TwinsTalk, a website where parents share tips, advice and stories about raising twins and multiples, at www.twinstalk.com. She is a member of the National Association of Women Writers and the Southeastern Writers Association.

Susan is married to Mike, whose ever-present support enables Susan to pursue a career she loves. They are the parents of four active sons, who are in elementary school, high school and college! You can reach Susan at susan@susanheim.com and visit her website at www.susanheim.com. Join her on Twitter and Facebook by searching for ParentingAuthor.

All in the Family

Thank You
About Chicken Soup
Share with Us

Thank You

We appreciate all of our wonderful family members and friends, who continue to inspire and teach us on our life's journey. We have been blessed beyond measure with their constant love and support.

We owe huge thanks to all of our contributors. We know that you pour your hearts and souls into the stories that you share with us, and ultimately with each other. For this book in particular, you really opened your hearts to us, sharing some very personal stories about your families, often for the first time. We appreciate your willingness to open up your lives to other Chicken Soup for the Soul readers. Your stories help so many people—we know because we get the letters telling us how the books have changed our readers' lives.

We can only publish a small percentage of the stories that are submitted, but we read every single one, and even the ones that do not appear in the book have an influence on us and on the final manuscript. We strongly encourage you to continue submitting to future *Chicken Soup for the Soul* books.

We would like to thank D'ette Corona, our Assistant Publisher, who seamlessly manages a dozen projects at a time while keeping all of us focused and on schedule. And we'd like to express our gratitude to Barbara LoMonaco, Chicken Soup for the Soul's Webmaster and Editor; Chicken Soup for the Soul Editor Kristiana Glavin, for her assistance with the final manuscript and proofreading; and Leigh Holmes, who keeps our office running smoothly.

We owe a very special thanks to our Creative Director and book producer, Brian Taylor at Pneuma Books, for his brilliant vision for our covers and interiors. Finally, none of this would be possible without the business and creative leadership of our CEO, Bill Rouhana, and our president, Bob Jacobs.

Improving Your Life Every Day

Real people sharing real stories—for fifteen years. Now, Chicken Soup for the Soul has gone beyond the bookstore to become a world leader in life improvement. Through books, movies, DVDs, online resources and other partnerships, we bring hope, courage, inspiration and love to hundreds of millions of people around the world. Chicken Soup for the Soul's writers and readers belong to a one-of-a-kind global community, sharing advice, support, guidance, comfort, and knowledge.

Chicken Soup for the Soul stories have been translated into more than forty languages and can be found in more than one hundred countries. Every day, millions of people experience a Chicken Soup for the Soul story in a book, magazine, newspaper or online. As we share our life experiences through these stories, we offer hope, comfort and inspiration to one another. The stories travel from person to person, and from country to country, helping to improve lives everywhere.

Share with Us

We all have had Chicken Soup for the Soul moments in our lives. If you would like to share your story or poem with millions of people around the world, go to chickensoup.com and click on "Submit Your Story." You may be able to help another reader, and become a published author at the same time. Some of our past contributors have launched writing and speaking careers from the publication of their stories in our books!

Our submission volume has been increasing steadily—the quality and quantity of your submissions has been fabulous. Starting in 2010, we will only accept story submissions via our website. They will no longer be accepted via mail or fax.

To contact us regarding other matters, please send us an e-mail through webmaster@chickensoupforthesoul.com, or fax or write us at:

Chicken Soup for the Soul
P.O. Box 700
Cos Cob, CT 06807-0700
Fax: 203-861-7194

One more note from your friends at Chicken Soup for the Soul: Occasionally, we receive an unsolicited book manuscript from one of our readers, and we would like to respectfully inform you that we do not accept unsolicited manuscripts and we must discard the ones that appear.

Chicken Soup for the Soul.
Count Your Blessings

101 Stories of Gratitude, Fortitude, and Silver Linings

Jack Canfield,
Mark Victor Hansen, Amy Newmark,
Laura Robinson & Elizabeth Bryan

This follow-on book to *Tough Times, Tough People* continues Chicken Soup for the Soul's focus on inspiration and hope in these difficult times. These inspirational stories remind us that each day holds something to be thankful for—whether it is having the sun shine or having food on the table. Power outages and storms, health scares and illnesses, job woes and financial insecurities, housing challenges and family worries test us all. But there is always a silver lining. The simple pleasures of family, home, health, and inexpensive good times are described. These stories of optimism, faith, and strength will make a great start to 2010.
978-1-935096-42-9

Check out our great books for more

Chicken Soup for the Soul®

Tough Times, Tough People

TOUGH TIMES WON'T LAST BUT TOUGH PEOPLE WILL

101 Stories about Overcoming the Economic Crisis and Other Challenges

Jack Canfield,
Mark Victor Hansen
& Amy Newmark

Tough times won't last, but tough people will. Many people have lost money, and many are losing their jobs, homes, or at least making cutbacks. Others have faced life-changing natural disasters, such as hurricanes and fires, as well as health and family difficulties. *Tough Times, Tough People* is all about overcoming adversity, pulling together, making do with less, facing challenges, and finding new joys in a simpler life. Stories address downsizing, getting out of debt, managing chronic health problems, dealing with loss, having faith, blessings in disguise, and finding new perspectives.

978-1-935096-35-1

Inspiration!

Everyone loves Christmas and the holiday season. We reunite scattered family members, watch the wonder in a child's eyes, and feel the joy of giving gifts. The rituals of the holiday season give a rhythm to the years and create a foundation for our lives, as we gather with family, with our communities at church, at school, and even at the mall, to share the special spirit of the season, brightening those long winter days. "Santa-safe" for kids!

978-1-935096-15-3

heck out our
great books for more